BREAKFAST
WITH
SOLOMON

Volume One

Gil Stieglitz

Breakfast with Solomon
Volume One

© Gil Stieglitz 2014

Published by Principles to Live By, Roseville CA 95661
www.ptlb.com

Cover by John Chase

All Scripture verses are from the New American Standard Bible unless otherwise indicated.
New American Standard Bible: 1995 update.
1995 La Habra, CA: The Lockman Foundation.

ISBN 978-0-9838602-6-6
Devotional

Printed in the United States of America

Dedication

The book of Proverb is the most concentrated revelation on living
as a wise person.

This book is dedicated to the wisest man I know – my father,
Norman F Stieglitz Jr.,
who taught me so much when I was a young boy and
continues to teach me with his life and words.

It is also dedicated to my children:
Jenessa, Abbey and Grace,
and to my grandchildren and great-grandchildren
as well as generations beyond them who I hope will sit at the feet of
Solomon and live a wise life rather than go down the fool's road.

Table of Contents

Preface.. 7

Introduction.. 9

January... 11

February... 77

March..145

April...211

May..279

June..345

About the Author...409

Other Resources..411

Preface

Many people need to be thanked for any book and especially when I am the author. I want to especially thank my wife Dana Stieglitz for being patient as I wrote and rewrote these pages. I want to thank Sandy Johnson for reading and rereading these comments over a number of years and helping them make sense and be grammatically correct. Many thanks go to Debbie Purvis who is my administrative assistant and has shepherded this project through to its completion or it would not have made it. I am also very thankful for the Board of Principles to Live By who allowed me to keep working on this project over the years.

I also want to thank all of the scholars who assisted me in understanding the meaning of the verses in Proverbs: the men and women who have done such fine work in producing the many Hebrew, Greek, and English dictionaries, commentaries, cross-referenced materials, and historical background materials that I poured over and which allowed me to understand the meaning and the intent of Solomon in these verses he penned so long ago. I hope that these devotional comments will encourage you to do your own study in the biblical text and draw out even deeper insights and applications.

Introduction to Breakfast with Solomon

A number of years ago I was asked to conduct a retreat for a dynamic church in Indiana. I met a godly grandfather at the retreat and he told me of a project that he was doing for his grandkids. He bought a new Bible each year and dedicated that Bible to one of his grandkids for that year. He did his devotions in the Bible and wrote extensive notes of what God was showing him and the meaning of the various passages. He also wrote personal notes to that particular grandchild about his hopes and prayers for the child. He scattered his notes throughout the pages of the Bible so that to read them all you would have to explore the whole Bible. He showed me the Bible he was working on for that year for one of his grandsons. At the end of the year he would give the Bible to that grandchild at Christmas that year. This Bible was now precious to that young boy or girl. It was full of wisdom from God and their grandfather. This was his way of speaking into each of his grandchildren's lives.

His unique way of speaking into his grand children's lives really caused me to spend some time thinking about how I was going to speak into my children and my eventual grandchildren. I know that God has led me to some key insights that I wanted my daughters and their children and their children's children to know. So a few years later I began a project that eventually took over 10 years. I began having my personal devotions in the book of Proverbs and allowing God to speak to me. I wrote down all the word study and insights that I received and wrote them for my three daughters and the children they would eventually have and even the children those children would have. This was just me try to share what God was teaching me to the people who I love the most. The wisdom in the book of Proverbs is so profound and so incredibly timely that I regularly marvel at Solomon and God for putting all of this wisdom in this book of the Bible. I wanted my children and all of their eventual children to have access to this information in a way that was personal to them. The level of people insights in the book of proverbs is astounding and I wanted my girls and their families to have the benefit of this information. So I began writing. Each verse was wrapped in the love of God for me and the insights that He was sharing with me and then I recorded it as how it might apply to my children and others not just myself. Solomon says in the proverbs that his father David sat down and shared with him many of these principles and gave him a love of wisdom. I was trying to do that for my girls and now for you.

I began to email these devotions to my three girls, Jenessa, Abbey, and Grace when they became teenagers. They enjoyed hearing my applications of the verses and the stories of when they were younger and the things they were learning at that time and that I was praying for them. Eventually other people saw the emails and asked to be on the email list. This process grew and grew until 7,000 plus people were receiving these emails every day. A number of people asked if I could put these devotions in a book so they could read it in the 'old fashion' way. We had to condense the devotions and work them through a process so that they were ready for publication, but here is the first of six volumes of Breakfast with Solomon.

This arrangement of the book of Proverbs is one verse per day. A verse from the first chapter of Proverbs on the first day of each month. A verse from the second chapter of Proverbs on the second day of each month. A verse from the third chapter of Proverbs on the third day of the month and so on through the thirty one chapters of the book. Some have asked if these could be put into a devotional commentary on the book of Proverbs in the normal verse one, verse two, verse three format. We are working on that format and those volumes and it will be released later.

Sincerely In Christ
Gil Stieglitz
November 2014

January

PROVERBS 1:1
The proverbs of Solomon, the son of David, king of Israel

The word *proverb* is the word *masal*, which means to become like or to be comparable to. The idea seems to be that a proverb is a way of declaring or seeing a truth by comparing it with something else. It is the comparison that brings a truth to full view.

In the book of Proverbs, all types of comparisons are used to bring the truth of life with other humans to light. It is amazing how many people want life to work like they want it to work. It doesn't; it works like God structured it. Working with other humans has rules. When you follow those rules, things go much better.

Notice that these proverbs are the proverbs of Solomon, the son of David and the king of Israel, which suggests that he wrote these before he himself became king of Israel, which would make these writings before the book of Ecclesiastes.

God inspired Solomon's insights into life: One, by giving him the wisdom to see them in the first place. Two, by allowing him to see the right comparison to bring out the truth. Three, by breathing into Solomon during those writing sessions only those truths that needed to be recorded and not writing those that did not need to be recorded.

One of the other things about this book is that it follows a Hebraic form with thought rhymes and not word rhymes. The ideas are connected by thoughts that are similar which gives them the context. They are hooked one to another until there is an obvious break in the thought. We are not used to thinking in this way, but it is the basis of the book.

Are you willing to listen to the wisdom of the wisest man who ever walked the planet? Are you willing to adjust your life when you find that you are at odds with that wisdom? Incline your ear for you will find great truth and helpful actions to avoid many of the common problems that derail others.

January 2

PROVERBS 2:1
My son, if you will receive my words and treasure my commandments within you

Notice the word *son*. This is a young man or a person who puts himself in the position of learner.

receive my words

Notice that the writer says that even the son must put himself into an attitude to receive the words of this book. Just because you are a physical son or follower or employee, it does not mean that you will automatically be willing to receive instruction.

How tragic that sometimes the very people we would like to have receive our wisdom are not open to it. A person must be open to receive words of wisdom. If they are not open, then the wisdom of these lessons will fall like water off a duck's back.

This is a word to parents that you should make sure, in every way you can, that your children respect you enough to be willing to listen to you. You should make sure that they are not given free rein to their selfish tendencies to blow you off. You must make sure that the nature of your relationship is close and supportive so that their receiving your words is a no brainer.

This is also a warning to us. Do we have the proper attitude to receive God's wisdom even when it says things we don't want to hear or comes through a person we don't like? God is pouring out wisdom to us. If we are willing to hear it, He will make us wise. Many times we must admit that our own selfish choices caused much of the problems that we now experience. Is your heart right to receive God's wisdom - especially through this book but also as we walk through the day?

treasure my commandments within you

What do you hold dear in your life? Is it a list of do's and don'ts that will show you the path of wisdom? Are we treasuring up useless trinkets when the real treasures we treat with disregard?

Remember our world system wants to get us to attach the wrong price tags to the stuff in our lives. They want us to have a high value on TV's, couches, cars, and homes while we put a low priority on God, family, Scripture, relationships, etc.

In this instance God is telling you to put a high value on the list of do's and don'ts that you will find in this book. It will be a healing and a life to you. There are very few things that are more valuable than a guide that will help you arrive at the right decision every time. The commandments in this book are that guide. Don't throw it away as worthless or too complicated.

The commandments in this book are over 3,000 years old and have shown their worth in every culture and every time. They are breathed with the life of God. They are inspired by God.

How many bad decisions have you made? If I could give you a list of things to think about before you made your decisions that would virtually eliminate bad decisions if you followed them, would that be worth something?

Now there is a difference between wise and foolish decisions and right and wrong decisions. Something may not be wrong, but it still may be foolish. This book will have us think about our decisions and actions at a much more fundamental level.

Three elementary guides that run through this book:

- Is this thing I want to do selfish? Am I the only one who will profit from this? Is there another decision in which God and others can also profit with me?

- Is what I want to do impulsive? Does it need to be done quickly without counsel or forethought? Impulsive decisions are almost always foolish decisions.

- Is this decision I want to do rebellious? Does it involve rebelling against proper authorities? Does it require disappointing their trust in me? Rebellious decisions are usually not wise decisions.

These three guides will help inform and educate your decisions if you will receive them. There is so much more in the book of Proverbs, but you have to have a heart to receive them and treasure them.

How tragic that many people have the greatest book on how to live life in their homes, but they do not value it enough to read it every day. Bibles on the shelf do not do any good. It is verses in the heart that build a great life.

PROVERBS 3:1

My son, do not forget my teaching, but let your heart keep my commandments

The significant aspect of this bit of wisdom is the depth of the keeping of the commandment. It must be kept by the heart – not just the outer man – to enjoy the benefits of length of days and years of life and peace. Some people seek to put a syrup-sweet coating over an unchanged heart and the power of the command is not activated. These commands deal with changing the heart or, as we would say, the attitude. The power of the internal attitude of the person is far greater than an external conformity to a rule.

The commandments that are being enjoined to be imbedded into your heart seem simple or trite, but they are incredibly profound.

- Do not let kindness and truth leave you
- Trust in the Lord with all your heart
- Do not lean on our own understanding
- In all your ways acknowledge Him
- Do not be wise in your own eyes
- Fear the Lord and turn away from evil
- Honor the Lord from your wealth
- Do not reject the discipline of the Lord

Many times in the reading of the book of Proverbs we miss the commandments in the midst of all the encouragement to embrace them. They are simple and profound and will change your life if you will bring them close and make them the way of your heart.

It is these commandments that I want you to embrace for they will ensure a successful, righteous life for you. God is so great to capsulate the righteous life in these statements. Solomon was remembering them from the teaching his father David gave to him. He decided to share them with the world. I want you to see the radical relevancy. We are too often trying to hear something new instead of spending time on the material from God that has proven itself true over the ages.

Remember that the words that are recorded in Proverbs were written down 3,000 years ago. Think about Solomon in a king's chamber writing down life lessons, little realizing that there would be people studying them 3,000 years later. They have force because they were breathed on by God. Don't miss these ancient lessons in how to have a better life.

PROVERBS 4:1

*Hear, O sons, the instruction of a father, and give attention
that you may gain understanding Hear, O sons*

The word *hear* is the word *shamah* which means to hear but also
carries with it the idea of hearing to obey. This is not just listening to
sounds but hearing so that you may do. You have not heard if you do
not do.

The word *sons* is the typical word for son or grandson. Notice in
verse 3 of this chapter that Solomon's father, David, sat him down and
taught him this information. This is Solomon doing for the whole
world what David, his father, did for him - sitting him down and trying
to give him life lessons that will allow him to avoid many of the
difficulties that will come at him. It is so hard for teens to listen
because they think they know all about everything. It is the
information in this book of Proverbs that they often know the least
about. In fact, most people are not wise and understanding and walk
right into problems, difficulties, and sorrows because they do not
understand.

However you do it, you - who are wise are responsible - sit down
with your children and grandchildren and pass on the wisdom and
understanding that you have. There is a shrinking amount of God's
true wisdom in the world. It is covered over with nonsense and
foolishness. I know one man who every year bought a different Bible
and made notes in it all year for one of his grandchildren. Then he
presented that Bible to that grandchild at the end of the year. These
notes that you are reading are really my attempt to record insights on
life for my grandchildren and great-grandchildren. I hope that my
daughters will keep them and present them to their kids and their kids'
kids if I am not around to do it.

the instruction of a father

The word *instruction* is the word *masar* which means instruction, training, even chastisement. This is not just lessons that Solomon is sharing; it is a training manual. This is training for life.

I am concerned that fathers are shirking their responsibilities as moral teachers and guides of their children. There is no one that your children would rather hear from about life than their dad. They need to hear from dad on these matters. Do not let mom be the only voice that children hear about morality and life. Don't think that the schools will teach this stuff; they won't.

Every time you read an article in the paper about something that your kids should know, clip it out. Every time you come across a verse in Scripture that would help them, write it down and bring it up. Every time you interact with a person and have an interesting interaction - whether it is good or bad - tell them about it. They need dad's perspective on life.

Too many fathers are being sucked into the world system way of thinking that we will make our biggest contribution at work, so put in your highest levels of energy and effort there. No, you will make your deepest impact and most long-lasting effect in your children. It will be a good impact or a lasting legacy of neglect and alienation. Your children are wanting to spend time with you; don't put them off until they are interesting to you. It will be too late. Enjoy them at every stage of life; but most importantly, constantly point out the insights that you have gained about life. These will echo in their lives forever. Be a dad.

and give attention that you may gain understanding

The words *gain understanding* are interesting because they are the words *know understanding*. God wants His children to really intellectually grasp and experientially realize the connection between behaviors, people, events, actions, etc. The key word in this phrase is the word *understanding*. It is the word *binah* and means distinguishment, power of judgment, perceptive insight. It is the ability to see connections between things - cause and effect - and to use that insight to make accurate decisions.

There are all kinds of connections between things that people miss. In the rest of the book of Proverbs, there are over sixty different types of fools mentioned along with their corresponding tendencies. Solomon also catalogues almost ten different types of positive characteristics that group around real wisdom. In other words, find the one and you find the others.

Why is this so important? Because young people do not always pick up on the subtle clues that tell them whether the person they are dealing with is lying or a cheat or using them. So they wander into relationships, enter into business connections, and get burned. God is trying to save us from this. He is saying that there is a connection between how a person carries themselves and what they are like. God is trying to get young people to make the connection between hard work and profit; between slothfulness and poverty; between borrowing and slavery; between planning and accomplishment; between teachability and success; between independence and failure and interdependence and success. Hundreds of these types of comparisons are in this God-breathed book. God had the wisest man who ever lived, other than Jesus, record insights on life in a book so we would enjoy Solomon's success and not repeat his mistakes.

January 5

PROVERBS 5:1
My son, give attention to my wisdom, incline your ear to my understanding

Solomon again emphasizes a crucial point to the man or woman who is willing to let him be their spiritual father. He has brought us various points of the wise life up to this point. Much of it has been positive in its orientation: honor the Lord; hang on to lovingkindness and truth, etc. But in this section of the proverb, Solomon - under the direction of the inspiration of the Holy Spirit - tells us one of the more difficult temptations that will come every man's way: the temptation to live a fool's life through illicit sexual activity. This particular temptation gets a lot of play in the Proverbs because it remains such a strong and lasting need and weak point - with men especially.

Men want and need physical intimacy. They also want and need emotional, mental, and spiritual intimacy. For many men, physical intimacy seems like the quickest path to have all of one's needs met. This is not true, but it seems that way especially to young men. Fornication, adultery, pornography, etc., seem like a great way to meet their need; but in reality they are get-rich-quick schemes for their soul which will bring ruin and destruction to their relationships and their soul. One does not build a great life by pursuing easy sexual relations. One builds a great life by developing discipline and sexual control and by pursuing a woman in righteousness and encouragement.

God, through Solomon, screams at us: Get ready for this temptation! It will come strong and will come often throughout your life. You must be ready for it. You must expect that the pull of this fool's pathway will seem like the right thing to do a number of times in your life. IT NEVER IS.

I have worked with a number of men and women who have committed adultery to try and meet some need in their life. It never does. It only seems like it will when you are under the cloud of emotion in the affair. Sexual foolishness and a lack of sexual discipline destroy relationships; it does not build up anyone.

God gives a whole section of advice to young people about this temptation. He details what will be said. He details what you will feel. He details what you will feel like after it is over. He details the thinking of your unfaithful partner. All of this was written over 3,000 years ago, and it is dead-on accurate.

To pretend that this temptation will not come your way at some point in your life is naive. Get ready because it is coming. Realize just as there will be numerous schemes to separate us from our hard-earned income, so there will be schemes to separate us from faithfulness to our spouse.

It is important to say that even if one is not married - maybe never having been married - one needs to abstain from sexual unfaithfulness because you will be staying faithful to the Lord and potentially your future spouse. When you hold back from these temptations, you are demonstrating faith in God that He will find you a partner and that He has a superior life for you even if it does not include sexual relations at present.

I have had the great privilege of performing a number of weddings in which the person, prior to getting married, presents to their beloved a purity ring that represents a pledge to save themselves for this day.

Notice that Solomon says you need to lean over and look hard at the connections that go on in this temptation. You need to understand how sexuality reaches into all areas of life and connects with men and women, with you, and with those around you.

Are you ready for these temptations - especially in the light of our culture? Are you ready for a seductive tone directed in your direction? Are you ready for someone to express real interest in you whom you know you cannot marry or cannot spend time with without restriction? Are you ready for increased pornography coming into your computer, coming across your path? How will you guard yourself against this?

January 6

PROVERBS 6:1
My son, if you have become surety for a neighbor, have given a pledge for a stranger

This is the classic passage against co-signing a note for someone, so that your financial health is in the hands of another person. Its application can also be stretched to be against borrowing in general, or striking surety, or making a pledge even for yourself.

One should not be involved in promising to pay the debts of another. If a person is not able to secure the necessary financing on their own, it is because they are a bad risk. It is this type of risk or exposure that leaves you completely at the whim, foolishness, or sloth of another.

PROVERBS 7:1

My son, keep my words and treasure my commandments
within you

This is the thirteenth group of instructions to the young learner of wisdom in the book of Proverbs. The master pauses and instructs his pupils in the ways of wisdom in short little groupings.

This is the second packet of instruction on the problem of adultery and how to avoid it. The last packet of information on this subject was in what we call chapter 5 but what was the 7th packet of wisdom information.

This particular pathway of foolishness called adultery is so tempting and such a sure way to be diverted from a fruitful and productive life that Solomon spends a lengthy period of time to give an example of a person he has seen be sucked into this errant path. This type of example or actual story is unique in the book of Proverbs, suggesting that this diversion from the path of wisdom is the most common or the most powerful. Those who would learn wisdom or live wisdom must be aware of the power and the danger of this foolish direction.

The point of this section of the proverb is to show the results of those who go down this path. Solomon even shares the nature of the conversation and the look of the woman. We are taken inside the foolishness so that its powerful, seductive energy will be known to us and thereby not as intoxicating. Solomon is saying: watch for this; watch for that; this is what it will feel like; don't get fooled by this. It is all the same and has been that way since the time of Solomon and before.

The young learner is to observe the interaction of adultery from a safer emotional distance. They are to see the trap being sprung and the effect in the individual. He wishes that he had not done it even though he wanted with all his being to do it before he did it.

treasure my commandments within you

The things I am saying are so valuable - is what Solomon is saying. You have to realize the value and embrace that value. This is not relative value; this is absolute value. If you want to have a life filled with riches, honor, and life, then do not go down this path. The seductions of the adulterous and adulterer are strong and seem incredibly valuable, but they are fake pearls and cosmetic jewelry. They have no real value compared to wisdom. Remember these lessons and do not give in to the pull of illicit sexual behavior.

In our day and age this type of lesson needs to be taught to young men from 11 to 65 years of age and maybe beyond. The spread of pornography and a loose culture adds to the acceptance of this wisdom-destroying action. Realize that if one is to make something of one's life and not get shoved into a dead end cul-de-sac in life, one has to practice self-limiting behavior. Only when we practice self-control and stop ourselves short of all we could do, do we prepare ourselves for great relationships and have the control and energy to excel at what is really important.

Proverbs 8:1
Does not wisdom call, and understanding lift up her voice?

What is amazing about this verse is that God tells us that wisdom is not unknown or mysterious. Wisdom is calling attention to itself; it is usually overlooked. According to this verse, wisdom is telling us what to do; we just don't hear its message.

The idea is that someone or something in your life is telling you the right thing to do. The question is - will you have the discernment to know which one that is and be willing to do it when lots of your own thinking says to do something different?

There are all kinds of reasons why we do not listen to the voice of wisdom; many of them are the reasons of a fool. It is not what we want to do. It doesn't feel right. It is a lot of work to do that. It means I have to work harder than other people. It means I have to be disciplined to pull it off. It means I don't get as much rest. It means that I would need to let others win and even promote their winning. It means that I will not get immediate credit for doing something. It means that I must let others win in order for me to win. It means that I can no longer just be the critic looking for the flaws in others plans. I must try to make a difference.

There are all these and many other reasons that any of us ignore the voice of wisdom that calls to us. The wise thing is never that far from any of us. It just doesn't sound easy or risk free or quick.

understanding lift up her voice

Remember that understanding is the connection between things. It is not a mystery why things happen as they do. We just often do not want to face the real reason - either politically, psychologically, or for some other reasons. We don't want to admit that a connection between one thing and another thing exists. In our culture people don't want to admit that there is a connection between pornography and child abuse.

People don't want to admit there is a connection between liberal enforcement of current laws and increasing violence. There are all kinds of connections that are real, but we do not want to admit that they are present. They scream to us, but we are often paddling on the river of denial.

Most importantly, there is a connection between the choices that you have made and the condition that you find yourself in. It is not a mystery why you have the career you have, the house you have, the marriage or children you have. These result from the choices that you make. If these areas are not what you want them to be, then make different choices starting now. Start listening to wisdom; start listening to understanding.

This is not to say that there is not injustice in the world where one person oppresses another person. This is present, but that also involves connections and choices. One should not submit to oppression, immorality, degrading conditions. New choices need to be made. It is true that the perpetrator of these things should be punished, but hoping they will be given justice will not make it happen. You may be the person who starts the wheels of justice turning. Potentially, just your act of no longer being under this immoral oppression may begin the change that will lead to justice, but at least it will change your situation.

PROVERBS 9:1

Wisdom has built her house, she has hewn out her seven pillars. She has prepared her food, she has mixed her wine, she has also set her table, she has sent out her maidens, she calls from the tops of the heights of the city.

The book of Proverbs - and especially chapters 8, 9, and 10 - are about the acquisition of wisdom. And this opening of chapter 9 notes a crucial aspect of wisdom. Wisdom is not in the speculation or talk or dreams of people. True biblical wisdom has actually produced something that has lasted. Notice the verb tenses of this section. Wisdom has built her house. She has hewn out. She has prepared her food. She has mixed her wine.

In other words, when you want to find wisdom, you look for those who have actually accomplished something and not the salesmen who can talk about what they will do and not the professor who spins logical fantasies. When you want to really lock onto wisdom, you ask yourself who has actually accomplished what I want to do. There is always someone. Wisdom is practical and real. Too often we listen to the dream weavers and wordsmiths who make it sound like their ideas will work, but they bring devastation.

Our culture has followed the visions of fools with open marriages, domestic partners, the children will be better if we divorce, junk bonds, stock speculations, all religions are the same or lead to the same place, completely free speech, pornography is not harmful and is protected speech, we evolved from monkeys and slime.

It doesn't matter which relationship in your life needs a dose of wisdom - God, Self, Marriage, Family, Work, Church, Money, Society or Friends. There is always someone who actually has a very together relationship; someone who has actually put that part of their life together. Listen to them. Ask them.

We all desperately need wisdom, and we are often deceived as from whom to receive it. Get it from those who have actually accomplished the wisdom you are looking for. If you wanted to build a building, would you talk with someone who has never successfully built a building or someone who has built a number of buildings and they are beautiful and functional. If you want to fix your marriage, would you talk with someone who has a broken marriage or someone who is living in a happy and contented marriage? If you wanted to become financially free and solvent, would you talk with the person who is deep in debt and working many schemes and plans or someone who is contented, solvent, and debt free? If you wanted to build a church that was healthy, growing, strong, and vital, you should talk with those who have grown a church that was healthy, growing, strong, and vital and not those who theorize about how a church ought to be. If you wanted to enjoy a great family life, you should talk to those who enjoy a great family life and not those who can make great speeches about family life but don't want to spend time with their families.

The Bible is clear: Wisdom is in the heart of those who over a significant period of time have demonstrated the type of wisdom that you are looking for. Do not be fooled by those who are merely rhetoricians - those who can make things sound nice but have not done anything in their own life.

I am greatly concerned that our culture is about to collapse because we do the opposite of this principle of wisdom. Most of our marriage counselors have failing or dreadful marriages. We are more interested in listening to actors and actresses who have played farmers or bankers than we are listening to successful farmers and bankers. We want to explore the boundaries of licentiousness so we let those who are mired in depression, guilt, and brokenness advise us about what is normal, acceptable, and desirable. We are unwilling to really look at the consequences of our actions but want to just keep telling ourselves that these problems we are seeing are normal. We do not want to admit that we are living with the consequences of our foolishness.

PROVERBS 10:1

The proverbs of Solomon: a wise son makes a father glad, but a foolish son is a grief to his mother

This chapter marks the beginning of a new section in the book of Proverbs. These are still inspired by God and written through the pen of Solomon, but these are more individual in their attention than the last section.

This section of the proverbs are insights into life and comparisons that point out unique and little-seen ways of finding and living out life wisely. Notice that Solomon will point out a truth by comparing it with another thing in order to highlight a particular truth. He will say that this is more valuable than that. In this way he is helping us establish priorities for our decision making. He will show cause and effect that is often overlooked in the ordinary course of life.

Remember, also, that he will connect these proverbs through thought rhymes. This Jewish device provides the context to the proverbs. In the west we are impressed with word rhymes, but in the ancient culture they used thought rhymes where each verse is linked to the verse directly before it or two verses previous by a similar thought. This insight hooks to another insight about the same or similar idea even though the application is in a completely different aspect of life. This is a very powerful form of learning called hooked learning. It is almost like a person is saying, "I found that insight fascinating; do you have any more insights about that truth?" The teacher then tells you about another place that truth applies.

a wise son makes a father glad

There is a question whether this is written for parents or for children. One of the things that all boys want to do is have their dads be proud of them. Solomon is saying that the surest way to have your dad be proud of you and burst with pride about you and your accomplishments is if you become wise. If a father can show how his son has beat the odds and is a wise man with others respecting his advice and demonstrating a real level of success through that wisdom, this will make a father proud. Solomon clues children in with this so that they do not have to guess as to how to make their parents proud. Become wise and your dad especially will be proud.

This proverb is also aimed at parents in that it is the parents who largely determine whether the child becomes wise. It is their shepherding and care that determines whether a child has any interest in becoming a giving, patient, team player. If a parent is never around and does not demonstrate the essential qualities of wisdom, then where will the child pick them up?

On a personal note, I have to say that a large percentage of the desire for wisdom that I have comes from being raised by my father who is one of the wisest men I have ever known. As I was growing up he constantly pointed out the difference between two choices and where the results would go. He was there to love, support, direct, and correct me. He also was an incredibly consistent role model of what a wise man looked like. My hope is that I make him proud in my attainment of wisdom.

Parents, there is nothing but grief waiting for you if you neglect to raise your children with love and wisdom. There are few things more painful than watching one or more of your children turn their lives into a train wreck. Put the time in to make sure they know that you love them. Point out the good and bad choices that are available to them. Correct them and nurture them. Listen to them and don't always feel like you have to have the last word.

Wise children are a wonderful gift that you have a big part in creating.

PROVERBS 11:1

A false balance is an abomination to the Lord, but a just weight is His delight

The essence of wisdom is contained in this little proverb. If others have to lose for you to win, then it can't be wisdom. The only exception to that is that the wicked will often lose when the righteous and the wise win.

Stealing through deceptive business practices means that one party is the winner and other parties are the losers. This is not the basis of a healthy economy. A healthy economy is the transfer of goods for a certain value that is agreed upon where everyone agrees on the worth of the item.

If a business is built on trickery and deception, it may prosper for the short term; but it will not make it in the long run. It will be discovered and cease to exist or pay a heavy price for its win-lose strategy.

When a person has an everybody wins philosophy in its business, then it is the delight of the Lord.

January 12

PROVERBS 12:1

Whoever loves discipline loves knowledge, but he who hates reproof is stupid

How much do you love to learn new ways to improve? How much correction can you stand? Do you really want to get better at your job, parenting, marriage, and living for God? Then you must be willing to be corrected so you can make progress in those areas.

It is not possible to make progress without change and realizing that there is a better way.

There are an awful lot of people who want better marriages, families, careers, and connections with God. They just don't want to change anything. If they are willing to change something, they are willing to add something. But they are often unwilling to eliminate anything. We act as though nothing we are doing is hindering any part of our life. We act as though maybe we aren't doing something we should but never that we are right now doing something we shouldn't.

This proverb says that whoever really loves knowledge also loves correction, rebuke, chastisement, and instruction in the proper way. It is the willingness to be corrected that tests our real love of knowledge.

whoever loves discipline loves knowledge

The Hebrew word translated *discipline* here in the NASB is the word *musawr* which means instruction, correction, chastisement, rebuke. In this context it seems to carry with it the idea of contrary information because of the parallel idea given in the second half of the proverb: but he who hates reproof is stupid.

In other words, the person who really wants to display that they are interested in knowledge and not just getting their own way will be open to contrary knowledge - knowledge that is a rebuke to the way that you have been living; knowledge that means you must change.

Think of instruction as feedback. All of us use and enjoy feedback. When we drive and turn the steering wheel, we need the feedback of where the car actually goes to give us feedback and what to do with the steering wheel next. When we are trying to convince someone of something or sell them something, we need the feedback of what they are thinking about what we are saying. Without the feedback, we will keep doing what we think is right even though it gets no results. There are all kinds of feedback experiments where people have been hooked up to monitors and they get to see how their stomach responds to particular stresses and thoughts. People have learned how to overcome their fears and the like.

What Solomon is saying is that instruction is feedback that is desperately needed and appreciated by the wise.

but he who hates reproof is stupid

This tells us that no matter what a person says about their love of truth or wisdom or knowledge, if they are unwilling to listen to correction or contrary information, they are really not after knowledge. The word *stupid* is the word *baar* which means brutish, dull, foolish.

The real questions for us to ponder are:

- Do you know someone like this? Someone who says they are interested in truth and knowledge, but they are unwilling to be given contrary information?

- Are you willing to listen while someone gives you contrary information?

- Are you willing to listen when someone - who clearly knows more - corrects you about your behavior? Or are you looking for a reason to disregard what they are saying?

One of the key characteristics of maturity I look for in my own kids is when they can take correction willingly and learn from it. Without the willingness to listen, gain from, and change appropriately from real contrary truth, a person is stuck in a fool's cycle having only themselves as the final judge of truth and stupidity.

The life of the wise person is re-directable by real knowledge. Therefore your life must always be willing to submit to real truth.

When was the last time you asked your boss for five ways you could be a better employee?

PROVERBS 13:1

A wise son accepts his father's discipline, but a scoffer does not listen to rebuke

The first verses of this chapter of Proverbs discuss speech and words. This is the context of this discussion. So much of what we experience in life is the result of what we say to others. Very few people really understand that. The type of marriage and the climate for our family are all created by the way we speak and the speech that we allow others to use. If the speech is harsh and biting or deprecating, then the environment is stormy and cold.

This section of the proverbs - as well as other whole sections - deal with paying attention to what people say to you and saying what you say well. We don't have the freedom to just say whatever comes to our minds. This will usually get us into trouble.

a wise son accepts his father's discipline

The actual Hebrew verse reads: *a wise son a father's correction*. There is no verb accepts or receives in the actual verse. It needs to be supplied. This is interesting because the whole of the book of Proverbs would suggest that we fill in a stronger word than accepts. We should potentially use the word *seeks out*.

Now the critical idea is that a son who is wise is connected to his father's correction. He doesn't push away at it. It is impossible to learn to play the game of life to win without being corrected. It is the people who we allow to correct us that determine how much and what kind of success that we will have.

Fathers have more experience and can look down the road of life further than their children in most cases. Fathers - in most cases - want what is best for their children.

This verse talks about two skills that must be developed: the father's ability to correct and the child's ability to accept or receive correction. Both must be present to produce a wise son or daughter.

There are issues in which a child must be willing to take correction: choice of mate; work habits; career; friends; attitude; temptations; use of time. We are, unfortunately, living in a culture that expects children to rebel against their parents' advice right at the time they need it most. The choices that children make in the teen years can set the tone for the whole of their lives. Many never recover from the selfish choices they make in these turbulent years.

In this process, parents, of correcting your children it is best to ask questions about the consequences of choices rather than just lay the law down as you did when your children were in the younger years. Ask questions like: What do you think happens to the typical person who makes that kind of choice? What are some other things that people could do other than that choice?

It is the skillful use of questions that allows a teen to accept their father's correction. I have found that most teens will come to good conclusions if they are given enough real facts about a situation.

Teens and young adults, it is absolutely imperative that you learn how to be corrected. I watch people all the time who cannot handle correction or even constructive criticism. Some fight back against any form of help, instruction, or training. They already know all that. Some blame others for anything that is pointed out. This is not a winning play. Learn to accept responsibility. Jesus says that one of the qualities of a blessed person is the ability to mourn. Some immediately impugn the motives of anyone who would dare suggest that their performance could be improved or had flaws. Some are in complete and immediate denial about the opportunity or need for improvement.

One of the ways to separate the young people who will make the most progress in life is those who can receive correction well and make appropriate adjustments.

On a totally different level, a Christian is always under His heavenly father's scrutiny. The book of Hebrews tells us that God chastises and corrects every person whom He loves. We should get ready for correction and training for better accomplishments. God loves us and wants us to be the most we can be. This means that God will put you in difficult circumstances. This means that God will, in a sense, spank you when you sin. This means that a good Christian who is learning to be wise does not run away when this happens. He or she does not blame God when God is trying to make them a better person.

but a scoffer does not listen to rebuke

The word *scorn* is the Hebrew word *lason* and means to be proud, haughty, ridiculing, and putting down. People who try to elevate themselves above others by putting down any criticism of themselves or others are fools. It is the cynical view that is so prevalent in our day. In fact, it is the ability to criticize that is held up as the intelligent and noble thing to do. Many of our best and brightest have become critics instead of producing any positive action. Don't become a scoffer. Listen to correction and training.

Now this does not mean that there is not a time for a critical analysis of any endeavor. There is always need for objective review. But just don't become a scoffer - that mocking cynic who has been jaded so badly by something or someone that they cannot see the good, the positive, the hopeful, and the helpful.

If a person is not willing to be corrected, that person effectively stops growing and life has become maintenance. Hardening of the viewpoint is deadly. Listen to the critic - especially when it is someone who really loves you and has your best interest at heart.

Learn the fine art of receiving correction well. "Thank you for sharing that; I will think about that." "You know I would have never seen it that way before. That is going to take some thought to really process what you just said. Thanks. I will spend some time thinking about it."

January 14

PROVERBS 14:1
The wise woman builds her house, but the foolish tears it down with her own hands

It is clear that the woman who is wise does those things that will build a flourishing home and family. The foolish woman, however, does that which is selfish and that which she wants and does not think about what it will do to her home, her family, or herself; just whether she wants to do it at the moment it presents itself.

Making the choices, actions, and the speech of a wise person is to think through the results of what you could do. If I do this, then my husband will be discouraged, mad, and distant. If I do this, the family will not have the money to do that. If I do this, then my children will have the sense that I do not have time for them.

The wise woman arranges activities that will build the family. These are often small decisions that slowly build a great family.

The verse is clearly suggesting that it is in each wife's hands to control her own destiny in regard to her home life. She can build a great family OR she can tear it down by her own actions. The environment that she lives in is really up to her. She is not a victim of her husband or her children but can, through looking for the triple-win, create a good environment for herself and her family to live in.

If it's to be, it's up to me is a great phrase. Wisdom does pay off. Too often we sacrifice long-term joy for short-term pleasure and end up with a heap of troubles.

We are not victims. We create our own environment. Many women and men are acting like they are victims of the circumstances around them because they do not realize how small choices that they can make can, in a relatively short time, change everything.

Ask yourself the question: Is what you are doing building the house and family and yourself or is it tearing it down? If it is purely selfish, then it is probably tearing it down. If it has multiple benefits for many, then it is a building thing. It is in your hands; start building.

January 15

PROVERBS 15:1

A gentle answer turns away wrath, but a harsh word stirs up anger

Chapter 15 of Proverbs is a whole chapter that has verses about the tongue, mouth, prayer, speech, lips, etc. It is the how-to-use-your-tongue-wisely chapter. Since our mouths get us into more trouble than almost anything else in our lives, this would be a great chapter to camp on. It is the positive counterpart to James 2 and the tongue being a fire.

This verse gives the solution to what to do when someone is upset with you. The answer is a gentle answer. To defuse a situation, your words must have a softness and tenderness. This means the tone as well as the words themselves.

Too often people will speak their mind when they are being attacked. They will let fly with the emotions that are raging within them. This is always a mistake. When someone is angry with you, you have to defuse the situation with your words and demeanor – gentleness. The natural reaction of anyone to another person's anger is to reflect back on their anger and stir up more. As one recent study showed, emotions are contagious. You can actually pick up the emotional climate from another person.

In the case of anger, you must keep from catching another person's mood and must re-infect the other person and people with a gentle, conciliatory, and adaptable mood.

When someone is already angry and you speak directly, forcefully, or even honestly, it usually produces more anger. Most people want to defend themselves or set someone straight in the face of the greatest emotion. This rarely, if ever, works; it only exacerbates the process. A person cannot let you win an argument when they are under the spell of anger; it only makes them angrier. The opportunity to reason will come later when tempers are calm.

Too often we only want to debate a subject at the worst time to debate it – when the topic is charged with emotion. If something is worth discussing, then it is worth finding a time when the discussion can be carried on without the emotions; and that requires that the angry person be defused. Many people are like the chess players who only thought about the move they were on instead of thinking five or more moves ahead. When dealing with an emotional topic, one has to think five or more moves ahead. Defuse the situation now. Listen to the kernel of truth in the blast. Plan a time to discuss the topic rationally. Develop a way of speaking about another viewpoint that will not re-stir the emotions. Create a positive climate of interaction – bring up the discussion in a nonchalant way as to keep it under the rational aspects of our being rather than the emotional.

January 16

PROVERBS 16:1

The plans of the heart belong to man, but the answer of the tongue is from the Lord

The whole of the first four verses of the 16th proverb is about the plans and direction that you are making. This is the way to discern what God wants you to do:

- First, listen to what you yourself are saying; it could be God trying to get through.

- Second, check your motives. Why are you planning to do a particular thing?

- Third, to make sure that you have God's best for you, pray a lot about it and actually go over the whole plan with God.

- Fourth, understand your purpose and that God has made everything else for a purpose. You won't find what you are to do until you understand your purpose.

the plans of the heart belong to man

There are deep questions to ponder in this proverb. Is God saying that He allows humans to think their thoughts and have responsibility over their own soul, but He is able to control its output under certain situations?

Is God suggesting that we should make our plans as best we can but pay attention to what we say as the Lord will reveal His will through the things we say?

The word *plan* is the word preparation or arrangement in the Hebrew. It means that part of one's life that one plans and seeks to set in order through arrangement. This is a crucial part of living life – making arrangements. It is not more spiritual or godly to just react and go with the natural flow. The natural flow may be sinful.

It is important to realize that this proverb is saying that God does not give us our thoughts to think. We are not puppets on a string in which God is the scriptwriter and the director. The plans that we have actively pursued are ours. There is a strain of Christianity that says that God has predestined everything that everyone will ever think, say, or do. This proverb says no. The thoughts and plans that you have are your own.

but the answer of the tongue is from the Lord

God does speak in those odd-between moments when you speak and out flows some of those things that even you did not expect. It is this ability that God has to interject into your speech – His thoughts and His will – that should keep us paying attention. This kind of thinking is contrary to much of our rationalistic and psychological thinking, but the Scripture declares that God can allow us to understand what He is saying or directing through what we ourselves say. It is amazing.

January 17

PROVERBS 17:1
*Better is a dry morsel and quietness with it than a house full
of feasting with strife*

The word *better* appears throughout the Proverbs as a means of
establishing value. Usually the things compared are reversed in their
value in the eyes of most. Wisdom is seeing the value in what the
proverb points out. Wisdom realizes that things are not always as they
seem. When you see the word *better*, remember that the proverb is
trying to get us to question what we value with this type of proverb.
Which item has a higher price tag in your world?

In the proverb before us, bread with contentment is contrasted with
rich parties with anger. Most people in Solomon's day and in our own
would choose rich parties with anger. Most figure that people will get
over their anger or that we can always get new friends or now a new
family. But Solomon presses us with the idea that if the relationships of
your life are not connected, you don't have a life no matter how much
money you have.

Solomon had experienced all of the parties and riches a person
could ever want, but he had also developed the anger and seething
bitterness that multiple wives and concubines can create. He testifies
under the inspiration of God to take the relational vitality and little
money over lots of money with anger and bitterness.

Now there is nothing wrong with big parties. The point in this
proverb is that if you have strife, it is not as good as being poor and yet
loved. There is a great joy that comes from relational peace where
everybody in your relational circles is okay with you.

There is another angle on this proverb, and that is that the words
translated *feasting with strife* is really the phrase *sacrifices of strife* or the
offerings of strife. In other words, you have been making sacrifices to the
god of strife in order to obtain the money that you have heaped up for
yourselves. This type of wealth will rot your soul. There are many in

our day that have chosen this method of wealth building. This type of wealth building is usually the product of an unbalanced life. This type of wealth building is not necessarily illegal or immoral; it is just relationship killing.

The thinking goes like this: I will work 20 hours a day for a period of time to make a lot of money and then spend time with my family and friends. This thinking says that I am sacrificing all of my time to make money for my family. I have to be rude to the family and my friends and co-workers now in order to close this deal, and then I can make nice when the money comes in. I have watched people be sucked into this type of short-term sacrifice – everything for a little extra money – for years. We are being lulled into this type of capsulated life where we focus on only one aspect of our lives to the exclusion of the others, hoping the other relationships of our life hold on until we are ready to give them some time. This is folly. Life is a whole; it has nine relationships in it and all must be constantly developed and recharged.

Don't be suckered into an unbalanced life by the pressure of our world. Be transformed by renewing your mind that God's ways are better. If I have to produce strife in order to have rich parties, then they are not worth it. If I have to betray my friends, family, and others to build up wealth, then I have the wrong way of wealth accumulation. There are career paths in our culture today that leave a man or woman wealthy but alone and often bitter. Don't go down that road or change the way you go down that career path.

Are there things that you can do today that will demonstrate that you believe in relational peace over riches and strife? Could you apologize to someone? Could you balance your life more? Could you invest more deeply in the people in your life? Could you find a new way of making money that does not require so much time away from home?

January 18

PROVERBS 18:1
He who separates himself seeks his own desire, he quarrels against all sound wisdom

This seems to refer to the person who, in the midst of a team-work type of interaction, breaks away and will not consider other people's point of view; does not want to be involved in the normal give-and-take of relationships; does not want to win some and lose some. This person wants to win every encounter with others. This is the person who will not reengage with people because it means admitting that they were wrong or selfish. They just want it their way.

This type of selfishness brings a temporary peace to their world, but it costs them dearly. If you cannot be involved in human relationships and the give-and-take that requires, then you cut yourself off from wisdom. Wisdom is about three people winning: God, others, and I.

This does not mean that you have to always be surrounded by people or you always have to give in to the demands or wishes of the group. The separation desire is usually a selfish desire and should be understood as such.

PROVERBS 19:1

Better is a poor man who walks in his integrity than he who is perverse in speech and is a fool

This is one of those value proverbs where God, through Solomon's observations, is trying to teach us the importance of something by comparing it with something else we would not expect.

This particular proverb is a very interesting and strange sounding comparison to our ears. We are essentially asked which do you think is better – this kind of person or that kind of person? We may not want to be either, but it highlights that right value that Solomon wants us to see.

The word *integrity* is the Hebrew word *tom* which means complete, perfect, finished. It can have the theological meaning of righteousness or perfection or being without sin. We have to be careful that we do not immediately apply the theological meaning to this word every time it appears.

The word *poor* is the word *ras* which means poverty or poor. The Hebrew word translated here *walks* is the word *halik* which means steps or movement in general. There are two different directions that this first phrase could mean. It could be understood that this is a poor person; a person who does not have enough to feed himself or his family; is complete or contented in his poverty and does not have the usual drive to feed his belly. Another possible understanding of the poor person is one who lives in the midst of his poverty or lack of basic necessity without going outside of law to try and gain what he needs. One interpretation focuses on the lack of drive in the poor person – his sloth or lack of industry – and the other interpretation focuses on his unwillingness to be sinful, even to gain basic necessity.

One has to understand the basic orientation of the proverbs and this period in biblical history toward wealth and poverty. The idea was that one's wealth was a sign of God's blessing upon your life. The richer you were, the more blessed and loved by God you were. This was a tangible way for people to see the strength of your faith. Abraham, Job, and David were all wealthy, righteous men. In our day and age we tend to see wealth and riches as a sign of greed and law breaking. Realize that from the biblical perspective, one who does not make money through the pain or harm of others; is generous with tithes and offerings; does not go outside the boundaries of the Ten Commandments to make their money; and is generous with their employees; and still has a growing pile of goods is not unrighteous. God has blessed this person and put them in the place where they can provide for themselves and others and even fund the movement of the kingdom of God.

The second clause talks about the perverse in speech. The word perverse is the Hebrew word *iqques* which means crooked, twisted, perverse. The normal use of words and speech has been abandoned for a twisted, sinful, crooked pattern of speech that in this case is all harnessed for selfish purposes. This would include those who flatter others to get what they want; those who use speech to con people out of their goods; those who talk their way into ladies' hearts; those who twist logic and argumentation to prove that there is no god or that we developed from slime. The "say anything" idea to get what you want. Notice that this does not necessarily mean that the person curses or swears.

Therefore, contrast is between a poor person who has no drive to get out of his poverty or is unwilling to break God's law to move out of poverty versus a person who has lots of selfish drive and uses words to fulfill it. In that day there was the natural tendency to excuse the fast-talking, selfish person but to see the poor person as lazy and unblessed. God, through Solomon, is saying to look again. If the smooth-talking salesman gains goods, hearts, trust, and position through lies, half-truths, and distortions, then the poor person is more blessed and of a higher value. It is not what you have but how you got it that God wants us to understand in this proverb. Value the process and the motive.

If you become rich or wealthy by twisting words and tricking people, then you are a poor person and will eventually be discovered as such – usually because those closest to you want nothing to do with you. They are tired of your word-twisting, lying games. Remember it is the richness of relationships that is the true riches that fill houses and bring life its joy and treasure. Someone whose words cannot be trusted does not build true rich relationships but only shallow surface interactions.

Make sure that you are a person who people can trust to mean what you say and say what you mean. If you have to lie or tell a half-truth to get what you want, you are impoverished when you gain it.

January 20

PROVERBS 20:1

Wine is a mocker, strong drink is a brawler, and whoever is intoxicated by it is not wise

This proverb is one of the basic lessons of a wise life. Don't get captured by alcohol. It is a selfish pursuit. Most people just assume that everyone knows this truth, but they don't – especially the young people who the proverbs are aimed at.

How much harm and heartache could have been avoided if this simple proverb had been heeded? Think of all the things that wouldn't have been said; all of the hurt that wouldn't have been done. Think of all the positive things that could have been done that weren't done because that time and energy was spent on drinking or recovering from being drunk.

People in that day – as in our own day – resort to beer, wine, liquor to take the edge off and to cause the troubles of the day to seem less intense. It will do that, but it will release levels of selfishness and even contentiousness that will not serve you well. I am amazed at the number of people who will argue for the positive result of the calming effect of alcohol but totally ignore the relational wreckage that also accompanies it. They do not want to see the whole picture – just one little positive to justify the activity.

Wine and strong drink are mentioned in this passage as intoxicants or those that lower social inhibitions and open the selfishness of a person's soul to the outside world. This is why wine is considered a mocker. All the snide and cutting comments that you would say – but social etiquette keeps you from saying – can come rushing out when you are drunk. The problem is that once you have said those things, you can't take them back. People don't say, "Well, he was drunk; he didn't mean it." They often think, "This is what they really feel."

The end statement of this proverb is clear and telling: *whoever is intoxicated by it is not wise*. The word that we translate *intoxicated* is the Hebrew word *saga* which means led astray or into error. Solomon lets us know that wine will lead us into error and that is not wise.

Drinking wine in order to be drunk is a selfish pursuit and will often lead a person into some form of error whether negative actions or lack of positive actions.

Just steer clear of this form of selfishness and your chances of wisdom improve dramatically. Notice that the proverbs advise us to steer clear of the sexually aggressive person, wine, the violent or angry person, the cynic. These are red flags in life's pathway. Spending time with these people or objects is a selfish pursuit that is better left unpursued. It looks fun, interesting, exciting, and enriching; but it isn't.

January 21

PROVERBS 21:1
The King's heart is like channels of water in the hand of the Lord. He turns it wherever He wishes

There are a number of observations to make here.

the King's heart

It is the leader's mind that is being discussed. We must understand that God can redirect the thinking of a leader anytime one of his larger purposes will be served by that redirection. It is a great comfort to realize that when my purposes line up with God's, then He is able to move those in authority over me to do things that they may not have been inclined to do before.

When I am the leader that is in question, I must realize that God is moving me to a place of recognizing His direction and His purpose. It is not by accident that we hear the things that we hear or see the things that we see. He really is able to give me the desires that He wants me to have. Psalm 37:4

I hope and pray that my children understand that they will not always get their way but when their plans, prayers, and actions line up with God, then He is able to change the thinking of their parents, government officials, husbands, and whoever is legitimately in authority over them.

Underneath the fabric of this text is the sovereignty of God – that wonderful truth that assures us that God has not lost control of the universe. Notice that the flow of the king was in a certain direction, but it did not line up with God's direction so God changes the way the leader thinks. There is something bigger than your getting your own way; there is the plan and purpose of God. The sovereignty of God allows for freedom and creativity within the purpose and plan of God;

but if your freedom will damage or destroy the larger purpose of God, He will control your choices and even your heart. What is fascinating – and at the same time difficult – is that God declares that He does mess with the leader's thoughts and emotions which is the equivalent of heart.

One of the larger questions is will we cooperate with the movement of God on our soul or will we fulfill the Lord's will from the negative position like Sampson? God was constantly directing Sampson as the leader, but it was through his sinfulness and Sampson had no joy or enjoyment of the victories that he won. David, on the other hand, was one who was tender to the Lord and when He was directed he stayed righteous and enjoyed the path that God had for him.

God has selected a path for each one of my children. If they adapt themselves to the pathway of God in righteousness in this life, they will have its share of joys and love. If they seek to find their own path outside of the will of God and righteousness, they will end up fulfilling His purposes but will not enjoy the journey.

One of the things I count on is that if I am going in the wrong direction, God will direct me like a channel of water to the right direction even though it may take me a while to catch up with the joy or reason for that change.

He turns it wherever He wishes

The phrase *He turns it wherever He wishes* could also accurately be translated *He inclines it wherever He delights*. The question becomes is it possible to rebel against this inclination that the Lord puts on our heart? While different theological camps have argued this one, it is the most helpful to look at this practically. Do not rebel against the inclination of the Lord even though parts of your being do not want what He is leaning you toward. You will have a miserable time fighting against God and end up fulfilling His purpose anyway.

The next verse would suggest that it is possible to rebel from the inclination that God puts on the heart for it states that God weighs hearts or judges them. It is not possible to judge or weigh hearts if the person has no say in what the heart becomes.

This suggest that we have the opportunity to develop our souls into wonderfully developed places where God and His inclinations are welcome or we can reject the inclinations of God as pious goody, goody impulses that should be ignored in a sinful world. The Bible is a whole book about the development of the soul and its effect on your life. If you give in to selfishness, then you get a shrunken negative soul. If you give in or follow God's inclination, then you enjoy an enlarged soul and the power and blessings of God in spite of what your outward circumstances may be.

PROVERBS 22:1

*A good name is to be more desired than great wealth, favor
is better than silver and gold*

Throughout life you will be tempted to surrender your good name
for a short-term gain - maybe a boyfriend or a girlfriend, maybe profits,
maybe prestige or power. Whatever compromise is required is not
worth it. Your good name and your best approximate at righteous
integrity is more important than any short-term gain.

In fact, your integrity will guide you by keeping you out of deals
that will in the short-run launch you, but in the long-run rob you of
real joy and peace.

People will try and get you to compromise your high standards, to
lighten up, to loosen up, to live like everyone else. But we have
watched countless numbers of singers, actors, politicians, and
businessmen go that path to their everlasting sorrow. They have shrunk
their soul for a short-term material gain.

What does it profit a man if he gains the whole world but loses his
own soul? Go for soul wholeness and not the short-term solution.

favor is better than silver and gold

The word *favor* is the word to grant a favor or to be gracious
toward. It is used of God in being gracious to sinners. The word,
therefore, carries with it the idea of being placed in a position of favor
even if one does not deserve it.

This proverb states that it is better to have others place you in a
category of favor in their mind than to have a lot of money or
possessions but have no one think well or favorably of you.

There will be many times you will be tempted to cut off a friend or
colleague for a short-term gain. It is not worth it. ***Life is relationships***.

If your relationships are a mess, your life is a mess. You have to have people give you grace and place you in a favored position.

Think through the implications of this proverb and act upon the truth. How do you gain favor in the eyes of your spouse or your employer or your friends or your children? It is these small actions you take that are the crucial building blocks to a great life. It is also your turning away from some material blessings in order to retain a good name that is required to have a great life.

I think of how many men and women have been seduced into giving all their time and energy to a job and regularly missing time with their children. Will those children be impressed with the overtime pay or a new job title? No, they want a parent who has time for them.

What would it take for you to have a good name in the eyes of those closest to you? There is a priority order to love. It starts with God and then moves out to spouse, then children, then colleagues, Christian friends, friends, and then society in general. There is a lie in our culture that being famous is extremely important. But being famous usually deals with the last priority group.

PROVERBS 23:1

*When you sit down to dine with a ruler, consider carefully
what is before you*

This proverb teaches conduct around a superior. How are you to
act when you are in the presence of a leader above yourself?

It clearly follows, as advice, the verse that ends chapter 22. If you
are gifted and skilled enough to be noticed by great men or rulers, then
be prepared to be ushered into the presence of luxuries and delicacies
that will be extremely tempting. This is almost like a warning: no
matter what you see and no matter how bad you want it, hold yourself
back; show restraint, moderation, and control over your desires or you
won't be in the presence of great people long.

The caution is that you should not act naturally or casually but
instead should realize who you are with, a person who makes decisions
about you and your future. A little forethought and self-control in these
instances goes a long way.

sit down to dine

This is a key phrase and needs to be explored. To dine with
someone in the ancient world of the Bible suggests a level of interest,
intimacy, or examination. It's as if you have been invited to have lunch
with your boss or have been asked to eat with a person who could
make or break your career.

ruler

This is a boss or king or someone who is clearly in authority over
you and eating a meal with you. This is past a business context and
offers an opportunity to relax and/or get beneath the surface.
Solomon's practical advice is that you do not seem too eager to
consume or have what they may offer.

The ability to control your desires is crucial to moving up in responsibility. Many people cannot understand why they do not get promoted or why they are not brought into the confidence of some very important person. It is often because they do not exercise enough self-control.

I fully expect that this will one day be read by my great-grandchildren whom I will never meet and whom I will not have the privilege of training on what to look out for and how to conduct themselves when they are invited to eat with a girlfriend's parents, when they are invited out by the bosses at the company, or when an agent offers to take them out to a meal. So I want them to realize that God has left this inspired, permanent record of what to do in all kinds of situations. God had Solomon – one of the richest and wisest kings in all of human history – record insights into how to live. Pay attention to what God is saying through Solomon. In this case Solomon says: Don't relax; remember who you are with, eat less than you would, and don't give into temptations.

PROVERBS 24:1
Do not be envious of evil men, nor desire to be with them

This is a strong prescription against this behavior. This is the same sentiment that is registered in Psalm 73: *I was envious of the wicked until I perceived their end.*

do not be envious of evil men

The word envious is a very strong word. It is translated zeal when directed toward God. *Zeal for Thy House has consumed me.* Envy when it is directed toward another person's goods. Jealousy when it is directed toward your own goods.

Notice that there are two prescriptions in this proverb: First, do not be envious of the evil person. Second, do not be desirous of being with them. Both of these actions happen on the inside but can spell disaster for a person.

The word *evil* in the proverb is equivalent of the word *wicked* – outside of God's moral boundary structure. His moral boundaries are clearly the Ten Commandments. When you become envious of the person who lives outside of the Ten Commandments, you move into a whole new territory. In fact, you violate the Tenth Commandment in doing this.

To violate the commandment to not covet means that you begin to look at someone else's life – especially the wicked – and want their life rather than exploring the life God has given you. To not explore the gifts, talents, and opportunities that God has given you and instead pine away for a future life that you could not have is coveting.

nor desire to be with them

There is a natural attraction toward the gain of the wicked. It is essential to define some terms as we look at this verse. First is the word *desire*. This is the Hebrew word *avah* and means lust, longed, covet, wait longingly. This means that you begin to dream about what life would be like if you were in their shoes. It means that you spend time thinking about ways to be with the people who have all the stuff and power and fame you would like. This hanging out with the wicked will begin to rub off.

How many teenagers have proclaimed to their parents that they would never do the stuff that their new friends are doing? Then one year later they are caught doing the same stuff. You can't hang around with evil people without having evil rub off on you. 1 Corinthians 15 – bad company corrupts good morals.

It is a terrible life to not embrace the opportunities that God has given you and instead keep wishing and hoping for someone else's life. This negative type of wishing and dreaming is even compounded when the type of life that is wished for is evil.

Desiring someone else's life means that we are missing the opportunities that God has presented to us. It means that we are not developing the skills and talents God has given us. It robs someone else of opportunities because we are pursuing things that should be left to others.

PROVERBS 25:1
These also are the proverbs of Solomon which the men of Hezekiah, king of Judah, transcribed

This is a historical reference to the discovery of a list of proverbs that Solomon, the King of Israel, had put together and that the men of Hezekiah had transcribed or translated for the public consumption of the people.

What is interesting is that many of the proverbs in this section are found in other parts of the book of Proverbs, but they are included here because they come with a different context so they have a different meaning or nuance. The context for the proverb is the proverb that precedes it or is two back. While many commentators declare that there is no context for the individual proverb, I do not believe that this is true or why would God repeat the same proverb in a number of different places. The context of a proverb is the proverbs around it. The wisdom contained in the one proverb triggers another proverb because the ideas can be related. It is this relationship that also brings insight and not just the truth of the proverb. This means that the proverbs are, in a sense, hooked learning. This type of learning is one of the best ways of causing people to remember and is, in fact, the basis of all catechisms in which a question is asked and then more questions are asked about the answer.

In order to become a person of understanding, one must develop the ability to see the connections between proverbs. There is a connection mentally, spiritually, relationally, and verbally between the one proverb and the next one. So one can ask what triggered this proverb to come to mind in connection with the last one and a whole new insight about and in the proverb comes to light. It is this different arrangement of the proverbs that gives the new insights in this section. Hopefully this view of the context of the book of Proverbs will allow you to see a whole new level of depth and beauty in the Proverbs. Why is this proverb here? What is its connection to the ones before it and after it?

There are sections of the book of Proverbs that are clearly marked off and form a larger context as well. This verse marks one of the sections beginning points.

PROVERBS 26:1
Like snow in summer and like rain in harvest, so honor is not fitting for a fool

like snow in summer and like rain in harvest

The focus is on appropriateness. It is not appropriate to add value to a person who is selfish, impulsive, and rebellious. When a person who is a moral fool has value added to him or her, it destroys that person. It adds credence to their already inflated opinion of themselves.

We make choices every day that will move us in the direction of foolishness or wisdom. Are we only thinking about what we want and what feels good at the moment or are we contemplating a world full of others who could win or lose by our decisions? Every one of us has talents that we have been given by God for the benefit of our families, churches, societies, and ourselves. If we do not develop our souls to the level of our talents, then we could easily be tipped over by the honor our talent brings. When the talent we have is not matched by a soul of humility, service, and love then the value, praise, and glory that comes through using our abilities will push us into a barren land of foolishness and aloneness.

so honor is not fitting for a fool

The word honor means to add value. To admire the ability or skill or gifts or actions of another is to respect someone, but to honor someone is going beyond just acknowledging their ability or action and to add value to them. This is appropriate for those who demonstrate righteous wisdom. If someone is valued past their ability, skill, or action when they are a fool (selfish, impulsive, and rebellious), it will reinforce their wrongheaded notion that the world does revolve around them. It will push them further into selfishness and pride.

This adding value to the already overinflated ego is a constant activity in our day and age. We flatter ego-bloated politicians. We have created Christian celebrities who have one talent but no humility. It is this honor that contributes to their destruction. When one allows people to praise you and value you for that which God should get glory and credit for, it pushes you in the direction of destruction.

Recently I became aware of a prominent pastor who destroyed his ministry through moral failure. Those who knew him state quite clearly that he came across as arrogant and playing at the edges of Christian or moral behavior. He was highly valued for his ability to speak. That skill contributed to his own inflated opinion of himself and led to his downfall.

Two lessons here for us: do not accept praise and honor as though you did it all but rather pass it on and realize that what you are is the result of what God and others have done to, for, and with you. Second, do not flatter a person who is a moral fool or you will contribute to their ultimate destruction. Also, do not allow yourself to be honored or praised when you are being foolish, selfish, impulsive, rebellious. It is inappropriate and it will be destructive.

PROVERBS 27:1

Do not boast about tomorrow, for you do not know what a day may bring forth

One of the great dangers is to begin to count too heavily about tomorrow – this is going to happen or that is going to happen.

When we boast about what we will accomplish tomorrow, it is even worse. All of our lives are under the sovereign control of God, and we do not really know what will happen tomorrow or what we will accomplish. We can prepare the best we can and we can pray, but ultimately the outcome of tomorrow is in His hands.

We all need a healthy dose of internal realization that it is all whether God wills or if God wills, we will do this or that.

Many people who had great plans on or after September 11 never accomplished them or had their lives forever altered because of the terrorist attack.

This verse is also about being overly proud and bragging about what you are going to do and acting like you are in total charge of your life.

do not boast about tomorrow

This is the practical advice in this proverb. It would seem like pretty obvious advice, but as always the Word holds some surprises and depth that we would not have expected.

Overconfidence about tomorrow and the future is what draws people into many types of foolish and evil behaviors.

The Hebrew word for *boast* is the word *helel* for which we get our word *halelu* which means to praise or exalt. The proverb is saying that one should not praise tomorrow or exalt tomorrow as though that were the solution to all your problems. Tomorrow is not the solution of your problems unless you do something in today.

There are some people who are always living in tomorrow as though that is when their ship will come in and fix all their troubles. Their ship is variously described as a lottery ticket, a handsome rich man, a beautiful woman, a new job, the death of a relative, etc. It is this idea of praising the advance of time as though that were more significant than the blessing of God today and the relationships that can be held and developed today.

While it is important to plan and seek to develop the skills and information that will make the future bright, Solomon is warning us not to embrace the notion that the future will necessarily be bright.

In fact, it is painfully obvious down through history that because of the effects of sin eating away at any and every society, the future becomes bleak when the effects of sin and selfishness reach their zenith in a society. I fear that our society is approaching a point where the moral decay is so great that the future will not be bright.

Some have trusted the future so much that they do not live in the present. Some have planned on money that is coming in the future and spend it multiple times. Some have counted on a relationship in the future and not spent time developing it in the present.

The question that we should ask is what can I do today to make the future bright and what must I do to prepare for the future no matter what takes place?

What is interesting about this proverb is that it speaks against a core value of Americans – trust, exaltation, and belief in the future. Many people have more trust in the future than they have in God. They trust the scientists to develop a cure for diseases and develop flying cars and reduce stress at work and a hundred other things. This trust can become praise and even worship of tomorrow rather than humility before our great God who holds all of our tomorrows.

do not praise tomorrow, praise the God of all tomorrows

Do not believe that tomorrow will actually be better just because it will be tomorrow. All types of things could take place that will make our yesterdays seem better than tomorrow.

Do not praise tomorrow. Instead, work hard to make tomorrow a better place within the moral boundaries of God. If tomorrow is not more moral, then it will not be better but instead worse. Whenever morality is sacrificed to achieve a goal, then the innocent and vulnerable suffer.

for you do not know what a day may bring forth

There are things that are out of your control; people, factors, and decisions that were made that did not consult you.

There is, throughout the proverb, the idea that God and His planning and sovereignty are behind all of our planning. There is something that will happen because you plan it and execute it. But that is not by any stretch all that will happen in the future. There are things that will happen that others plan and execute. Some of those may have an impact on what you plan. There are things that God plans and executes that will happen that impinge upon your plans.

We must maintain a certain level of humility, realizing that the universe does not revolve around us. God did not check with us as to whether it was okay if He allowed this or that or if He did this or that. There will be days when everything you wanted to do will be thwarted by the events of the day. Are you willing to laugh and submit to God who has planned your schedule differently than you did?

January 28

PROVERBS 28:1

The wicked flee when no one is pursuing, but the righteous are bold as a lion

the wicked flee when no one is pursuing

Those who live outside of God's moral boundary structure are always in a position in which they could be caught doing something that society finds wrong. Therefore they are ready to take off or scurry away at a moment's notice. They even take off when no one is following them.

The word for *flee* is *nus* in Hebrew which means to retreat, wander, flee, or moving away in a hurry from the scene. At the slightest little disturbance, the wicked are gone because they fear the inspection of the light.

The word *pursuing* is the word *radap* in the Hebrew which means to follow behind, to pursue.

Who wants to live a life of looking over your shoulder to see if someone is following?

but the righteous are bold as a lion

The word translated bold is the word for confidence or security. This suggests, in contrast to the wicked, that the righteous welcomes inspection and truth. When you have nothing to hide, then you are bold and moving forward.

The interesting point to notice is why would Solomon put this proverb here? What triggered this truth? The section of Proverbs that immediately precedes this verse is about good, sound financial management. The verse that follows talks about sin in the land causing many people to claim leadership. The idea here seems to be that the confidence and security – that those who act righteously enjoy – is obvious. They are putting down roots. On the other hand, the wicked are ready to take off at a moment's notice.

January 29

PROVERBS 29:1

A man who hardens his neck after much reproof will suddenly be broken beyond remedy

hardens

This is something that the person does; their self-will rises up and stiffens them against counsel – both friendly and divine.

There is a point in which God will just say "ENOUGH" and will severely limit a person's potential, ability, opportunities, etc. Realistically they did it to themselves, but they will be broken and unfixable. Grace will come and work its wonderful work, but one cannot go back when the hardening is of such a nature that a breaking had to come.

There will be no remedy. This is so strong, but it is truth. There are some consequences that are unrepentable. Things will stay broken. We are a society of second and third and fourth chances, but at some point they run out. Even the God of lovingkindness and mercy and grace at some point pours out His wrath. At some point in the righteous ruminations of His mind, He is able to say "no more" and the person pays a heavy price for their refusal to submit to the gentle tug of God.

PROVERBS 30:1

The words of Agur the son of Jakeh, the oracle. The man declares to Ithiel, to Ithiel and Ucal.

the oracle

This is the Hebrew word for burden or load. The person whom God selected to carry His message had an extra heavy load – especially because it was usually a word of rebuke; a word that would not be received well. This oracle was a spiritual burden, a soul burden, and a physical burden. You could not refuse to say what God had put on your heart. You carried the burden of the Lord, and it weighed on you until you unloaded it on His people. Jeremiah says that it was like fire in his bones. He tried to shut it up within him but he was unable. When God has chosen you to be a spokesman for Him, you carry a burden. And that burden must be delivered to the right people and unloaded.

Agur: **this name means gathered**

Jakeh: **this name means blameless**

Ithiel: **this name means God is with me**

Ucal: **this name means devoured**

This was a message from a prophet of God - one carrying the message from the Lord. This was a message to two people: *Ithiel*: God is with me and *Ucal*: devoured. This was a message from *Agur*, son of *Jakeh*: gathered blameless. This would potentially translate out as a message from God to two kinds of people: those whom God is clearly with and those who have been devoured by life. It comes from God through His specific servant who wants to communicate that He wants all people to know that they can be gathered to Him (God) in a blameless fashion through the son that He will be offering for their sins.

The first part of the oracle or burden from the Lord is that God has a son who will allow his people to be gathered blameless in His presence - those whom God is clearly with and those who have been devoured by life and by the choices that they made.

The Jews might see this proverb about the son to be about them - gathered blameless in the presence of God; those who walk with God and those who have been devoured by life. His people will clearly be called sons of God, but I think this points to its ultimate fulfillment in the true and only begotten Son of God, Jesus the Christ, the Lamb of God who takes away the sins of the world.

PROVERBS 31:1

The words of King Lemuel, the oracle which his mother taught him

King = leader, authority

Lemuel = for God

Oracle = a burden or message from God or another spiritual entity that is a spiritual, soul, and even physical weight on your being until you deliver it to the intended parties.

This proverb is a burden from God which came to the mother of Lemuel for all those who would be leaders for God. You must understand the way God sees leadership and your responsibilities.

This proverb sets out priorities and orientations for those who would be leaders for God. They were not to use their power and authority to pursue immorality or collect women. The position of power draws certain kinds of women and this temptation is real – to be diverted from leading for God to collecting immoral conquests. He was not to desire strong drink or become a drunk or a person who was always after the next party. He was to remember the laws that had already been passed. He was to remember tradition and not believe that he could just change everything just because it was more convenient for him. He was to make sure that the defenseless were protected and that their rights were not abused or neglected. He was to speak up for those who could not speak. He was to champion those who had been oppressed. He was to make decisions that clearly reflected an understanding of the Ten Commandments. He was to defend the biblical rights of those who were easily taken advantage of - the afflicted and the needy.

This was what a leader for God was to do. A leader for God was to lead in the place of God and see with God's eyes and not with their own eyes or with fleshly, sinful eyes. A leader for God was to clearly demonstrate that God loved His people and had an eye to the poor and downtrodden. A leader for God was also clearly to demonstrate an understanding of the moral boundaries of life, the Ten Commandments, and to use them on the society that they governed - especially those who, through wealth, were taking advantage of those who had none.

February

PROVERBS 1:2

To know wisdom and instruction, to discern the sayings of understanding

to know

The word *know* is interesting in that it is the Hebrew word *yada* which is expressed in all the different verb forms in the Old Testament but is always a form of knowing that involves that which comes through the senses – experiential knowledge; almost Aristotelian knowing, growing out of sense experience or other's sense experience. Solomon does not want to give us theories about how to live life, but he wants to pass on what really works and how to make the best choices. He wants us to know that this way that does not seem right to us is the best way - the wise way. Because of the experience we have had in watching others, hearing his words, observing life, he does not want us to have to wait until we have experienced the negative consequences of being a fool.

There are three crucial tasks in this verse that Solomon lets us know this inspired book is designed to accomplish.

Wisdom is the first and the foremost. It is often defined as the application of knowledge in a proper or ethical way. While this is true, it is a much broader, richer term in this Hebraic understanding. Wisdom throughout the book is that action or choice or speech which is difficult to find – not instinctual – that causes God to win or be glorified, others to win, and us to win. There is a choice or action in every situation which is the wise one. It may cost us in the short term, but it will pay off in the long term. Consistent actions of wisdom – finding the triple-win choice or action consistently is a rich life. It will have setbacks and difficulties, but there is much protection and reward. This book, inspired by the Holy Spirit and penned through the writing of King Solomon, is the distillation of how to find and live the triple-win choice or wisdom.

The second thing that this book is designed to accomplish is that it is self-instruction – not in the simple sense of a set of instructions but in terms of training. If the plans and actions of this book are followed, it is the training manual for an unbelievable life. You will not just intellectually know the right thing to do, but you will be trained to respond that way in the various situations of life. Constant attention to this book and its sayings will train your mind to perceive what you do not perceive at present and to react and act in a way that now you find impossible. This is the course on people dynamics and applied moral ethics. It is this book that will form the role-playing manual for a new way of living.

instruction

To know instruction is to know how others would rebuke you if they had the chance. The idea of instruction is education in what you don't know or don't see or don't want to see. To become a wise person is to be willing to look at yourself honestly and work where the work is needed, not just where you want to work. The wise person seeks instruction and seeks realistic views of himself or herself. An interesting question to ask yourself is: If God were to openly rebuke me right now for three things, what would they be?

The third aim of this book is an ability to perceive the sayings of understanding. This phrase is lost to modern hearers because we do not see its incredible power or claim. The word *understanding* is the word *bina*. It carries a relational connotation with it. It carries a sense of interconnectedness – how this relates to that in ways we don't suspect. This book is claiming that you will be able to see the hidden relationships between saying this and this other thing happening in your life. Why when this happen, friends come or flee. When you do this, it strengthens your marriage or destroys it. There are invisible strings or webs of relationships between things that we would not normally perceive or see, but biblical understanding means seeing these cause-and-effect devices. The book of Proverbs consistently tries to open peoples' eyes between seemingly independent actions and choices.

The book of Proverbs is worth spending great time in – over and over again – because it offers to help us find the triple-win choice or action in every situation. It offers to train us so that our natural reaction is no longer going to subvert our way; and it offers to show us the invisible connections between actions, relationships, and choices that cause everything to change on the chess board of life with a single move.

This is valuable stuff and we need it.

February 2

PROVERBS 2:2
Make your ear attentive to wisdom, incline your heart to understanding

One of the main messages of the book of Proverbs is that wisdom is all around if we would just look for it and be sensitive to it when it shows up.

make your ear attentive to wisdom
Solomon tells us that we must make our ear attentive to wisdom.

The word *ear* is the Hebrew word *ozen* which means ear or the part of the body that interprets symbolic language or a person's responsiveness to commands or information. It is this last aspect that catches our attention. In a Hebraic mindset, one has not really heard what another has said unless there is obedience or appropriate response to it. When the Scripture says "Hear the word of the Lord," it means obey the word of the Lord, not listen for the sounds God will make or take notes on what He just says. So in this same way Solomon says you have to make yourself ready to respond positively to wisdom when you come across it. You are not really a student of wisdom if you just say, "Oh, that is interesting" or "I will save it for later." It must be imbedded in your person so that you act in accordance with it.

We have a storage-tank approach to information and wisdom, filling ourselves with information and good actions that we call wisdom to be pulled out of the storage tank and used when appropriate. This works in some cases. The Scripture has a different view when it comes to wisdom. When you are faced with a decision or course of action, you are looking for wisdom. You will not find wisdom if you do not pre-commit to doing it once you find it for it may be somewhat painful to do in the short-run. Remember that wisdom is the triple-win choice – that action or choice in which God wins, others win, and I win. This is opposed to the choice in which I win and others lose or I win and some others win but God loses. Therefore if I am facing a decision, I need to pre-commit to doing the triple-win option when I find it. If not, I will be tempted to go for the quick, selfish choice in which I am looking out for number 1.

The point Solomon is telling his young learner is that wisdom must be done or it is gone. It cannot be found if it will not be obeyed. I have counseled many people who have asked me to save their marriage or help them financially or stop their children from rebelling, but then they tell me what they are unwilling to do. Usually what they are unwilling to do is the direction that wisdom is in. They will say things like, "I have already tried that" or "Don't ask me to apologize or give more of my time or live on a budget or something like that." What they want is for everybody else to change but themselves. They want to continue to be selfish and get different results in their marriage, checkbook, and family.

Make a pre-commitment to wisdom. It may seem difficult to lessen your personal win to have others win and God get glory, but it pays rich dividends in the future just as making small investments over time in a reasonable investment option. It gets better with time.

I recommend that you tell God every day, as you are studying the Scriptures, that you want His wisdom and are ready to do it. Also, when you are facing a major decision in your work, marriage, family, church, or any aspect of your life, start by telling God you are looking for wisdom and are right now pre-committing to it.

incline your heart to understanding

This is a fascinating concept that we think we comprehend but we don't.

The word *heart* is the Hebrew word *leb* which means the actual physical organ of the heart; it means the center of the person or the place of decision, volition, and emotion. And some would connect this with the immaterial part of man called the soul.

The word *incline* is the Hebrew word *nata* which means extend, lean over, incline, bend. This word carries with it the idea of leaning to the point of falling in a certain direction; going beyond what is normal and natural and balanced. One could say that Solomon is advising us to unbalance our mind, will, and emotions to grasp this thing called understanding.

The word *understanding* is the Hebrew word *bina* which means distinguish between, between the power of judgment and perception. One of the quick ways I like to understand this word understanding is as the connections between things; to grasp how things are interrelated. In other words, if I do this, then that will happen. If I say this, then so and so will feel these things and probably react in these ways.

It is tragic when a person does not have any understanding of the connections between what they say and do and how other people react. They just see what they want and go after it, regularly amazed at the idea that other people may have had designs on that thing themselves or could have a reaction.

This is the place where many people in our society are today. They do not realize that all actions are interrelated with lots of other people. If a person chooses to smoke, they are doing a lot of things beyond just putting smoke in their lungs. They put smoke in the lungs of those around them; they damage their lung's ability to breathe; they increase their risk for cancer; they decrease their life expectancy; they are perceived differently; they smell different. If a person chooses to be proud, a whole host of connections and reactions are set in motion. If a person commits adultery, a massive amount of connections and reactions are set in motion. If I own a company and choose to pollute the river or air, a huge number of reactions and connections are unleashed in the society. We live in a society in which people basically want permission to do what they want to do with little regard for what will happen to all those who are impacted by their actions.

If you and I are going to be wise, then we will need to stretch out for or not rest until we see the various reactions and connections that our actions will have. If we were to just stop and think a while before we acted - What will happen if I do this? - we would be inclining our heart to understanding. It is like putting a chess piece in the place we are thinking about moving it but not taking our hand off it. We can then survey the various possibilities and countermoves that our potential move makes possible.

Too often we just grow weary of this type of hard thinking and want to do what we want before anybody can stop us. This is the fool's way. If we want a great marriage, a satisfying career, an enjoyable family, devoted friends, then we must take the time to lean over and see the various reactions and connections that our actions will have on these very important parts of our life.

If this is hard for you, then ask someone who is wise to help you. Give them hypothetical situations and say, "If I said this, what do you think my spouse would say; my children, my boss, my friends?" Keep doing this type of thing until you begin to grasp understanding for then you will be wise and most likely a lot less quick in speech and action.

At various times you will be caught completely off guard by the reaction of others. This is an indication that you have some growing to do in understanding. A person who has understanding can anticipate the reactions and interactions of others and decide beforehand whether they are worth it.

February 3

PROVERBS 3:2
For length of days and years of life and peace they will add to you

length of days

One clearly gets the impression that God's principles in the book of Proverbs are able to lengthen your life; that God's ideas on how to live life are valuable extenders of life.

There is a corollary to the ideas of this verse: It is possible to extend one's life if the principles and ideas in this book are followed. In other words, you will live this long if you do xyz stuff; but if you live out the ideas in this book, you will 10, 20, 30 years longer. You and I get to choose whether we extend our life. And not only that, we get to decide whether it will be extended with a sense of completeness, wholeness, and peace.

Think about the opposite of what is being said. To ignore the principles in this book means that your life will be shorter, harder, and constantly incomplete. Who would want that? But many choose that road because they ignore the wisdom in this book from God.

years of life

It is consistent with the understanding that not only the actual time you have on earth will be extended but the life in those years.

Life is something to be enjoyed and used for the Lord God. We are in the midst of a training assignment here on earth getting ready for the real assignment in heaven. How well you learn to love and care and trust Christ here will determine the opportunities that you have there. It is important to extend your life, if possible, so that you can do more good works for the Lord.

But even if you have a short time on earth, let them be filled with life. Invest heavily in wisdom and righteous relationships. Life is relationships – it is not about heaping up wealth or power; it is about building and sustaining key relationships first with God then with others that God has put before you.

peace

This is the Hebrew word *shalom* which means peace. It comes from the root which means completion or fulfillment. It seems to carry with it the idea that one has stopped the harried acquisition mode and has the treasure that can be enjoyed. Too many people in our day are constantly in the acquisition mode and never have a sense of completion or rest. So they are never at peace.

It is possible to live life but never acquire those things that will actually bring a sense of completion to life. It is relationships that will bring peace. It is strong vibrant righteous relationships that will bring a sense of completion to life. If the crucial relationships of life are missing, then one is never satisfied.

Notice that in verse one of this chapter Solomon states that he has commandments to follow. In verse four he states that if you follow his commandments, it will bring favor with God and man. Therefore, the by-product of listening to and living by the wisdom of the book of Proverbs is completed and strong relationships which are peace. One can then live fulfilled without the constant acquisition mode of most.

It is tragic to constantly be in acquisition mode and then be completely unsatisfied when the acquisition is made, unable to enjoy the latest acquisition, unable to feel completed by the acquisition that one has poured so much energy into achieving.

The key acquisitions that bring peace are strong, vibrant relationships with God and man. It is these relationships with spouse, children, self, colleagues, believers, neighbors, and friends that bring peace to life. One's life is not complete until you have these. You can't have these if you violate the principles in this sacred book penned by Solomon but authored by God and breathed into by His life.

The fool constantly asks the question: What would make me happy? What do I want to do? The fool asks selfish questions. But the wise person asks: How can I enter into a deeper connection to the key people in my life? It may mean that I throw myself into a less pleasurable activity so that I can have a more intimate link with this other person. There is greater joy in deep connection with another key person while doing an uninteresting activity than the selfish pursuit of my own desires.

Selfishness, sin, and a materialistic focus rob the ability to be completed by one's gains.

The New Testament idea of peace is harmony or matching the key frequencies of the lives of those around you - primarily God but also the key relationships in your life. If you constantly are living out a melody that is out of tune and radically different from those around you, then you will never have peace. If you are unwilling to play the tune that God has laid out for you, then you will constantly be in a state of unease and lack of peace.

God wants to be the completer of your life; the one who brings you peace; the one who makes you whole. He does that differently than we would initially think. We often think that he could make us whole by giving us all the wealth that we would want and by giving us people who will do whatever we want. He does not, however, become our genie in a bottle. He becomes our God and directs us in the paths of life. He presents people, situations, and opportunities that - if embraced - will complete us and bring a sense of wholeness and therefore peace to our lives. He also presents Himself as the key completer of our lives - our guide, corrector, instructor, friend, father, judge, confidant, attorney, and object of reverence. All this is needed in a completer - one who brings peace to the restlessness in our souls.

February 4

PROVERBS 4:2
For I give you sound teaching, do not abandon my instruction

This proverb speaks of a deep fear that many parents have - that their child will listen to them and agree with them when they are at home; but at some time later when they are in college or sometimes even earlier, they will abandon all the rules, ideas, and values that their parents have taught them.

Solomon is acting as a spiritual father here and wants to anticipate this dynamic. Don't get rid of this stuff later. What I am teaching you is sound teaching; it is the stuff that will last. Don't think that it was okay when you were a little kid but now you need to follow the "modern" ways of looking at things. In whatever century or period of time all the way back to Solomon's time, the "modern" way has been another name for the selfish way. Now there are advances in knowledge, but these advances do not abrogate moral knowledge especially that given by revelation of God.

sound teaching

This phrase *sound teaching* comes from two Hebrew words *tob* and *leqah*. They literally mean good and learning. The idea is that what Solomon is teaching is beneficial and it is new information. Solomon is saying that I am giving you information that you have not had before, and it will significantly benefit you. You will rejoice if you follow it, but do not make the mistake that many people make in later moving on to some other new information that happens to tickle your intellectual or moral antenna. This is the stuff you should stay with because it is good, beneficial, and righteous.

abandon

This is the Hebrew word *azab* which means leave, forsake, loose. The idea is clearly this tendency for young people to forsake the teaching that gave their life meaning when they learned it at home and in the community that shaped them. They grow up a little and they need to update their learning about God and begin to trust Him and find Him reliable at this new age, but they do not need to scrap all they learned to embrace some new philosophy that seems more adult and able to handle the dog-eat-dog world. I am tired of seeing young men and young ladies destroy the innocence and joy in their lives for some selfish, secularized values. Often these same youth come back to God and church and their parents when they have a family of their own, always ashamed of what took place during their period of rebellion. Some never make it back from their rebellious years. It may be average to rebel, but it is not normal. Normal is what God says ought to happen. Too many kids stop using their faith and the values that God injected into their life and then they say that Christianity didn't work for them. Christianity was not tried and found wanting; it was not tried.

The power of God's wisdom is sufficient for every age and stage in your life. Your understanding of God's wisdom and what to do in particular situations may need to be expanded and understood in new contexts, but it is still worthy of your trust. DO NOT BELIEVE THAT YOU HAVE GROWN PAST YOUR FAITH. No, you have only wanted to become more selfish and your faith will not allow you to do that.

instruction

This is the Hebrew word *torah* which means law and is where we get the title for the first five books of Moses. Now it is important to talk about the nature of law more than a minute. Laws are boundaries in which individuals in authority and society say that behaviors beyond this line are not allowed. Laws are by nature negative. They are trying to boundarize the selfish impulse inside of each person. God has said in the Ten Commandments that individual behavior becomes a threat to the individual, others, and the society as a whole when it goes beyond these ten places. It is not because God is an ogre and He wants to limit our fun and enjoyment of the world. He just knows how He set up the world and the tolerances of the moral order for selfishness. It will not sustain order when selfishness is pushed past these limits. We see the consequences happening all around us as people believe they have the right to be as selfish as they can get away with: children permanently scarred by the divorce, abuse, adultery, and anger of their parents; women and children permanently scarred by the selfishness of men; men permanently scarred by the selfishness of the men and women around them. When selfishness is allowed to reign, love grows cold, the innocent suffer, and the society becomes morally polluted and begins to break down.

In this case Solomon is stating the fact that he is going to give moral boundaries that his pupils should follow. They may seem restrictive, but they will benefit you in the long run. These are his laws or boundary markers.

On this note, every family has boundary lines which they say people should not do this or not do that. Sometimes it is these restrictive boundary lines that the children rebel over when they leave the home. This is often the attempt to differentiate themselves from their parents. This is fairly typical and does not have to constitute rebellion. Each child needs to be able to establish the personal boundaries they will adopt that will keep them from violating God's law. Some children will adopt a different personal boundary than their parents had. This is okay as long as it is still inside of God's clear moral boundary.

Coming back to the point of this proverb - have you needlessly abandoned a Godly philosophy of life only to find the new selfish out-for #1 philosophy is not working out like you thought? Abandon it and come back to God and accept the forgiveness that is in the person and work of Jesus Christ.

If you are a youth, drink deeply of the wisdom in this book called Proverbs. There is no need to learn a different or better philosophy of life later. This is the only one you will need.

February 5

PROVERBS 5:2
That you may observe discretion and your lips may reserve knowledge

observe

This is the Hebrew word *samar* which means to keep guard, observe, give heed to. This is a fascinating insight that Solomon shares in this verse. He is saying that young people can flush their ability to make their own choices and plans through sin. How many times have I watched as men and women have made idiotic decisions that don't make any sense until you factor in some relationship, some sin, some addiction, some illicit activity. They were protecting or guarding the foolish thing, the sinful thing, and flushing their own life.

Solomon is screaming at us: DON'T BE SUCKED INTO FOOLISHNESS (especially sexual foolishness)! YOU WILL FLUSH YOUR ABILITY TO CHOOSE WISELY.

discretion

This is the Hebrew word *mezimma* which means purpose or plot. This is the ability to make plans, to set goals, to make decisions both in the short term and long range. Solomon is saying that if you do not embrace wisdom, you will lose your ability to plan and make decisions. You will be robbed of your ability to make a wise decision by other factors.

The translators have chosen the word *discretion* because the English word means the ability to make responsible decisions and the power to make free decisions within an acceptable range. The idea here is that when one gives up their discretion, they no longer have the ability to make a free choice. There is someone or something that is influencing their choice so that it is no longer really free and uncoerced. In this case it means that getting involved in adultery robs one of this crucial ability.

You are no longer free because you have been hooked. You are asked to make decisions that you shouldn't even face. You feel pulls in directions that you shouldn't even be considering. You are conflicted and stretched in ways that will clearly distort your ability to make a wise decision.

Watch what you allow into your life; it may rob you of the ability to have a life – your ability to choose. Most people think they are still the captain of their ship, the king of their life; but many give away the ability to make wise choices to the vices they invite to live with them. They are held by the cords of their own sin as Solomon says at another point.

and your lips reserve knowledge

reserve

This is the Hebrew word *nasar* which means to watch, guard, keep. Solomon is saying that you will not be able to retain the knowledge you have gained or need if you continue to give in to sin. You will begin to shape the truth to fit the world you are living in - the world of self-indulgence.

knowledge

This is the Hebrew word *daat* which means information and skills. Solomon is saying that it is possible to let information and skills slip through your fingers if you get involved in adultery and other forms of foolishness.

February 6

PROVERBS 6:2
If you have been snared with the words of your mouth, have been caught with the words of your mouth

This verse is the continuation of the idea developed in verse one – namely, that you have promised to pay the debts of another person. But it also carries a nugget of wisdom about the use of the tongue that is surely independent of co-signing and borrowing. Namely, that one can be put into a snare by what they say.

if you have been snared with the words of your mouth

The word *snare* is the Hebrew word *yaqosh* and appears first in the sentence. This emphasizes the word and the importance of the concept in the sentence. The writer is trying to emphasize that promising certain things is a trap or a snare which you make yourself. This is foolish talk.

The second word in the Hebrew sentence is *speech* or *words*. And the third word is mouth. In other words, the sentence reads: *A trap built with words out of your mouth.* This is the definition of foolishness. Who would build their own trap? Who would build a trap for themselves using their own words that everyone knew came out of their own mouth? Who would walk into a trap to be caught? Who would walk into their own trap that they themselves designed? The answer to each of these questions is A FOOL.

In trying to appear big and generous, the fool has built and stepped into a trap. How impulsive and lacking sense.

Let's expand the application of this idea a little further. How many of us have used our mouth to spin a tale that is really not true but makes us look good? This is also a trap built with our own words. We then are forced to openly admit our fabrication or to protect our tale with greater fabrications. Don't build a trap with your own words. Tell the truth. Don't try and have people be impressed with you because of what you say or what you do. Just do the right thing and the appropriate praise will come to you. When we try and make ourselves look better, through loaning people money or stretching the truth, it is a trap that will be an uncomfortable prison.

If you have built one of these traps, before it springs closed verse 4 tells us to get out by telling the truth and canceling the contract. Don't allow yourself to be caught.

have been caught with the words of your mouth

There is a difference between the first phrase and the second phrase. The first is a snare that has been built but it has not been sprung. The second is the trap that has been closed and caught someone – namely, you. The first phrase refers to before the problem has occurred and the second is after you have been caught by what you said and made to pay for another.

In either case the person must do the same thing: seek deliverance from the trap. It is obviously better to be delivered before the trap has sprung shut.

The picture is of a person who is walking down the path of life and stops to build a steel cage on the side of the road to impress his friends. Instead of making progress on the path, he is busy building this cage. Then he walks into the cage and waits for the door to be thrown closed and locked. It is the friends that you have been trying to impress who will throw the door closed and imprison you. Don't let this happen. Keep moving on the path of life.

When we make a pledge to cover the debts of others, this is a fool's trap. Only a fool needs us to cover their debts, and the goods purchased by such an arrangement did not need to be purchased.

I have watched as people have derailed their marriages, families, and even careers to help out a friend, relative, or boss. Often these include bailing a person out of prison or co-signing for a car or starting a business. When the debt becomes due, it totally destabilizes the helper's life while the person who needed the help moves forward without them.

Do not do this...

PROVERBS 7:2
Keep my commandments and live, and my teaching as the apple of your eye

What commandments are being mentioned? Clearly the whole, but specifically a group of commandments that are the capsulated summary of what will be said in the whole of the book – Proverbs 3:3-11.

- Do not let kindness and truth leave you
- Trust in the Lord with all your heart
- Do not lean on your own understanding
- In all your ways acknowledge Him
- Do not be wise in your own eyes
- Fear the Lord and turn away from evil
- Honor the Lord from your wealth
- My son, do not reject the discipline of the Lord

These commandments form the core of what God is trying to get people to do in life. These are simple rules, but many get sucked aside from the paths of life by violations of these simple rules – adultery, pride, get-rich-quick schemes, hoarding, greed. The next few verses will detail the problems of adultery. It looks like it is all sweetness and light, but instead it is a narrow well.

February 8

PROVERBS 8:2
*On top of the heights beside the way, where the paths meet,
she takes her stand*

Wisdom wants to get the word out to people to live a different way. She does not hide what she knows in some dark place reserved only for the special few who will spend years looking and recite some bizarre incantations. Wisdom is right out in the market place.

Wisdom is in a prominent place. When life is not working the way you have put it together, then look up for there is a wiser way of living. And right around you - in a prominent place - are the people who will give you the answer.

There are a few things that are interesting in this verse:

One is that wisdom is prominent - on the tops of the heights, right beside the way, where the paths meet.

Two, she calls for people to turn in and listen to a different way of life. She does not call out what to do. Wisdom does not spew her pearls to everyone. You must turn in and be willing to listen before you hear it. Some people are just not ready to listen that there is a better way than working harder and doing what seems best.

Three, the place where wisdom stations herself is the same place that the elders of a town station themselves or where the supervisors of a crew or company station themselves. There are people who have gone down the road you are on that would love to share the secrets of how to get ahead, but you must be willing to listen. You must turn in. In other words, you must be willing to listen and submit to those who have been down the road farther than you.

Now it is important to say at this point that wisdom – as delineated in the next few chapters – actually has succeeded at the area being considered. Unfortunately in our day we have a host of "experts" who offer their ideas on how to live, but they have not succeeded in that arena. They have degrees and the ability to lecture convincingly. This kind of academic learning is not necessarily connected with wisdom. It is important to recognize this distinction because we do have people tell us to learn from them, but they have not been wise themselves. We have pseudo wise people who have studied all the different things to do and then begun teaching the one they like – not because it worked but because they like how it sounds.

Do not be fooled. Those who have raised great kids should be listened to. Those who have succeeded in business without blowing out their marriages and kids should be listened to. Those who have amassed wealth without becoming greedy should be followed. Those who actually have a righteous walk with God should be listened to. Those who have a great marriage should be followed.

As you are reading this, it may be that some aspect of your life is not working. It could be your marriage; it could be your family; it could be your money or your career. God has stationed people around you who understand wisdom in the area you are lacking. If you ask, they will tell you. It requires humility and a willingness to change the way you live your life. If you are unwilling to do things differently, then any wisdom they would share with you would be worthless.

Four, wisdom is not internally discoverable. You can't just think about things yourself and come up with the better way to live. You need to read a book or talk to people who are wise. Many times we try and appear self-contained, not needing anyone to help us figure things out. This is the fool's plan. Wisdom is calling all around you about how to build a better life, but you do have to be humble enough to listen and change.

February 9

PROVERBS 9:2
She has prepared her food; she has mixed her wine; she has also set her table

Solomon mentions three aspects of the preparation of wisdom to receive guests. These give us a metaphorical picture of what wisdom does when you become its student.

- It has food prepared
- It has drink prepared
- It has a table prepared

she has prepared her food

The word translated *prepared* is actually the Hebrew word for slaughter. In fact, the actual Hebrew phrase *is she has slaughtered her slaughter*. The idea is that real meat has been prepared for this wisdom banquet. The question is raised as to what the food is when pulled out of this analogy. It is clearly wisdom. Wisdom offers to its students meaty chunks of wisdom to nourish the soul and to give strength. In many ways the book of Proverbs is the meat for it is deep wisdom that must be meditated upon and contemplated and used for energy and action.

she has mixed her wine

This is interesting in that it can mean that the wine was diluted which was the typical Jewish custom as straight wine would be too strong for the average Jewish taste and sensibilities. Or it can mean that wisdom has mixed wine with other juices or alcohol to make it stronger as in Isaiah 5:22. It would seem that in this analogy that wisdom prepares wine in the common way just as the slaughter of meat is in the common way. Therefore, this is most likely a diluted wine which was the custom of that day. What is the wine? It is also wisdom and/or understanding or counsel or prudence or one of the other aspects or partners of wisdom.

she has set her table

Wisdom is not impulsive and unprepared. There is a table set. This speaks of preparation and desire to entertain. This is contrasted with the impulsiveness with the woman of folly. She counts on the impulsiveness of desire to draw her guests. Wisdom has been planning to have students and she has a table prepared. Also note that in Proverbs 7 the woman of folly prepares her bed and not a table. Wisdom does not do illicit things, and the preparation is for discussion and at a table where relationships and information are gained.

The point of this section is that wisdom wants people to learn how to live better. There are results to show that have stood the test of time. Wisdom is projecting potential but has real wisdom to share that comes from the rough and tumble of real life. There are real discussions about how it applies in business, at home, in friendships, etc.

Too often what is passing as wisdom in our colleges and places of higher learning today are new theories that have not been proven. When you are listening to teachers and the supposed wise, keep asking yourself whether what they are saying has really been tried in the real world. Has it accomplished something? I grow weary of theories and ideas about leadership, marriage, families, business, friendship, normal life that has never been tried or comes from a person who has only failed at the very thing they are trying to help us with.

- Don't get your marriage wisdom from someone who has been divorced three times.

- Don't get your parenting wisdom from someone with rebellious kids who hate their parents.

- Don't get your business wisdom from someone who keeps failing in business even if they do it spectacularly.

- Don't get your view of meaning in life from someone whose life is a train wreck of marriages, failed business, abandoned friends, and addictions.

- Don't get your spiritual advice and wisdom from someone who has no prayer life or who is more greedy than godly.

Get your wisdom from those whose lives have stability and look like what you want yours to look like. They will have something to say that is meaty and worthwhile.

February 10

PROVERBS 10:2
Ill-gotten gains do not profit, but righteousness delivers from death

The three-word phrase translated *ill-gotten gains* here in the New American Standard Bible is actually in the Hebrew two words: *wicked treasures.* The idea is that there is a treasury of wickedness or material gains that can be had from the storehouse of wickedness, but it does not profit a person.

This is such a valuable lesson to learn. The younger that a person learns it, the better it will be. All of us will be tempted to gain money, wealth, possessions, power, prestige, popularity, etc., in ways that are just not right and we know it. But we can see how what we want can be had by just a little cheating, by just a little lie, by just a small theft, by just a little sexual license, by just a little greed or anger or intimidation. Riches and prosperity look like they are there for the taking, and in many ways they are there and they can be had. But they do not really profit. They will, at some point, destroy you. They will at some point – if not immediately – suck out your soul so that the very things you wanted are no longer enjoyable.

I think of politicians who plagiarized others' speeches and were never prominent on the national stage again. I think of football coaches who lied on their resume and had to give up dream jobs they had just won. I think of executives who are behind bars today because they played fast and loose with the books and lied to investors. I think of pastors who had huge churches and incredible ministries and then were selling used cars because they committed adultery. I think of stockbrokers who made billions of dollars using illegal schemes and were drummed out of their profession. I think of accountants who went along with schemes to fool investors who destroyed their whole company. I think of bankers who cheated in investment schemes to line their own pockets and who, in the process, brought down companies that had been in business for hundreds of years. I think of sports heroes who took steroids and other drugs to win and when exposed, lost everything.

Remember in the game of life you will be given opportunities to cheat. It does not matter what field of endeavor you find yourself working in. There will be chances to cheat and shade and take shortcuts. Don't do it. For even if you do gain, it will not profit. It is better to be poorer and have your integrity. For the life of a person who makes withdrawals out of the treasury of wickedness is not the life you think it will be.

but righteousness delivers from death

Doing the right thing instead of the cheaty, wicked thing causes you to escape the death that is stalking the one who has profited by the treasury of wickedness.

Notice that Solomon uses the word *death*. He is saying that some form of death is following those who play on the wicked side of the street. There may be profit there, but there is also death. What is death? It is separation from: Physical death is separation from our bodies. Spiritual death is separation from God. Emotional death is separation from our emotions or from our feeling; going dead in the sense of enjoying our feelings or having real joy. Mental death is separation from coherent thoughts and logic. Each of these forms of death stalks the person who uses the treasury of wickedness as their personal bank account. When anyone crosses the lines of righteousness and makes a profit by doing what is against God's Ten Commandments, they ask death to follow them and cling to them. They may not die physically for a few years or a few decades; but emotional, mental, or spiritual death is also following them and attaching itself ever deeper to their lives.

Notice that one of the benefits of righteousness is that it delivers from death. When we act righteously and refuse to go along with wickedness, then life wins and death loses. I think of the businessman whom I heard was involved with a business that unbeknown to him was cheating people. When he discovered what this business was doing, he told the person what he had discovered and said you will either quit or I will completely pull out. The wicked person refused to stop, so the righteous businessman withdrew from the arrangement at considerable cost to himself. In a few short months the government came and arrested the wicked man and was amazed that the righteous person had removed himself from that business. The wicked person went to jail and the righteous person received a commendation and escaped jail and fines because of his refusal to participate in wickedness.

This proverb is a way of saying to us: Don't be tempted to gain in the wrong way. It is not worth it. Gain in the right way. Make progress on building up a pile of goods for yourself the right way.

You may be tempted to cheat at school or lie about your age to get into a place or be tempted to lie on a job resume or be tempted to be wicked in a thousand other ways that this world, your own selfishness, and the Devil will come up with. DON'T. It is not worth it to have the milky film of death begin to coat your life, your emotions, your mind, and your spirit.

I must say at this point that the only thing or form of righteousness that will deliver from the spiritual death – that is the condition of all of us – is the righteousness of Jesus Christ, the Son of God. The New Testament tells us that Jesus Christ lived a perfect life and was perfectly righteous, completely satisfying God's demands for entrance into heaven. He willingly gave up that perfect life and submitted to death on a cross to be able to substitute His perfection for the sins of all who would embrace Him as Savior. Each one of us is being stalked by spiritual death and, in fact, are already separated from God because of our sins. But Jesus Christ and His righteous life and sacrificial death makes a way back to a living relationship with God.

February 11

PROVERBS 11:2
When pride comes, then comes dishonor, but with the humble is wisdom

pride

The basic idea is pride, a sense of self-importance, which often is exaggerated to include defiance and even rebelliousness.

What is interesting about this proverb is that it proclaims that the one thing the proud person wants is exactly what this person will not receive. The person who is proud wants to be noticed and to have attention focused on them for who they are or what they do. This person wants their accomplishments trumpeted; they want even just their presence at an event or place trumpeted. They must be noticed. They want honor – the added value that is given to the truly deserving. Their pride, however, causes them to seek attention in a disruptive and obnoxious way.

When the aspect of any person's personality shows up that has to be noticed or on top, etc., then dishonor is on its way. Hold back those impulses that make you want to focus attention on yourself - that moves you to want to be noticed just for being there.

dishonor

This root signifies the lowering of another's social position. When we seek to elevate our social position or standing through power plays, rebelliousness, bizarre attention, getting devices or stunts, we may get what we seek; but it will come with a lowering of our social position. In other words, the very thing we seek we will not have. This is a pulling away of social esteem and favor. When we seek to be noticed or gain attention for ourselves, we are moving into a place of foolishness and away from wisdom. You can't find wisdom clamoring for the spotlight. When you seek to be noticed and have attention on yourself, you will be devalued. Your goal is negated by the search. Honor is a by-product of a loving life.

humble

The verb means to be modest or humble. The Septuagint translates this Hebrew word with a word that means low-lying. This could be taken to mean calling attention to ourselves – a notice-me spirit. When we seek after the acclaim, fame, or attention of others rather than doing a great thing for the simple sake of its needing to be done, we will find it brings shame. A test in a sense is set up. Can we do something and not demand notice or point out that we did something? If you make too big of a deal about yourself or what you have done, then it will be your downfall. It seems to be that God would have us be noticed for what we truly do, not what we do to be noticed. It is not wrong to be noticed and even to be strong or forceful in our personality. But when we seek out the fame, attention, power, and prestige that accompanies real honor, then we get the opposite of what we wanted. To seek after the results of doing something positive without doing the deed is the essence of pride. It will result in dishonor. I may not know my great-grandchildren at all, but I do want them to know that whatever the world looks like at that point, it is still God's universe and pride will not help you for long and it will eventually hurt you. Do good things that really help people and the honor you seek will come to you.

wisdom

Wisdom is again that triple-win choice. What type of choices are you making? Are they choices where everybody wins? Does God win? Is He pleased? The fear of the Lord is the beginning of wisdom, so start looking for the wise thing to do by asking what would please God in this circumstance. That is a much better starting place than starting with what would please me or others.

February 12

PROVERBS 12:2
A good man will obtain favor from the Lord, but He will condemn a man who devises evil

This proverb is the essence of moral living, but it also hints at at least one of the problems of viewing moral living from a foolish perspective.

This proverb says that the person who does the good thing – the morally helpful thing and not just abstaining from the selfish and/or morally reprehensible thing – will receive favor, blessing, and grace from God. At the same time, the person who plots and schemes to accomplish selfish and sinful ends will be guilty and receive a compensation or consequence because of it.

One needs to spend some time thinking about the idea of goodness. This is the opposite of evil. Evil and wickedness in the Old Testament is behavior that is beyond the Ten Commandments; therefore, stealing, lying, adultery, blasphemy, idolatry, rebellion, murder, coveting others property are all forms of wickedness. Much of morality has been discussed and framed as stopping before one commits these violations of the Ten Commandments. That is true but it is not being good. Good is a positive, not the absence of a negative.

One could make a case for the boundaries of morality being in the place they are because it is at that point when the selfishness-track that the person is on begins to do significant societal damage. The actions that are being perpetrated at that morality point are now going to collect damage and difficulty to the person and others at a point where it begins to destabilize the individual's life and the peace and security of the society at large.

Goodness is doing the opposite of the negative and, thereby, benefiting society and another person. Being good or doing good is worshipping God and putting Him first. Goodness is speaking blessings into others' lives. It is adding value to authorities rather than rebelling. It is meeting the needs of others rather than being angry and violent. It is developing a strong and loving marriage rather than being selfish and unfaithful. It is being generous and charitable rather than stealing. It is being truthful instead of lying. It is being content rather than covetous of others' blessings.

We must make sure that we do not begin to define being a good person as one who didn't do really bad stuff or being a nice person. That is not a biblical definition. Goodness is doing really good stuff. This means that we need to set out each day to do positive things into the lives of the people that we meet that day. I am amazed at how many well-meaning Christians never escape thinking about themselves every day. They somehow have not gotten this idea of being good – doing something positive and need-meeting into the lives of people. They believe that if they are nice and not overtly evil or selfish that this somehow is okay and good. It is not; especially for the person making a claim to godliness.

Pour into the lives of the people and relationships of your life positive, helpful, need-meeting activities, words, and attitudes so that people will know you as a biblically good person.

One must also realize that this is not good in the ultimate sense as God is good. That would require perfection in goodness. No one but God has that level of goodness and because of that, no one but Jesus Christ has ever earned a place in God's presence with their life.

One of the hints or subtle truths of this verse is how long it takes for the favor of the Lord to show up. This is not talked about in this verse directly but think through the process of goodness and foolishness. The fool is one who lives for self and immediate gratification. They want what they want right now with no waiting. If they do not personally see a benefit to an action immediately, they will rarely do it. This is the opposite of the person of wisdom. They are motivated not by self but to glorify God. They are able to be patient and wait for the personal benefits that come from righteousness and goodness. Because of how the wise person and the fool approach benefits and results, it is obvious that the favor that the good person receives will not come as a candy motivation to keep doing good things. Instead, the favor the Lord bestows on those who do good and slowly builds up and envelops the good person. They may not even be able to point to specific benefits as to why they came; they just surround the good person. For while God rewards those who live righteously, it is not a Pavlovian reward but instead a higher more patient benefit.

In other words, realize that the benefits of the good actions you perform will come to you over time and by the hand of a good and benevolent God who knows how to reward those who seek Him. Do not do something good and then look heavenward for where the candy reward will fall.

PROVERBS 13:2
From the fruit of a man's mouth he enjoys good, but the desire of the treacherous is violence

Solomon noticed that it is not essentially a man's talent or ability that causes him to prosper but his people skills. That is what this nugget on wisdom tells us. You can have tremendous abilities, talents, and gifts; but if you are a jerk, you will not succeed. We must all learn how to talk to other people in a positive and constructive way. It is what you say that causes people to want to be around you.

One of the studies that consistently strikes me was done a number of years ago. Engineering firms were asked to rate what were the causes for engineers to be hired, retain their job, and get promoted. Their findings were that 85% of an engineer's ability to be hired, retain their position, and be promoted was their people skills – their ability to work with others. It was not their technical skills or brilliance at math; it was people skills, the ability to work on a team, the general likability factors that are considered soft sciences. If this is true for engineers, then it is even truer for all other professions. It is, as Solomon says, in the mouth that a person enjoys good.

There are two verses in Scripture which push this analogy further: Proverbs 1:31: *They shall eat the fruit of their own way* and Hosea 10:13: *You have plowed wickedness and have reaped injustice, you have eaten the fruit of lies.* This sentiment is very similar to the statements of God in Galatians 6:7: *Do not be deceived, God is not mocked whatsoever a man sows that shall he also reap.*

Watch what you say and how you say it. Learn how to be positive, helpful, constructive, and encouraging. Let me remind you that any idiot can point out things that are wrong with Watch what you say and how you say it. Learn how to be positive, helpful, constructive, and encouraging. Let me remind you that any idiot can point out things that are wrong with others or their work. NO one responds to that unless it comes from a boss and even then it is usually resented. It is recognition of the strengths and successes of another person that is most appreciated and remembered. It is the fruit of a person's mouth that will produce what a person lives off even if that person is not a salesman. We often think that only sales people have to speak well or be positive when they really want to tear into someone. But this is not true. It is a principle of life that Solomon shares here. He even says it stronger than the translators. The original Hebrew states that the fruit of one's mouth is what a person eats. If you do not use your mouth for the right things, you will not eat well.

One of the things I try and stress to my children is that we must know how to get along with all kinds of people. We do not need to point out everything we disagree with a person about. In fact, we are usually better off not to focus on where we disagree with a person. We should look to see where we agree with a person; where we can connect with others. There will be time to talk about where we disagree. When it comes to that, it will be better received if we have a history of looking for the places of agreement. This is one of the dangers in our current culture. We attack not just the ideas of people we disagree with but the whole person. It is entirely possible for a person to hold a wrong notion about something and to still be worthy of human dignity. But our society has become hardened into camps which cannot see anything good in the other person who has a different perspective on certain ideas.

but the desire of the treacherous is violence

The word translated *desire* is the word *nephesh* which means soul. The idea here is that the deceitful, treacherous person internally thinks only of what he wants. They cannot divert what they want from occupying their mind. It seems foreign to think about what other people want or need. It is abhorrent for them to think about giving up what they may want in order to help someone else get what they need.

The word *treacherous* is the Hebrew word *bagad* which means transgressor, unfaithful, deceitful. It is clearly a person who regularly goes outside the boundaries of the Ten Commandments to accomplish what he wants. He finds no limit in these moral guidelines from God. He deceives others about his having crossed them in order to have them believe that he is playing by the rules that they have to abide by. But he does not live by any rules but "I want what I want." Therefore he does violence to others.

This is contrasted to those who produce fruit from their words for others. The one is selfish to the core. The other is a servant and a lover of others through kindness, goodness, and civility to others.

The word translated *violence* is the Hebrew word *chamac* which means violence, cruelty, wrong, damage, injustice. What Solomon is saying about the person who deceives with their words is that following behind them is a wake of damage and destruction. These people use words to get what they want, but it produces violence and destruction. The righteous person instead produces fruit that they themselves and others feed off.

What are the results of your words and speech patterns? Health, energy, joy and relationships or damage, hurt feelings, emotional bruises, feeling used. One person produces words that are edifying and helpful; the other deceives people to get what he wants. The second person does not care that what they want will hurt others and leave a trail of destruction. These people just want what they want.

February 14

PROVERBS 14:2

He who walks in his uprightness fears the Lord, but he who is devious in his ways despises Him

There is something motivating righteousness. People don't stay within the guidelines of God's morality without a reason. That reason is a mixture of positive and negative reasons called the fear of the Lord. It is a shame that we no longer teach the fear of the Lord in our churches or our culture. And as a result, no one has the proper incentive to stay within the boundaries of morality and decency.

What is this cryptic motivator called the fear of the Lord?

It is positive in that it is reverence and awe and delight in the Lord. It is the realization that God exists, is great, and is worth seeking. Hebrews 11:3. There are positive benefits to maintaining one's self in righteousness. God will reward those who trust Him and, by faith, carry out His directives.

The fear of the Lord is also negative in that everyone will face consequences for their actions and judgment day in the future. God has so structured the universe that there are consequences for all actions. The consequences for morally wicked actions build up and destroy the joy of life. The wrath of God is right now being revealed against all ungodliness and unrighteousness of men. Romans 1:18. Our society has become willingly blind to the consequences of cursing, lying, stealing, adultery, and murder. They have wanted to pursue a course of action that will take them past the morality of the Bible, so they have stopped detailing what happens when people live this way.

The fear of the Lord also means that there will be Judgment Day at the end of life. All that we have ever done, said, or thought will be replayed for evaluation. Romans 2:5,6; Proverbs 24:12; Matthew 16:27; 2 Corinthians 5:10. Believers and non-believers will face this type of judgment. Those who have not accepted their need for the sacrifice of Jesus Christ will face a judgment in which God will be looking for mistakes, wrongs, and selfishness. Those who have embraced Jesus Christ as their Savior and Lord will be looking for that which He can reward, that which is done trusting Him and at His direction. All that we have ever done will be on display before the righteous judge of the earth.

This should persuade us to not do some things that we could do. It should cause us to not think certain things but instead embrace wholesome thoughts. It should keep us from saying some things we would like to say but know that we shouldn't.

Only when one has a healthy and constant understanding of the fear of the Lord – both positive and negative – will one have the proper motivation for being righteous.

One must regularly remind oneself that everything we ever think, say, and do will be on God's video tape and will be played back at Judgment Day. It is your choice whether the events recorded on the video tape record actions of faith and righteousness or events that Jesus had to die for on the cross.

Realize that there is a reward for living a life of righteousness. It is a life of deep and enjoyable relationships. God does bless those who follow Him. Enjoy His blessings without guilt and do not chase the "blessings" of the wicked.

but he who is devious in his ways despises Him

The word devious is the word deviation or crooked or turn away. It really means so much more than a person who is just devious although that type of person could be included in this person. This, instead, describes one who turns away from morality; one who lives outside of the boundaries of the Bible and, in many cases, outside of societies. This is a person who basically says: no one tells me what I can't do.

This type of person is described as a person who despises God who is the ultimate authority in morality. This proverb does not say anything about what happens to this person; it is just a statement about their motivation. They despise God. In our growing pagan culture it is easier to see this type of person's contempt for the God of the Bible. They actually believe that belief in God and biblical morality has harmed society. This proverb tries to get the wise person to understand that this is the way the unrighteous person thinks. Realize this and understand it. Appealing to God and the Bible will not work with this person. Unless they have a radical conversion, they will not submit to God and His rules.

This proverb does not state how the wise person should use this insight into the motivations of the wicked. But there are a number of obvious applications.

Do not expect them to accept appeals to God's revealed morality.

Expect them to ignore the consequences of sin.

Their only motivation for change is self-interest.

There are people who do not want any authority to be over them.

PROVERBS 15:2

The tongue of the wise makes knowledge acceptable. But the mouth of fools spouts folly.

Notice that the mouth of the fool gushes forth with selfishness, anger, hatred, criticalness, and impulsiveness. This is very normal for each person to let their sin nature show. When sin grabs you, this is what comes out of your mouth. You become a fountain for selfishness.

A great question is: Would you want to deal with you the way you are acting? Answer: No!!!

When you are trying to persuade someone that your expectation is the valid one, then you will need to be much wiser. You must figure out a way to make it a win for them. If your words make it a win for you and a loss for them, then you will always have the other person reject your advice. Making knowledge acceptable is a part of saying things in such a way that the person will see how they benefit from doing it the way you like. It means that you think about how to present the information or the expectation in such a way that everybody wins. The word acceptable is the idea of well pleasing. It is more than just acceptable but desired. When wisdom is used, the person wants and desires to do it the way that you have presented it. They see what you are saying as clearly a win for themselves.

There is much foolishness in the idea that "I won't let anyone tell me what to do. I will not follow your rules. I will be a difficult case unless it goes my way. I will be completely selfish and see things only from my point of view." The wise person realizes that everyone just wants to win. And the real leader and wise person show how everybody wins through following what God wants and, hopefully, they want. There is a level of selfishness and pride in the fool that is unmistakable. I watched a man at a swim meet clearly act like spending time with his family was beneath him. He had to be there, but he clearly protested every minute. He kept trying to demonstrate how in control he was and how irritated he was. He just kept saying things that were meant to make others see him in a positive light but just made him look more bizarre.

This type of tongue and words can grab a hold of anyone and turn them into a fool. All they have to do is let selfishness take over. All they have to do is let a wound fester. All they have to do is let pride take over. All they have to do is let the fact that they didn't get their own way take over. These temptations to become a fool are all around us.

PROVERBS 16:2
All the ways of a man are clean in his own sight, but the Lord weighs the motives

This is one of the numerous passages in Proverbs and through the Scriptures that speak of Judgment Day. There will be a judgment day for every person who has ever lived. It is this sure judgment that allows for the scales to be balanced properly in the end. There will be some things that will not be settled until then. You will see some who are evil prosper while some who are righteous suffer. Don't despair. *God will not be mocked whatsoever a man sows that will he also reap.*

Everything we ever think, say, do – every attitude and every motive – is being permanently recorded for evaluation at the judgment.

Think about everything you have ever done being exposed to God and others and there will be a profound sense of humility and a cry for mercy. It is only in the death of Christ on the cross that we have any hope of favor with God.

Judgment day is a sobering thought, but God continually wants us to focus on its reality.

all the ways of a man are clean in his own sight

Mankind has a fascinating ability to rationalize even the most heinous sins and actions. We just believe that the reasons we did something are weighty enough to give us excuse for that action. The reason why we put off that thing. The reason why we never finished school or were rude to that person or looked at pornography. All our actions have reasons and something internal to our self-focus beliefs that our reasons are sufficient and excuse the behavior.

What this proverb states is that this is not true. God has a higher standard and will judge people not from an outside perspective but from the very depth of their being.

but the Lord weighs the motives

The word translated *motives* is really the word *ruach* which means spirit. The Lord is weighing and judging the spirit of the person and what they are in the deepest part of their being.

This is why the early church established a pattern of confessing sins every night before a person retired to bed. The seven deadly sins became a favorite as well as the Ten Commandments. These were confession guides to evaluate from an outside perspective what we had done that day. I highly recommend this practice. It is an application of Jesus' principle of daily foot washing in John 13.

As you are going to sleep before you have dozed off, go through the seven deadly sins (Pride, Envy, Anger, Lust, Sloth, Gluttony, Greed) slowly, asking the Lord to bring conviction if you have committed any of these sins that day. If God convicts you that, yes, you have done one of these, then agree with God that it was wrong.

Thank Him for the forgiveness that is in the blood of Christ. Ask Him to apply the forgiveness of Christ to that sin. If any restitution or apology to a person is needed, then plan to do that the next day.

PROVERBS 17:2
A servant who acts wisely will rule over a son who acts shamefully, and will share in the inheritance among brothers

acts wisely

The word *wisely* is the Hebrew word *sakal* which is a synonym for understanding but includes the idea of understanding the reasons for events and not just distinguishing between. It can also be thought of as having insight and comprehension.

The proverb states that the person who is just an employee can find positions of authority and prosperity if they learn how to act with insight and comprehension. All leaders, owners, and directors are looking for sharp people who are really loyal that will grow their business under them.

This proverb screams that you can rise beyond minimum wages; you can have real authority; you can be trusted with significant assignments and personnel; you can be given parts of a company. All you have to do is act with insight and comprehension. Act in such a way that shows that you understand how things really work.

It also screams that if you are only offered minimum wage jobs or you never get promoted or you do not get significant assignments, then you have not acted wisely. No matter what you think you have done or acted like, it has not been a demonstration of wisdom, insight, and comprehension if your compensation has not risen, your authority has not grown, the projects have not increased in significance.

acts shamefully

This is the Hebrew word *bos* which means shame, disappointed, and also carries with it the idea of failure.

The idea here seems to be that the favored person who fails will not be as highly regarded as the servant who succeeds. Actions speak louder than failed bloodlines. Yes, who you know or are related to will open a door but wise actions speak louder. Learn to act wisely.

Most businesses operate as meritocracies. Whoever merits the raise or the promotion will get it. If this basic rule is not followed, then a political, social, contentious mess develops. The people in the positions know who works hardest and who has the best attitude.

will rule

Rulership is based upon the ability to lead well. Some people are leaders, but they do not lead well so others are reluctant to put them in the next level of leadership.

God is saying that if you learn how to cause others to do your expectations in a non-confrontational, non-manipulative way, you will be given leadership positions even over relatives and favored employees. The story of Joseph is the classic example as is the story of Daniel and his rise through the ranks of Nebecanezzer's court.

will share

This is the Hebrew word *chalaq* which means to divide, to share. Those who do a great job of leading and managing will divide the profits and even the inheritance. We see this with Eleazar and Abraham.

Just because you were not born into a privileged family does not mean that you cannot get ahead. If you learn wisdom, you will be able to share in the inheritance; but if foolishness still guides your actions and words, then you will be constantly frustrated by your lack of promotions and lack of inclusion.

PROVERBS 18:2
A fool does not delight in understanding, but only in revealing his own mind

The word *fool* is the Hebrew word *kesil* which means dull or obstinate – not in their intellectual gifts but in their moral and volitional gifts. This is the selfish, rebellious, and impulsive proud person. There are three words used in Proverbs for fool: *kesil*, *ewil*, and *nabal*. Each of these words emphasizes a slightly different character trait of the same type of person. *Kesil* emphasizes the obstinate rebellious person who makes consistently wrong choices. *Ewil* is the word which emphasizes that this person does not respect moral boundaries, only his/her own wants. *Nabal* focuses on the anger and meanness of this type of individual, forcing others to try and get their way.

The proverb opens with what the fool does not take great delight in which they should. The word *delight* is the Hebrew word *hapes* which means to feel great favor towards something. The person who is wise takes delight and finds great enjoyment in discerning the reasons things happen – the quality of understanding – *tebuna* in the Hebrew. The fool only cares about getting their own way. They do not have any curiosity about how systems work or why things happen the way they do. They only care about what they have become fixated upon – their own selfish desires.

Have you become fixated upon what would make you happy and refuse to probe into what would make your marriage better or your family more enjoyable or your career move forward?

The great danger is that we all feel the impulse that the fool does. We all want to talk about what we are thinking about; what we believe about something; what we want; how things impact us. But that is not what a wise person does. The wise person investigates and pursues insight and discernment. The wise person makes sure that they have the facts. They take great delight in finding the real reasons things happen.

Stop and ask yourself: Do most of your conversations involve telling others what you already know or do they involve asking questions, listening, probing, etc. If all you talk about is what you already know, then you are well down the road to becoming a fool. Learn something new and take delight in penetrating beneath the surface. Do not fixate upon yourself; there is a whole world of delights that don't involve you. God's world is full of surprises. Become wise; it will be a great time.

February 19

PROVERBS 19:2

Also it is not good for a person to be without knowledge, and he who hurries his footsteps errs

This verse gives a good definition of hurry: proceeding without adequate knowledge. No matter how fast or slow you are going, if you don't have the right knowledge then you are hurrying. On the other hand, no matter how fast you are going, it is not hurry if you have adequate knowledge.

The quest then is for the proper knowledge. Usually in every endeavor there are certain bits of knowledge that must be obtained. Without those bits of raw data or information, it is unwise to move forward. In order to move a project or decision along, one must move along the acquisition of this crucial knowledge.

Each person is tempted to move ahead with only part of the information needed. We want to guess on the rest or project that those bits of information are not critical to the decision. But they are and will sink the endeavor if they go against the decision you want to make.

There is another foolish thing that some are prone to do. That is to go into the knowledge-acquisition mode to such a degree that even after the crucial bits of information are gathered, there is still no decision to move ahead because there is always more information to gather. This is killing an idea through study.

The crucial question is: Do you have all the information that you really need to make a decision? Should you wait until you have another bit of information? If you have the crucial pieces of information, then move ahead and make the decision. It is not hurrying if you have knowledge you need.

February 20

PROVERBS 20:2

The terror of a king is like the growling of a lion; he who provokes him to anger forfeits his own life

The idea is that the leader of any venture has a plan and an expectation; and the person who blocks, interrupts, redirects, or cancels that expectation of the leader will provoke the wrath of the leader.

Anger is the reaction to unmet expectations. It is not the only reaction, but it is a major reaction to unmet expectations. Every leader has a preferred future – a vision of how things would be in a perfect world. It is these future pictures that form the expectation and battle plan of the leader. Do not get in the way of that or you will be seen as a mutineer. You will be forfeiting your life within that organization.

Leaders expect to have their expectations carried out even when they are not communicated clearly. They still expect people to just somehow know what they are interested in. The anticipation of the leader's expectation is the key to promotion in any organization. The quickest way to stalled development – or even being fired from an organization – is to cross the expectation of the leader.

February 21

PROVERBS 21:2

Every man's way is right in his own eyes, but the Lord weighs the hearts

every man's way is right in his own eyes

This is a statement of the basic perspective of people "under the sun" or from their sinful or selfish position. If I didn't think it was right for me, then I wouldn't do it. This does not mean that everyone thinks their way is right in the eyes of God.

All of us have a natural tendency, since Adam's fall, to live from the selfish or foolish perspective. It is this perspective that God asks parents to drive out of their children. It is the orientation to only or primarily look at a situation or choice for what we can get out of it. How do we win in this situation? It is this that the Bible calls foolishness. It could also be regarded as the natural outgrowth of original sin. We were originally created to have a different default setting. God created mankind to automatically think and act from the perspective of what does God want, then what would cause others to win, and finally what would cause me to win. One of the effects of the fall is that this order is exactly reversed and self becomes primary in our heart.

When we are restored at the return of Christ, it is this self-focused tendency that will be fixed or we would never enjoy heaven. In fact some people say, "Won't heaven be boring?" "How long can we sing praises to Jesus?" "Won't we grow tired of playing ping pong or resting?" All these questions represent a self-focused position. We will not have that in heaven. It is hell where the self-focused stay. God will fix it so that we will naturally be inclined to what brings God glory, what would God want, and what would please the Lord Jesus. We will think of wanting that first. Then we will naturally, and with great delight, want the others in heaven to win and gain and profit next. This will not be drudgery or difficult. It will be our natural inclination. The wonder of heaven will be that others will truly be looking out for our best interests as well as God. It will not be like here where it is unnatural for people to actually truly, from no ulterior motive, be looking out for your best interest. And then and only then will we consider what choice or action would benefit us. But truly we will not have to think about that much because God and others will be naturally thinking about that for us. We will enjoy the wonder of their love and concern for us constantly. We will profit and gain and enjoy immensely because we will not be self-focused.

Now interestingly enough, the same thing can happen here that will happen in heaven and that is that we can stop being so self-focused and selfish and really think of God's glory and others' profit first. When we do that, it will always result in a better life here for us. In fact, this is the kind of life that God wants us to live.

God wants us to get out of the natural, selfish, and foolish way of living by reminding us that He weighs hearts. The Christian does not come under the judgment for life or death. But the Christian does have to face the judgment seat of Christ (2 Corinthians 5:10). We are reminded that we will be judged whether our deeds are good or worthless. Did you do what was selfishly profitable or did you love God or others with your actions today? Have you added to the glory of God through your actions today by putting Him first? Have you added to the glory of God by looking out for the best interests of others ahead of yourself? The Christian should be the one who realizes that he profits only when God and others profit. The Christian is not allowed to pursue the win/lose scenarios. He left that kind of life when he came to Jesus Christ.

This proverb reminds us that we all have a natural tendency since the fall to baptize our own perspective and our own selfishness as correct and good. The key perspective is: Would it stand muster under the Lord's gaze? Would it stand under the evaluation of the first and second great commandment?

To draw this down to a finer point. It is my job as a husband to make sure that my wife wins in the choices I make and the actions I take, before I win. It is my job as a parent to make sure that my girls win in the choices I make and the actions I take, before I win. It is their job to escape their natural selfishness and make sure that I win. It is my job as an employee to make sure that my employer wins before I make sure that I win. We are living in a devolving world in which selfishness is increasingly becoming the order of the day. It is called a dog-eat-dog world in which you need to get yours before other people eat your lunch. This is the path of personal and societal destruction. There is a similar verse in the book of Proverbs which gives a different point on the idea of your own "right" way. Proverbs 14:12: *There is a way which seems right to a man but the end thereof is the way of death.*

February 22

PROVERBS 22:2

The rich and the poor have a common bond, the Lord is the maker of them all

This is a proverb that is easy to overlook. Solomon is speaking really to the heart of the person who is rich. The rich are not made out of different stuff than those who are poor. God is the maker of both.

What He really says is also hidden under the translator's words. The actual Hebrew words read *rich and poor meet maker all The Lord.* The most readable literal translation would be *rich and poor meet, the Lord is the maker of both.*

The word *maker* is the word *asah* which is to make, to do, to produce. There is richness that can be seen in the implications of these ideas. Remember that this seems obvious, but there is a reason why Solomon took note of it and why God thought it was significant enough to make the Scriptures.

There is a tendency on the part of the rich to forget two things: One, that they are the same as the poor person; they just have abundance while the poor person has less than they need.

Second, the rich person tends to forget that they will meet the poor person in front of the judgment seat of God. There will be a judgment day in which their deeds and the poor person's deeds will be evaluated for their selfishness or sin content. They both will face the same God and money will have nothing to do with it.

The rich person tends to forget these two things. It is important to remember these and not believe that you are somehow fundamentally different from the person who cannot generate an abundance of money.

The definition of poor is that they have less than they need to live. It is not that they have less than they want or less than an arbitrary amount that society says is enough. They have less than what they need to eat, clothe, and shelter themselves. The rich are those who have more than they need to eat, more than they need to clothe themselves, and more than they need to shelter themselves. According to this definition, there are many more rich people in this culture than people think. It is important for them not to believe that they are somehow better or fundamentally different from those who are poor. It is also important for all to realize that there is a judgment day coming when all a person's thoughts, motives, words, attitudes, and deeds will be evaluated by the Almighty. It is a sobering thought – which should make us run into the arms of our Savior, Jesus Christ.

February 23

PROVERBS 23:2
And put a knife to your throat if you are a man of great appetite

This proverb is the actual command of what to do when dining with a leader when you are in the presence of luxuries and desirable things that only the very rich or powerful have available to them.

Solomon uses very strong imagery. Put a knife to your throat so that if you were to swallow, you would cut your own throat. Your swallowing mechanism should be closed to the opportunities that will be available to you.

One of the greatest tests of a person's character is success. It is easier to be moral and controlled when there are few other options. But when the whole world is offering itself to you and you can have every type of temptation, this is when your character shows through. Solomon says you must make sure that you do not let your guard down just because it is free; just because it is being offered. Food, sex, money, and power can all be traps which hold their prey in an ever tightening embrace.

Solomon is trying to get you ready for any and all eventualities. If you are successful at the skill development that God has given you, then you will be in front of great men; but you must know how to be there without letting that environment destroy you. This is one of the few sections of the Scriptures that deal specifically with gluttony, overeating, and the temptations of food. In America we have become the young stewards let into the king's chamber who could not control ourselves. We have become fat – feasting on all the wonderful pastries, desserts, and wonderful tasting goodies that are plumbing us up for ill health and inactivity.

Taking a broader perspective on this verse, we see that having self-control with our eating is crucial to maintaining our place of leadership and success. Don't be fooled; you can eat your way out of the center of God's will.

The most highly successful weight loss program in America and the only one to stand up under scientific study is Weight Watchers which emphasizes, through their points system, portion control – or in Solomon's parlance, putting a knife to your throat. Realize that living anywhere in western civilization is to be in the king's chamber where delicacies are available to you that are not good for you. You have to learn how to tell yourself NO. You have to, in many cases, eliminate whole types of foods as not to be consumed: Cookies, Ice Cream, Cakes, Pies, French Fries, Fast Food, etc. The healthy way to go with eating seems to be vegetables, fruits, whole grains, lean meets, and lots of water.

The ethical adage is appropriate here. Just because you can doesn't mean you should.

It would be a shame to go to all the work to develop a skill and gain information that vaunts you to making a significant impact, only to be shut out of using it because you could not control your weight. I know that shouldn't make a difference, but it does. It did in Solomon's day and it still does today. Put a knife to your throat – control how much of the bad stuff you are consuming.

February 24

PROVERBS 24:2
For their minds devise violence, and their lips talk of trouble

This is a very important proverb describing the thinking of those that God describes as evil. We all find ourselves tempted to give into this kind of thinking, but it will surely move us in the direction of evil and a non-satisfying life.

for their minds devise violence

The word *violence* is the Hebrew word *sod* which means havoc, to spoil, maltreatment, etc. What one has to see in this word is often the idea of vengeance or payback with a violent or escalating element. The evil person is the one who gives voice and place to the thoughts that come across everyone's mind when they have been crossed: How will I make them pay for doing this to me? If you give into this kind of thinking, then you will become evil or have already become evil. The constant defense of your own ego or plans against others ends with a person in a very evil place. You are the embodiment of selfishness gone to seed.

I remember watching a man literally challenge every driver – who did not yield to his explicit right-of-way – to a fist fight. This man was unable to work because of his inability to get along with anyone except those who totally submitted to his thinking. He destroyed his own family and every relationship that he touched all by loudly and violently exerting his rights, ego, and ideas. When selfishness takes over a man or woman, they will end up across the line of the Ten Commandments; and what they will become once over there is a person who will become consumed with payback and competition. This may be actual violence or it can be political, reputational, emotional, mental, or vocational revenge and havoc.

Don't go down this road where every wrong must be redressed. Don't feel as though every slight and every injustice must have an answer. Life is not always fair to you or supportive of what you want to do. Get over it and move forward and find another way. Seek justice for the big things, not everything.

By the way, if you find yourself working for a person who needs to keep track of every aspect of non-support or perceived disloyalty and then make the person pay, this is an evil person who bends the rules in all sorts of ways to fit his/her own situation.

Don't let your mind go there. It will be tempted to engage in this type of havoc and destruction. Let it go.

and their lips talk of trouble

The evil people are always talking about the trouble they will cause to others - especially those who cross them or who do not help them or who oppose them. There is this idea of themselves as the necessary good and all others need to get out of the way and or help this irresistible good. This is selfishness at its core - to believe in every case that your ideas need to be implemented; that your plans and ego need to be dominant. Everyone has a measure of this, but those who choose to live outside of God's moral boundary structure have huge doses of this selfishness and of this "here is what I want to do to the person who got in my way."

Get out of the revenge business and into the promotion of good ideas and helpful products. There will be others who will oppose you as competitors without needing to see them as enemies. Do not believe that everyone who does not openly support you needs to be taught a lesson.

Do not keep talking about how wronged you were and what you are going to do about it. This type of vengeance will eat you alive.

God, through Solomon, is making an observation that evil men have over time allowed themselves to become the sum total of what is right and good and necessary. This leads to the need for vengeance and trouble for those who do not go along. Everything is seen as either for us or against us and what will be done to those who are against us.

It is interesting that the next verses deal with building a house with wisdom and filling the rooms with treasure. The connection is that if you are spending your time thinking and talking and planning how to pay people back, you are not going after building your own house and treasure. Go after the positive rather than seeking to make sure that the other person is punished.

This type of payback threatens to infect every sphere of life - politics, work, church, home, marriage, friends, etc. Don't let it infect you. Don't let payback and destruction dominate your mind; let wisdom and the building of a positive future become the goal and focus of your thinking.

PROVERBS 25:2

It is the glory of God to conceal a matter, but the glory of Kings is to search out a matter

One is immediately struck with the question, why? Why would it make God greater and more glorious if He hides what He does or has done? Is it that He gets glory when the building blocks of the universe and the laws of nature and the wonder of creation are not readily discernable but must be studied and explored. He should get great glory for the intricacy of design that He wove into the fabric of the four-dimensional space time that we inhabit. The difficulty is that with evolution being the persistent and dominant lie in our age, He gets no glory as we uncover the brilliance of His work. Instead, chance and nature get the glory. Amazing to hide the glory of God just to escape the moral implications.

I still want to ask, though, why doesn't He have His glory more on display? Why does He make it so difficult to discern the wonder of His creation? This question may only be understood in a day and age which has a perverted cultural lens through which to look at all the wonders of God.

The second idea in this verse is that it is glorious for leaders (kings) to search out a matter and that it gives leaders great prestige and honor to do their homework. It is a prestigious thing to uncover the real info behind something. It is a powerful form of honor and respect when a leader doesn't just accept the typical or surface explanation of things. The leader must dig deeper and make sure that he/she knows and understands the real reasons why things have happened individually and happened consistently and/or collectively.

This would suggest that God, at times, hides or conceals some or all of the purposes of the situations, circumstances, and events in our life. It is up to the leader to search out why did this happen. Is God trying to say anything to me? How does this fit into God's work in my life? What lessons or knowledge or understanding could God be trying to weave into my life through this episode or situation?

This principle is not universal because it has been to God's glory to reveal a matter in a number of instances. His nature, the Ten Commandments, His Son, salvation – all types of things especially about Himself that we would never have uncovered and the more that we searched the further off we would be.

The verse really deals with the nature of forgiveness and justice. That it is the glory of God when He forgives and allows a person to redeem his life from the pit and make a new start. It is the glory of leaders to search out a matter and make sure that justice is done and the guilty do not go free. In this sense it is not to God's glory when He who knows everything exposes and constantly reminds us of our sin. It is His glory and exaltation that He can conceal or forgive or cover a matter of sin. That is an amazing thing that our God allows us the privilege of forgiveness and redemption after our sins. He could rightly enforce the dictum: every soul that sins shall die; every deviation from the God-directed norm would mean death. It is God's glory that He forgives us and gives us room to repent and love Him.

It is the glory and honor of rulers, leaders, and kings to search out the guilty and punish them – to not let the guilty go free.

This may be the more correct nuance in the text because of verse 5. Take away the wicked before the king, and his throne will be established in righteousness. It is the king's responsibility to root out wickedness through justice, background checks, accountability, etc. The more wickedness he allows around himself, then the less respect they will have. It is God who forgives.

We are seeing this lived out in the pedophilia scandals of the Catholic church in our day. The leaders of the church were not ruthless in their rooting out of wickedness; they erred on the side of forgiveness and kept priests in positions of influence and power even after they were known to be perpetrators of vile wickedness. It is not to their glory and the scandal is rocking the church. They leaned too heavily on the mandate of the church to forgive and not enough on the need for leaders to search out a matter and remove the wickedness from around the leader.

February 26

PROVERBS 26:2
Like a sparrow in its flitting, like a swallow in its flying, so a curse without cause does not alight

The great danger that this proverb points out is not to give too much credence to every negative thing said about you. All kinds of people will say all kinds of things about you – most of which are not true or some twisted incomplete view of what really happened. We cannot afford to respond to that or be emotionally worked up about it. In fact, in many cases it would be better to not hear it.

I was talking with a woman the other day who was being critical of another person just to cover up some issues that she was dealing with. I thought how difficult it would be for the person she was speaking about to ignore what was being said, but that is what would need to be done.

The analogy is a sparrow and a swallow – two birds that are always flying through the trees and around the house. What effect does their flying and wandering have on the occupants of the house? Answer: NOTHING. So you pay them no mind even though they are always around. In the same way realize that the process of living causes people to be upset with you for all kinds of reasons and, therefore, to say all types of things about you. Don't be bothered by these.

The proverb says we should only worry about those things that people say that are true. It is the foolish person who wants to correct everything that is said. I have watched people spend all kinds of time to correct what people are saying and only increase the untrue things people are saying in the process.

Remember, you do not want to know all the things that are being said about you. Much is not true. If any of it is true, then fix it. If you hear a bunch of inaccurate things about you, just let it go, especially when it is said by a person who does not really know you. Live your life as a righteous person; do the right thing every chance you can. That will, over time, speak for itself.

If you hear people saying things about you that are blatantly not true, it will not stick so let it go. If you, however, get all upset and go after everything that is said about you, people will begin to wonder what kind of person you are.

Be righteous and enjoy the people God has put in your life, realizing that even some of your close friends might believe things about you that are not true.

February 27

PROVERBS 27:2

Let another praise you, and not your own mouth; a stranger, and not your own lips

One of the ways to make yourself really obnoxious fast is to constantly be talking about how wonderful you are. It is best when others recognize that you are doing good. This is a very difficult thing at times when you feel that others are not recognizing what you have done. But if you are always boasting about what you have done, then people get tired of you.

Now it is all right to tell people about things you have done and that you did a good job. But don't praise yourself.

I saw one of my daughters grappling with this aspect of wisdom. I heard her say that her parents and other adults don't always see all the good things that she does or comment on them. This is true and discouraging at times. But it is good that she continues to do good things even when they are not noticed. They are noticed by God and will be praised by Him in heaven. It is my job, as her father, to strike a correct balance of pointing out the wonderful things she does as often as I can without giving her a proud or superior mindset. By the way, all of us will naturally move in the direction that we are receiving praise. So if your children are receiving more praise from their friends than their parents, they will naturally move in that direction. Be lavish in your praise and generous in your appreciation.

When your good deeds just continue to mount up, then they will be talked about.

PROVERBS 28:2

By the transgression of a land many are its princes, but by a man of understanding and knowledge, so it endures

Each sin against a people is remembered in the collective consciousness and causes people to be distrustful of that type of problem. There are collective sins where leaders abuse people. This happens in churches, in civic organizations, in business, in political parties – anywhere there is leadership over a group. If the leader is not willing to lead toward righteousness rather than selfishness, then there are offenses and new leaders spring up to pull the group back toward the righteous action that should have been taken.

The word land is the idea of a group of people. If the leader of a group of people becomes corrupt and uses them for his own personal gain exclusively instead of for everyone's benefit and God's glory, then this transgression will mark this people and they will develop champions for their own causes.

There must be a sense that the leader is concerned and leading with the best for everyone in mind, not just the best for himself or the political party or the best for the company. The people must sense and see that an everybody-wins strategy is being employed. If not, it is like personally growing factions and factious leaders.

No leader wants to have factions and lots of small-time rivals. The answer is clearly: Lead with a righteous everybody-wins agenda and they will be silenced and diminished. One expects, in a church, to have a leader who has a bigger scope than selfishness; but it is not always the case as men build empires instead of God's church.

If politicians are ever going to go beyond a fractured landscape, they must go beyond their own ideology and support what is truly wise. If a leader is going to really bring unity, there must be a clear sense that this person is not out for himself or herself but instead has the best interest of everybody on their mind.

by a man of understanding and knowledge, so it endures

This is the answer to how a leader keeps everyone moving forward together. The good leader must be constantly aware of relationships between people and things – which is understanding. Also the leader has accurate information and appropriate skill to hold people together. There is a lost art of leading a larger group, pointing out the rightness of the various causes that make up the group and their linkages but also having the skill to have people unify behind a larger vision than just the one issue. In every group leaders must learn and demonstrate these skills. If they don't, then there will be an endless number of factions and cliques.

March

PROVERBS 1:3
To receive instruction in wise behavior
Righteousness, Justice and Equity

receive instruction

Notice that one has to receive instruction in wise behavior. It takes learning, concentration, and new information. We don't come equipped since the fall with this orientation. Since the fall of man in Adam, even though we may know the right thing to do, we are oriented toward the selfish thing.

The Hebrew word translated *instruction* is the word *musar* which means instruct, chasten, train, discipline. Therefore the idea is that one must come to the place where one is ready to enter into a training course to become a person who acts wisely. Wisdom does not automatically flow from us; in fact, we are automatically oriented toward self.

This suggests a picture of a learned master beginning a rigorous training process with a young disciple who wants to learn to be wise. The youngster has heard and watched the actions of the master and presents himself to be schooled so that he will not longer make life-killing, foolish decisions. The book of Proverbs is the ancient manual of that old master. It is Solomon's text book for the school of wisdom.

In fact, I write these devotional comments for my grandchildren and great-grandchildren that have not even been conceived yet so that they would be willing to enter into the school of God's wisdom. I want them to know that I was thinking about them years and decades before they were ever around. And that God knew everything about them before the world ever began. God had Solomon write this book so that in God's grace each of us could overcome our natural bent towards selfishness. Young men and young women, realize that wisdom is a rich treasure that must be learned.

So many times we must admit that we have acted foolishly and could wish that we would have thought through what we did with greater insight – that is what this book is for. It helps us realize that what feels right at a given moment is not necessarily the right or wise thing to do.

When a person who has learned wisdom has finished their life, they sit in their chair surrounded by people who love them preparing to go home to meet face to face the Supreme Being who they have been relating to for a long time.

Never forget that the ultimate goal of wisdom is living out the two great commandments: *Thou shalt Love the Lord your God with all your heart, soul, mind and strength and your neighbor as yourself.* Life is relationships and wise people build them.

wise behavior

The word *wise* here is the word *sakal* which is close to the word understanding in the Hebrew. It emphasizes the intelligent understanding of what certain behaviors will do and what others won't do. It is sometimes translated insight (Jeremiah 3:15). It is clear that the goal of Proverbs is for one to look past his/her own urges or cultural impulses and examine all the potential actions in any given situation and choose the one that will result in God being honored, others being benefitted, and the individual being blessed. Wisdom looks for this action, and it is not ready to move until it finds that action.

Wise behavior always promotes relationships. It deepens and strengthens connections between people. Unwise behavior is selfish behavior. If unwise behavior were known, it would immediately weaken connection and bring disconnection between people.

The term "wise behavior" is broken into three sub terms in this opening lecture in the inspired school of wisdom. Wisdom's component parts are righteousness, justice, and equity.

righteousness

This is the first of the words that describe the larger term "wise behavior." This is the clearest moral action term. That which is right. The straight measuring rod. The commandments of God are the definitions of righteousness and the individual would be wise in working them out in his/her life. The Lord is described as righteous in all His ways and holy in all His works. What is interesting is that at times it is difficult to discern how God is being righteous in a particular action, so righteousness is at times a complex and daunting behavior. But the book of Proverbs is the training device for the task.

That which is right or righteous is not just inside the boundaries of the Ten Commandments; it is the opposite of the violation of the Ten Commandments. Look at each of the Commandments and go to the core of that command – or in most cases its opposite – and you find that which is truly righteous.

- No other gods. True full-hearted worship of the Almighty.

- No graven Images. Awesome reverence for the boundariesness of God. He cannot be contained or explained by anything in the three-dimensional, space-time world.

- No taking the Lord's name in vain. Powerful and positive verbal worship on a regular basis.

- Remember the Sabbath Day to keep it holy. A day set aside to pursue God and His demands and commands – desires and person.

- Honor your Father and your Mother. Adding true value to your parents through your conduct, interaction, and speech

- No murder. True love of your fellow man. A commitment to improving the lot of your fellow man, not just not destroying a person.

- No adultery. True faithfulness. Deep committed love to one spouse all your life, creating an environment of committed love.

- No stealing. Generosity of spirit. Hard work and saving in order to give to others.

- No bearing false witness. Truthing in love.

- No coveting. Contentment with God's provision and desire to fulfill the full measure of your lot in life, not someone else's.

Each of these are expressions describe what it means to be truly righteous. Righteous can never be a negation or defined as what one doesn't do. It is a positive in even a greater sense than wickedness is positive action in an evil direction.

justice

This is the second of the descriptors of "wise behavior" stated above. The word is the Hebrew word *sapat* which means to lead or exercise the power of governance. In the ancient world there was not a separation of the powers of government into three branches, but instead there was the leader. When the Proverbs speak, it is designed to help the leader make the type of decisions that will be right. The Proverbs are a course in how to be a righteous king or a leader with integrity.

Thus the ability to govern or be a leader is critical to this discussion. That is why the Proverbs are full of references to the king. This is the supreme leader within an Old Testament setting. If a person understands how to deal with a king and how to act like a wise king, then they will be a great leader. We would say that the book of Proverbs is a course in leadership. Notice that the book refers to leadership and to comparisons: This is better than that; that is worse than this. It is in part in these comparisons that the foundations for wise decisions are made.

The book of Proverbs is designed to be a course in leadership development. How to rule well. How to be a good and wise leader. If one can see the truths of the book of Proverb being lived out, then it will begin to be true for you in your life. The book of Proverb was designed to be a course on how to be a great leader.

equity

Each one of these words is a partial definition of wise behavior that is stated as the goal. This word *equity* carries with it the idea of moral uprightness. How to fully follow the Lord's commands. To be upright in every situation. The word comes from the idea to go straight ahead or to proceed on a level place. To apply uniformly or smoothly. Some have suggested that this is the idea of fairness. What is equitable is what is fair or balanced. The fact that this word is associated with leadership and governance would suggest that there will be some very difficult calls in leadership. That there will be times when two good things are demanded that seem to be in opposition to one another. Other times it will seem that the only choices are evil choices. But the book of Proverbs guides us around and through these conundrums towards the correct course even if it takes a while to see that course of action. Enter into this unique training program that was instituted over 3,000 years ago with the official stamp of God's breath. Begin growing in wise behavior so that you will enjoy all the life that God has for you.

March 2

PROVERBS 2:3
For if you cry for discernment, lift your voice for understanding

discernment

This word translated in the NASB here as *discernment* is really the word *understanding* – where the person is crying out for perception into the relationship between events and knowledge. The cry is for insight into what is behind just the raw facts.

understanding

This is the only place where both words for *understanding* are used in the same passage which adjusts the meaning of these usually synonymous terms. The first reference carries the usual meaning for the word understanding – insight even discernment. The second is a cry for the object of understanding – the carrier of key information that unlocks the understanding or relationship.

This is a very interesting bit of information. One must gain the understanding through a deep and open desire for the insight about what is the relationship between events, circumstances, people, etc; but one must also be just as hungry for the object or means through which that information will come. Understanding does not just pop into one's mind; it is conveyed through someone or something and one must be ready for the teacher or the insight will be missed.

In other words, one must be very interested in understanding why things happen and the relationship between events, and one must realize that God will teach you these insights through a teacher from whom you must equally be prepared to learn.

PROVERBS 3:3

Do not let kindness and truth leave you; bind them around your neck, write them on the tablet of your heart

This is the basis of all horizontal relationships: lovingkindness and truth. The word translated kindness is really the word love *chesed*. It is the idea of commitment to mercy, meeting needs, kindness, compassion, etc.

This pairing of love and truth takes place throughout the Bible. Speak the truth in love in the New Testament. The message of Proverbs in terms of successful relationships is to be loving and truthful. Do not be so naive that you believe what everyone wants to tell you; but also do not be skeptical and cynical that you forget to have grace, mercy, and love for others. It is the combination that brings the best situations.

Notice the permanent attachment. These principles you will never outgrow. It is these and these alone that stand the test of time and relationships. Learn how to be in harmony with lovingkindness and truth. When you vibrate in harmony with these two pillars, then you will have found wisdom.

This is to be permanently etched on your soul. You must visualize to do that. They must go beyond simple words you memorize. You must see yourself living out these qualities in various situations until living out of these qualities is second nature.

Notice that you are doing the binding to your heart. Notice that you are doing the writing. There is not a holy zap that can do the writing for you. Now it is true that in the New Testament, God the Holy Spirit writes the New Covenant on our hearts, but you must write its application to the situation in your lives. Too often we want to learn about what these blessings are, but we do not see that we must live out the implication of these truths by yielding our bodies to these qualities.

March 4

PROVERBS 4:3

When I was a son to my father, tender and the only son in the sight of my mother

then he taught me and said to me

This is one of Solomon's tenderest memories – when his father, King David, took time to instruct him in the ways of God's wisdom. It was those lessons that were imprinted on his soul. There is not enough emphasis on the instruction responsibility of fathers to take time and direct their children in the way of wisdom.

Notice that David did not try and instruct when Solomon was older and could interact with him. No, David taught Solomon when he was tender and the lessons would make the greatest impact.

It is too often that we wait to teach valuable lessons, thinking they won't understand. But if you teach when they are still in the elementary years, they internalize the lessons much deeper. Later the lessons may be met with more cynicism and resistance.

If you are a father, schedule time every week – even every day – to teach your young children the lessons of life that they will need. Impress on them the need to acquire wisdom. Become a person who discerns between possible decisions and chooses the one that causes many to win.

Notice that this teaching took place between David and Solomon before Bathsheba had any other sons.

PROVERBS 5:3

For the lips of an adulteress drip honey and smoother than oil is her speech

The key word is the word *For* – Solomon has just been telling us that one has to be careful that wisdom doesn't slip through your fingers. It is possible to be disoriented and to miss the plan that God has for you. And then he tells us the source of the disorientation: the lips of the adulteress. When you are in the midst of adulterous love, you believe the words that you are being told. They have no basis in long-term reality, but you believe them.

What is interesting is that God tells us through Solomon's words that the only antidote to those words is not to hear them and to stay far away from the door of her house. Verse 8 Even if you know all the bad things that will happen to the person who commits adultery, the promised affection is so intoxicating and disorienting that you may do it anyway if you allow yourself to be captured by the words, beauty, or touch.

It is the lips or words of the adulteress or adulterer that carry the great drawing power. The words of the adulteress always suggest that you are wanted, you are admired, you are fascinating, I enjoy listening to you talk, I could listen to you talk for hours. The fact that the adulteress has such drawing power through her words and listening ability says that these areas are huge needs for men and women. Men especially are drawn toward the person who admires them, wants them, listens attentively to them, and follows those conversations with sex. Solomon says that the power of those needs in men is so strong that it will draw men out of their marriage vows, so it is best if they never hear those words. Notice that later Solomon says to find a way to increase the depth of your relationship with your spouse. He is counseling that you find a way to have those needs met by your spouse.

It is too disorienting to have someone even pretend to meet your deepest needs. The drawing power of these needs is so strong that all your moral training can be overcome in a short period under the wonder of these needs. If one looks at the top needs of a man, six of the seven could be met in these encounters: Respect, Adaptation, Intimacy, Companionship, Attractive, Listening. These six pull too hard at the fiber of a man to resist if he has been caught by the power of her words. It is better not to even listen to the words. Stay away; you can't resist. Go home and strengthen the ties to your wife.

PROVERBS 6:3

Do this then, my son, and deliver yourself, since you have come into the hand of your neighbor, go, humble yourself, and importune your neighbor

deliver

This is the Hebrew word *nasal* which means deliver, rescue, even save. Solomon here acknowledges that, at times, everyone will make mistakes. We all need to know how to undo something that we should not have done. How can we rescue ourselves before our mistake becomes permanent or complete?

Too often we have this idea that we must finish what we know is a mistake. If you discover something is a mistake, then stop and seek to deliver yourself from the problem. It takes humility – which is hard on our pride – and a willingness to be vulnerable in the admission of our mistake and request for a change.

humble

This is the Hebrew word *raphas* which means to stamp, tread down, humble, trampling under foot. It is a word of lowness and submission. In this instance Solomon suggests that you do this to yourself. Make yourself low and under the level of the person you are approaching. It is a shame that many in our day do not know how to approach another person from this position. Even children are taught to power up and try and connect with people through a power position. When you have made a mistake, take the humble route. Don't try and justify how you were tricked into the problem. Don't try and blame others. Don't try and threaten what you will do if you are not let out of the problem. Just humble yourself. Step down on your pride, admitting that you made a mistake when you said what you said or when you did what you did. This will not be easy and your pride will give your suggestions on how to stand up and be powerful. Refuse to listen to the impulses of your pride. They will not help you; they will only make matters worse.

importune

This Hebrew word is a surprise and the strength of the word is shocking and fascinating. The word is *rahab* which means storm, boisterously or strongly or boldly. The idea is that this is a request that will not go away. It comes on strong and will not take no for an answer.

From a very humble position Solomon is saying that you strongly ask to be let out of your mistake. *This is not a could you please if it is not any trouble for you.* It is a *please, I need to be released from the mistake I made. I should not have agreed to do that; I just cannot do that.*

In one sense the idea is that you become a storm upon the person until he/she releases you from your mistake. You are open and humble about your mistake, but you must be released from your own stupidity. This word importune is a strong word.

When you make a mistake either through what you do, what you say, or what you sign, then be willing to admit that you made a mistake; but go after being released and stay humble but stay after it. Just like the unrighteous judge says about the woman who importuned him. She was like a relentless storm at his court until she received justice. So persistent, humble relentlessness has its place in the arsenal of the wise person. They need it to get themselves out of the stuff they do when they are not wise.

PROVERBS 7:3

Bind them on your fingers; write them on the tablet of your heart

bind them on your fingers

This seems to refer to a physical way of reminding. It could have been how our culture got the idea of tying a string around your finger to remind you of something. The idea is that every day one needs physical reminders to prod us to remember the biblical truth that will be the focus of the day. The soul needs training and a template for the day. Give it Scripture. Each day write down a verse, phrase, or word from Scripture that God can use to direct your actions, speech, and thoughts that day.

write them on the tablet of your heart

The word heart expresses the deepest inner recesses of a person – both the material and immaterial aspects of a man's being. This is the soul and the mind.

What is interesting here is that the soul is open to new programming. Humanity is not just the result of random chemicals or the reactions to those who act upon it. God declares that a person can program his/her soul to follow a righteous set of instructions. In our day of evolution and naturalism we have almost completely ignored the soul as an aspect of mankind. We believe that there is nothing beyond the brain and the firing of the nerves in it. This, however, is not true. Mankind has a soul – an immaterial part of their being that is not dependent upon the physical. Studies done on those who have gone through various surgical procedures and have been pronounced brain-dead have been able to recount memories of the time during which they were brain-dead. This suggests that those memories were stored in something beyond the brain. It is the strongest purely physical evidence of the existence of the soul.

We must be roused from our naturalistic stupor and re-embrace the fullness of what we were created to be – mankind body, soul, and spirit. It is in the soul that the programming for the life you live will take place. We are not only the product of our environment, our genes, and the universe as a whole. God declares that we can be different than the flow around us. We can program the soul to respond to different stimulus than the natural.

We don't have to be proud, selfish, greedy, power hungry, immoral, and lazy beings; but instead we can take the Word of God internally and use it as an operating system for our lives to orient us to God and run the hardware of our body.

We have largely given up on moral training because we have bought the lie of being only physical chemical beings. Moral training is essential to have a civilized society. Instead of moral training, we have substituted advertising and have bombarded our body and soul with messages of materialism, lust, selfishness, greed, and envy until it is these messages that form the dominant operating system for our lives.

This is tragic because we already had an orientation toward these things in our fleshly nature anyway. Since the fall of Adam, mankind has been oriented to selfishness and rebellion. And added on top of that is the orientation toward activities that will destroy relationships with God and others – further immoral training is tragic.

This is a long way of saying that what we think about and repeat over and over again programs us. What we hear repeatedly, sing, or watch in the movie theater of our mind creates an orientation to the world. If that orientation is not godly, then we will go in that direction. Jesus stated this when He said: *If your eye be single then your whole body is full of light... but if the light that is in you is darkness... how great is the darkness.* If the internal messages that are guiding your life are all materialistic, sexual, selfish, haughty, and angry, then your life will be constantly directed toward destruction.

God's way is different; it orients us toward relationships, not against them. It guides us to submission to God rather than rebellion.

We have a constant need to hear again these counter-intuitive messages or we will never make the right choices.

Let's get practical. This proverb would suggest that one needs to have a phrase or verse that you are repeating over and over again that day which will be your moral prod that day. It could be one of the two great commandments. It could be one of the Ten Commandments. It could be one of the Proverbs. It could be the fruit of the spirit. It could be a particular word from Scripture that you are focusing on that day.

If you don't have a verse or phrase of Scripture to ruminate on, then most likely you will be left with some advertising slogan you hear or a song on the radio you like or a phrase from a character on TV. These are rarely, if ever, moral training. These phrases will not keep you out of trouble. In fact, the phrases from advertising, music, and TV often encourage impulsive, selfish, and rebellious behavior.

What is your godly phrase today? Write down your phrase each day at the beginning of the day in a conspicuous place so that you will see it throughout the day. You might want to put in on a card or a Post-it note. If you don't have a phrase for today, use a major theme command of Proverbs and wisdom. Do not let lovingkindness and truth leave you. Listen for the guidance of the Holy Spirit moving you toward living out these ideas.

March 8

PROVERBS 8:3

Beside the gates, at the opening to the city, at the entrance of the doors, she cries out

The place described is the place that the elders of the city sat to conduct business and to govern the city. He is saying that wisdom resides in and near the place where the elders and successful businessmen are. They have done it. They have accomplished a level of success that has put them in a position to advise others who have not done it.

The key idea is that you should listen to what the leaders who have done it would say about your idea. You should be willing to listen to what these highly respected leaders say about success and prosperity and life. Wisdom is not hidden; it is out in the open in these men. They want to advise you. Listen to them.

These men have made many of the mistakes you are thinking about and have overcome those mistakes in order to have a level of prosperity that does not require them to be out in the field or store every day. They can dedicate a high level of their time to governing the city.

Now the type of thinking in this proverb is that those who have been successful and have lived life should give back to the community by governing. In this time the governors or leaders were highly revered people; not reviled as lying politicians. If you have a question, make sure you get the counsel of those who have already successfully navigated the waters you are about to sail in.

Wisdom is the triple-win: the win for God, the win for others, and the win for yourself. The kind of choices that result in this type of winning and understanding requires that you listen to the voice of experience. The choices that result in real winning over the long term are not always easily determined.

PROVERBS 9:3

She has sent out her maidens, she calls from the tops of the heights of the city

The characteristics of wisdom are personified as a king with servants. It is to allow us to see when we are listening to wisdom and how to find it when we need it.

Verse 1 of Chapter 9 is clear that wisdom has accomplished the thing we seek. It is successful, over time, with a balance of Glory to God, help and honor for others, and personal development and enrichment. Too many charlatans can talk a good game but cannot show any real evidence of their success. Wisdom has results to show.

Verse 2 of Chapter of 9 is clearly another characteristic of wisdom: it has figured out how to present its wisdom in a way that others can grasp. It wants to share its information, but it has thought through that presentation in some detail. Notice prepared food, mixed wine, set table. It is true that many are successful, even wise, who cannot communicate the essence of what they know to others in such a way that others can grow from their knowledge. It is either too deep within or its presentation is too muddled and thus indigestible.

Verse 3 is clearly another dominant characteristic of wisdom. It wants to have others gain from the wisdom it has learned. It sends out maidens. It seeks to enlighten others. True biblical wisdom does not have to be pried out of the hands of those who truly have it. They want desperately to communicate it. It is just few who really want it. Notice that there are others beside wisdom itself that are enlisted. It is developing a communication strategy.

she has sent out her maidens

Wisdom wants to help. The message from these verses is that you cannot do this alone. One person totally alone, even with a book of wisdom, cannot discover and maintain a life of wisdom all by themselves. They need to be shown the way to do things: "mix their wine."

There is a complexity about life that demands that you need others helping you, advising you. Do not be so selfish and proud that you are independent and will not accept help.

she calls from the tops of the heights of the city

Wisdom does speak from a place of superiority and accomplishment, and it means that you must put aside your own pride to listen to the message. She is saying that there is a level of complexity and sophistication between where you are and where I am, and I would be more than happy to show you if you would listen. Are you willing to be humble enough to listen?

Too many times we see the rewards of wisdom – the prestige, the prosperity, the power – and we believe that we can get to that place on our own without help. Or we think we see the way that you get there: a straight line. But that is not true. That is a simple person's approach to life.

PROVERBS 10:3
The Lord will not allow the righteous to hunger, but He will reject the craving of the wicked

This proverb contains a very important clarification on some myths that exists in Christian circles. Many people will read this proverb and then draw direct applications to the lives of people they know or people they read about. If the person was truly righteous, they would not be hungry. If this person is going hungry, then they must not be righteous. If they are going hungry, then it is their fault and we do not need to be concerned with what God is justly doing to them. The problem is that this is not what this proverb actually says. The actual Hebrew sentence reads: *The Lord will not allow the soul of the righteous to hunger, but He will thrust aside the cravings of the wicked.* This proverb deals with how God responds to the internal needs and impulses of people.

the Lord

This is the Hebrew word *YHWH*, the unspeakable name of God. It was the name that God gave to Moses at the burning bush. The Jews, in order to protect themselves from violating the Third Commandment and speaking the name of God in vain, outlawed speaking the name completely. Every time they see this term in the Hebrew text, they say Adonai which is the word for Lord in Hebrew. What is interesting is that this is the personal name of God. When God is acting in the most intimate caring ways, He gives Himself this name. The actual definition of this word is that it is a derivative of the verb *to be* or we understand it as God saying that He is the great I AM. He is the ever-present one. There is no past, present, and future to Him. He is outside our time domain and exists in the eternal now. It is this One who has no time constraints and who wants a personal relationship with His righteous worshippers.

165

will not allow

God does allow a lot to happen to people that is not His perfect will for them. He allows the individual to make choices that result in devastating consequences. He allows unjust governments to build evil, oppressive systems to treat people unjustly. He allows other people in your life to treat you poorly or even do evil to you. One of the problems that we, in the modern world, have with God is how much He allows to happen. How come He is not the overprotective grandparent keeping all the bad stuff from happening to us? This type of question would not have come from the Ancient World. They understood that their choices mattered; that the choices of their leaders mattered. They understood that God was looking for people who would choose wisdom and who would choose to honor Him. It was in the next life that God would remove the evil influences and sludge of sin.

There are some things that God will not allow, but they are not what we assume they would be. This verse contains one of those things. He will not allow the soul of the righteous to hunger.

the righteous

As we have already stated, the actual Hebrew phrase is the *soul of the righteous*. God is promising, through the lips of Solomon the king, that He will not allow the person who is righteous to hunger or to be without what they basically need. The righteous in the book of Proverbs is contrasted with the wicked so that the definition of what it means to be righteous could be understood to be the person who stays within the boundaries of the Ten Commandments. However, we know that it is not possible for anyone to stay within this boundary perfectly (the only exception was Jesus). The Jewish sacrificial system was put in place to deal with the righteous who sinned. So righteousness is something deeper. The Old and New Testaments state that the righteous man shall live by faith or trusting in what God has said to do. In Abraham's case it was trusting that a child would be born to his wife

Sarah who was too old. In Rebekah's case it was trusting and favoring that God wanted to bless and honor the younger son Jacob and not the older more manly son Esau. In the life of the Jewish believer it was bringing their offerings to atone for their sins because God said this would fix the problem. Therefore the righteous one is the one who trusts God and thereby acts in accordance with God's commands and in the New Testament the guidance of the Holy Spirit.

The proverb says that God will not allow the soul of the righteous to hunger—hunger being defined as actually going without the needed thing to the point that death occurs. The soul of the righteous needs different things than the body. The soul needs relationships and it requires connection to God, to others, and to emotional support. God says He watches and will make sure that those who trust Him will not suffer soul-hunger to the point of the death of their faith. Notice this proverb does not say that God will keep a righteous person from ever going hungry physically. I would suggest that I have heard and seen God do this in a number of different ways. I have read reports of those who were locked in concentration camps or prisons where God sends an angel to minister to them or even gives them a new level of vision of His presence. I have seen God send new friends to those who were cut off by those who should have been their support and encouragement. I have watched God draw a person deep into His presence in the midst of disastrous, emotional trauma happening to them or around them. I have read reports of God actually calling a person home to heaven because there was not an adequate way to meet the needs of that person's soul here on earth.

We as a society have become fixated on the health of someone's body and their physical well-being – in many cases as though that were the issue of supreme importance. The body is important, but it is only the tent that houses the soul. And the soul will enjoy at least one other house. I have begun to think about the soul as an operating system and the personal files on my computer that I can download and transfer to another computer when the computer that I am on begins to fail. I collect programs and files and information and the software gets bigger and bigger and defines MY computer. But my stuff is not the computer; that is just what runs my stuff. I have changed computers a number of times and all my stuff is still there running on a new computer. One of these days we are all headed for an upgrade in terms of our hardware. God is going to take our soul and cleanse it of the parts of our operating system that orients it to selfishness and sin and put it into a new body to enjoy a new life and in a new place with a new level of relationship with Him.

Just remember, it is more important what we put in our soul than what we put in our body. It is the soul that lasts for eternity. It is the soul that God will make sure does not hunger to destruction.

March 11

PROVERBS 11:3
The integrity of the upright will guide them. But the crookedness of the treacherous will destroy them.

The word *integrity* means wholeness or undivided oneness. The idea in this verse is that if you are always the same person in every situation and every relationship, that oneness – that undivided type of thinking – will tell you what to do in each new situation.

If you would not cheat in business, then you should not and will not in golf. If you would not utter swear words in the family, then you should not when your team loses the game or you hit your thumb with the hammer. It means when you don't know what to do, you look at the decision before you and ask yourself if you would do this kind of thing in another context. If the answer is no, then don't do it. If the answer is yes, then move ahead.

There are too many people who are duplicitous – people who act one way at church or around friends and a different way in business and sports. What is amazing is that even though people try and play a deceptive game of "I will only be like this in one area of my life," it always bleeds over and they cheat, lie, steal, swear, are unfaithful, and angry in every relationship.

Strive for wholeness... be the same way... always aim to stay in the Ten box – INSIDE THE TEN COMMANDMENTS

will guide you

The interesting thing is that this phrase *will guide* you can be understood in two ways. It could be the idea that when a person does not know what to do and is righteous, he/she should look to that which is full of integrity and in line in every way with the Ten Commandments. This is a reasonable application of this idea. What is consistent with righteousness is the right question when one does not know what to do and then do that particular thing.

The second way of looking at this phrase is what will happen. Your integrity will guide you. In other words, that which you do consistently will guide you. The only question is whether you will be guided by the best advice. I have watched person after person do what seemed right to them or what was consistent to them even though it made no sense. This is the principle that we make a series of choices and then those choices begin to make us. It is the accumulation of our choices that determine what we will do in almost every case.

Notice that integrity and crookedness are parallel to one another in this proverb. One either acts in a way that is consistent with the path of righteousness or one acts consistent with twisted or crooked, selfish dealings. It is the accumulation of these choices that will guide each person and seem right to them.

Ask yourself the question whether your typical solution to a problem results in good being accomplished. Does it have the ring of what is inside of the Ten Commandments? Or does it come out wrong consistently even though it feels like the right thing? You are either being guided by what is outside the Ten Commandments or what is inside the Ten Commandments. This guidance is either building your life or it is tearing down what is really wonderful about life.

PROVERBS 12:3

A man will not be established by wickedness, but the root of the righteous will not be moved

What an encouraging insight. It seems in our day and age that any business can go out of business; that no one's pension is secure; that no one's marriage is safe; that even one's convictions can come under assault.

But this proverb declares that one never really built a lasting enterprise on the violation of God's law or basic selfishness. Understand that wickedness is living outside of the Ten Commandments. Solomon is stating a truth that many do not think about: You may go outside of God's moral boundary structure to establish your life, but it will not lead to much for your family, your legacy, and the society as a whole. The gaining by wickedness is a short-term proposition.

All of us would like our lives to have a lasting impact and count for something way past when we are alive. This is possible when your life is built on righteousness. This is how you build a lasting legacy. It is not quick nor necessarily fancy, but it is an unmovable root. You bless generations when you begin today to be righteous.

Too often we do not think about what we are doing to ourselves ten years from now; our children or grandchildren twenty years from now; or society thirty-plus years from now. But we need to do this kind of thinking. When anyone voluntarily lives within the boundary structure of the Ten Commandments, they begin at that point to establish a righteous root and develop a legacy.

It is your decision. Are you going to start a legacy today by living by God's grace righteously or are you going to continue making the same selfish choices that you have been making – living largely only for yourself at the present time. Only thinking about today is a fool's choice. Be righteous.

March 13

PROVERBS 13:3
The one who guards his mouth preserves his life; the one who opens wide his lips comes to ruin

Oh how much this proverb needs to be taught, grasped, and applied.

The word *guards* is the Hebrew word *nasar* which means to watch, guard, or keep. The word *preserves* is the Hebrew word *samar* which means to keep, guard, watch. What Solomon is pointing out is that when you are careful about what you say, you are really protecting your life. Keeping watch over your mouth is keeping watch over your life. This is a very important idea and relationship that many in our day and age do not understand.

If a person says whatever they want to whomever they want, they are invariably damaging relationships. That relational damage will come back to haunt them. What God continually points out is that life is relationships and what damages relationships instead of building them up, damages your enjoyment of life.

We have this naive opinion of who we are in this world; that we are this disconnected, solitary person. And we should be able to say whatever we think or would like to say, whether that is about someone or something or really anything. Our culture has elevated free speech to a right. It is, in reality, the right to be foolish and the right to destroy the most important things in our life by our own hand. God gives us a more accurate perspective of who we are in the world. We are one person who is connected to lots of other people and every advance that we make in life is the result of one of those connections. If we knowingly or flippantly damage one of these connections with others, we damage our own potential.

Most of us have to admit how stupid we have been at times by saying something to our spouse or friend or boss or colleague that we shouldn't have said. Then we have to go to the trouble of trying to repair that relationship when if we had just listened to this proverb and put a guard over our mouth, we would have guarded our life.

LIFE IS RELATIONSHIPS – the better your relationships, the better your life. If you have a lot of stuff but no deep, loving, and positive relationships, then your life is not much of a life. But even if you have very little stuff but have lots of deep, loving relationships, then you have a wonderful life.

the one who opens wide his lips comes to ruin

The word *opens* is the Hebrew word *pasaq* which means open wide. Let everything that is behind the partition out. Or as my fourth-grade teacher used to say: "Does every thought you think have to just come out your mouth?"

The word *ruin* is the Hebrew word *mehitta* which means destruction, ruin, terror. In other words, your life can become a living nightmare – everything you hoped wouldn't happen – if you don't close your mouth. I wonder how many people have ever thought that the life they are presently living is often the direct or indirect result of whether they guarded their mouth or just let fly.

Too often we have just let fly with words that we can never take back. Once they are out there, they can never be taken back and the weight and damage they cause continues to crash around in the minds of those who heard it. Don't say everything that you could. Don't comment on everybody and everything; it doesn't need to be done.

Every job you have received is because of a relationship with someone; it was nurtured through what you said. Every friendship you have ever had was nurtured through things you said. Every evening you have enjoyed at home with family was nurtured long before by things that you said. Realize that what you say is the bed you will sleep in your whole life.

Now it is best to say positive things; but if you are not at that point, then just cut down on the destructive things that you say. Stop gossiping; stop running people down; stop providing negative commentary about everyone or everything. You only destroy your own potential. Set a guard over your mouth.

If you argue with your parents each time they make a suggestion, it diminishes that relationship. If you have a sarcastic comment about everyone at school, pointing out the flaws and weaknesses in everyone, you don't enhance how much people like you. If you let every opinion you have be known, you will run the great risk of having few friends and a limited potential.

Make a commitment today that you will set a guard over your mouth and not talk negatively today.

PROVERBS 14:3

In the mouth of the foolish is a rod for his back, but the lips of the wise will protect them

in the mouth of the foolish is a rod for his back

There are three possible directions that God could be going in this proverb. One, that the selfish and impulsive person says things that eventually act like a rod and punish him. As the foolish woman in 14:1 who has to live in the midst of the relationships that she destroyed, she has torn down her own home or dwelling place. If this is the idea, then the contrasting proverb would mean that the words of the wise man would not create the relational damage that foolish words create.

The second possible intent of the proverb is that it is the things that the foolish person says that can be used against him to discipline or punish him. The contrasting proverb would mean then that the wise man does not say things that will get him in trouble later.

A third possibility shows itself from a more literal translation of the verse. The most literal translation of the proverb is the *lips of the fool is a rod of pride*. This suggests that the fool really thinks of himself in a very high manner and believes that he is above others. And the contrasting proverb would be that the wise person's words protect him from the foolish person's verbal blows.

March 15

PROVERBS 15:3
The eyes of the Lord are in every place watching the evil and the good

This is a very important concept. Nothing escapes the purview of the Lord of the heavens. He does not fail to see the evil, and he registers every good.

This is one of the big things that we, who are truly Christians and theistic, must prove – that there is a judgment day coming; a time when every action of every man will be evaluated from a truly objective point of view.

One of the great problems for meaning and point to existence is where is the recorder of our deeds that is outside of us and beyond our universe? If no one sees what we do or the bravery or cowardice that we demonstrate, then it does not matter which one we do. If there is no ultimate recorder, then there can be little meaning to our lives except that which we live in front of others and that will perish with them.

But if there is an ultimate recorder that cannot perish and who sees and records everything that we think, say, and do, then life is full of meaning in every choice that comes before us. This is especially true if that recorder is somehow connected to a reward for the correct actions.

The one question that this verse does not address is: Why does God only watch the evil and the good? Why does he not immediately stop the evil or encourage the good? Numerous theories have been advanced throughout the ages. The one most often advanced which seems to make the most sense is that in this world – being a prelude to the next one – God must test our true choices to see if we would love Him and righteousness even if it is not immediately rewarded. He is looking for those worshippers and lovers of righteousness who will embrace truth and goodness even if it does not have an immediate temporal benefit. It is easy even for the unrighteous to be good when there is an immediate tangible benefit. God is testing us to see what is in our heart – whether we will call this world our home or continue to search for the better one which is beyond this one. Jesus does declare that those who follow Him will receive many times more for their obedience and suffering both in this world and the next.

It is clear that Christians are banking their lives, their destiny, and their choices on the fact that there is a next world in which the wrongs of this world are made right; that the wonder and splendor of the next world will marginalize any pain and suffering that we have experienced here in this one. This common theme that all justice will not necessarily be accomplished during our lifetime here in this world is important. It is a truth of the Christian faith which must not be abandoned to the "this is all there is" thinking of our modern day. If this world is all there is and there is no God in heaven watching and recording, then live as you please for there is no meaning to anyone's existence except what little bit you can conjure up yourself. It will die with you and your meaningless life will have accomplished nothing, no matter what you did.

I am deeply saddened that many Christians in the West have diminished this truth or embraced its secular opposite. When we forget the basic truths of the Christian faith, it is almost impossible to live the Christian life with any vigor. I believe we have been sapped of Christian strength by the lie that this is all there is and when you die, it is over. It is not over; it is just beginning and the choices you made here will make all the difference about what you enjoy there.

March 16

PROVERBS 16:3
Commit your works to the Lord and your plans will be established

Commit is the word roll or we might say have God evaluate as well as make sure that He has approved and or has your permission to shut down these plans.

The idea seems to be that if you do not put your plans in the hands of or through the approval system of the Lord, then they will never really be solid; they will remain fluid and slippery.

Also, why would you want to work really hard on a set of plans for which God is not willing to open doors?

There is an interesting nuance in this verse that is often missed. He says that if you commit your works – the things that you already have done – to the Lord, honor Him out of them, glorify God through them, see God in the midst of them, then your plans for the future will be firm. But if you will not honor, commit, and glorify God with your present works, then your plans will remain slippery and inadequate.

There is backwardness in this concept. If you acknowledge God and give Him glory for what you have already done, then He will firm up and work with the plans that you have. It is the same idea as: *In all your ways acknowledge the Lord and He will make your paths straight.*

It must be clear that what you are doing and have done is for the Lord and to honor the Lord and in doing that He will make your plans firmed up. We don't know whether that means that He will make sure you add the little parts to the plan that will make them work or whether He will make sure that the things that need to happen to make the plans work will happen or He will adjust your plans to the ones that will work out like in Psalm 37:4: *Delight yourself in the Lord and He will give you the desires of your heart.*

The word *plan* is a word that means thoughts about a particular direction and can also mean motive or purpose. There is the clear idea that God will bring out of the swirling mass of your thoughts, certain ones, and will firm them up when your present and completed works have been dedicated to the Lord. If this is not done, then the implication is that the swirling mass of your thoughts will remain a swirling mass of potential directions. It is the firming up of thoughts into actual reality that is being promised here.

We also need God to take the good thoughts and provide some fixity to those and let the bad ones or evil ones pass by. Why does one idea that we have come to reality and another remain a thought? Why do some ideas seem so good and yet they will not fly in the real world? God is saying, I will fix that problem if you will learn to commit your works to Me. To dedicate to roll on to... to Honor Me with...

Oh God, I give you everything and dedicate it to you and for your service. I want you to bring out of my mind the thoughts and dreams that should come out and would succeed. I want you to pass over the thoughts that flow through my brain which are not for me to do and / or are not good ones.

March 17

PROVERBS 17:3

The refining pot is for silver and the furnace for gold, but the Lord tests hearts

Clearly the Lord will subtract certain things from your life and add other things to put you under stress and to bring to the surface what is in your heart. God wants to bring up the gunk so He can get rid of it, and He wants to refine the good stuff that is in your life.

The idea that God monkeys with the blessings of your life is hard for many to believe or fathom, but clearly God will bless you in many areas and withhold blessing in another area so that you will have to trust Him.

Understand that the word *heart* is not your emotions alone, although that is clearly a part of the idea. Heart in the Hebraic mindset is the mind – what you are thinking about and the way you will reason through a problem.

He is really saying that He is going to test you to see how your mind works. Who do you go to for problems? Where is your confidence? How ready are you to ask for help? When you face a problem that you cannot solve or looks in every way impossible, what do you do? Do you give up? Do you get lured into temptation? Do you pray? Do you wait?

He is looking for clear evidence of how you are wired for the purpose of rewarding you, and so that it can become obvious to you that a rewire job is in order.

PROVERBS 18:3
When a wicked man comes contempt also comes, and with dishonor comes scorn

This is an interesting lesson in people and wisdom. What God is telling us is that if you have a person who violates the Ten Commandments (wicked), they will also bring with them contempt. In other words a person who would curse, dishonor parents, murder, commit adultery, lie, steal, covet will also downgrade others.

They may be joyful and full of life when you are sharing their sin, but they will bring a level of contempt into your life by their presence. This concept of linkage is a crucial understanding for wisdom. What comes with doing this or that? Many people only see the first activity or the sin and do not think through that action's relatives.

The real key to understanding is to look for and realize the linkages between things.

One must ask questions like: *If I marry a person who cheats, what else will I get? If I go into business with a person who lies or is unfaithful, what else will I get in the business and my dealings with them? If I become close friends or marry someone who does not believe in God or acknowledge His primacy, what else will I invite into my life?* It is these linkage questions that are so often not asked. Or they are discovered after the fact when the contempt is already there and the scorn is rampant.

Another interesting linkage is the backwards linkage. There is a lot of contempt in this business, this family, this church. Where and who are the wicked who bring it in? If contempt is here, then wickedness is also here?

This kind of linkage must be handled with great skill, but it does give you a great leg-up in understanding and solving people problems.

March 19

PROVERBS 19:3
The foolishness of man ruins his way and his heart rages against the Lord

Foolishness is a moral quality in the Hebraic understanding; not a level of one's mental acumen. To be a fool is to be self-focused, selfish, impulsive, rebellious, and morally deficient.

It is the sin nature in each one of us that makes us fools. Each person has the natural tendency to see every situation from a self-focused point of view. This tendency must be overcome by wisdom, knowledge, prudence, and understanding.

This verse declares the basic truth of the whole book of Proverbs. If you let your natural foolishness, impulsiveness, and rebellion direct the course of your life, you will ruin your life.

The result of this type of foolish, sinful action is that you will be angry at the Lord for not making your life better; but it is you who has destroyed the life that God gave you.

The Septuagint, in a rough translation, says that a fool destroys his life and he accuses God in his heart.

PROVERBS 20:3

Keeping away from strife is an honor for a man, but any fool will quarrel

This passage is a continuation of the idea discussed in the previous verse (20:2): the anger of the leader. The fool is the person who just constantly needs to point out the other point of view; who needs to be right; who needs to be noticed even when it is not helpful to be right.

When you do not have to cross swords or expectations with those around you, then you would be wise to avoid it even if you do not completely agree with the direction or idea or topic. There is no need inherent in any relationship – especially the relationship of leader to follower – that requires a person to come up with, point out, or develop alternative points of view. In fact, it is the fool who usually does not understand that moving down a different path than what was declared as the goal is the clearest way to provoke the leader to anger and lose your life in that company or organization.

But the fool sees it as honorable to constantly criticize and constantly point out the other point of view. Do not constantly be disagreeing with people; let it go. Work hard to avoid criticizing people. Only when you are forced to do it should you do this.

We often play the fool in this way. We want to make ourselves look good or we disagree when we have a valid point, but it will not cause the other person to change his/her point of view. It will just cause this person to hate you.

March 21

PROVERBS 21:3

To do righteousness and justice is desired by the Lord more than sacrifice

Which is more desired by God: to obey or to repent when you do something bad? Clearly it is to obey and do the thing right the first time.

One of the things that my children did not completely grasp is that saying "I'm sorry" did not fix a relational problem especially when the "I'm sorry" was said half-heartedly. I wanted my daughter to realize before she hit her sisters or tried to trick them that there was probably a positive or encouraging thing to do instead. They seemed to think that there was always "I'm sorry" as a way out of relational trouble. This is not true with God and it is not true with other people.

This verse tells us that God does not want you to be breaking the laws and principles and then counting on the sacrifice to make it right. God really wants you to surrender to Him before you do something. What would bring the greatest amount of joy, peace, love, and encouragement into this situation? What does God want me to do?

Are you relying on apology rather than just doing things right the first time?

March 22

PROVERBS 22:3
The prudent sees the evil and hides himself, but the naive go on, and are punished for it

Solomon is trying to help people see a truth that is always raising its head. In a world full of sinful, selfish people – a fallen world – stuff happens that is bad. Are you prepared for those eventualities? The more naive a person is, the less they prepare and then they will pay a heavy price.

When you enter into an agreement or begin enjoying a situation – especially one that has long-term designs – one has to ask, "What are the safeguards if this whole thing goes bad?" or "What are all the ways that this could go bad?" If you are not prepared for the evil that could and will most likely eventuate, you will be naive and pay a heavy price.

the prudent sees the evil

The word *prudent* is the Hebrew word *yaruwm* and means crafty, subtle, shrewd. It is often used negatively for one who is devious. It can also be used positively for one who plans and really thinks through the details of how things will happen. In this case it seems to be that the prudent person looks at all scenarios and the possible good and bad outcomes. The one who is thorough thinks through all the ways this situation could go bad and finds a way to protect himself.

and hides himself

The word *hides* is the Hebrew word *sathar* and means to conceal, hide, hide carefully, be secret. The idea is to be out of the way when the evil that is coming in the first part of the verse is happening; to be protected from that evil happening to you. There are all types of ways to protect oneself from situations when they go bad. These could be in a signed, legally binding contract; could be in running away; could be physically hiding oneself; could be calling to check references; could be in having a savings account; could be in not entering into an agreement or relationship.

The key idea is that the person who is wise and who is growing in their prudence does not just leap into situations, relationships, or deals but examines what could go wrong as much as what could go right. In business it could be the hiring decision with no thought about how to fire the person. At church it could be putting a person into a leadership position too quickly without having thoroughly checked them out. In romance it could be too quickly saying "I will" when the person's character has not been examined.

This is a key principle in life. Do I have a way to hide myself from the trouble this will bring if it all goes bad? If the answer is no, then you are not being wise.

Some people take this to an extreme and live only for the hiding. They only plan on things going bad. This is also poor judgment and does not allow a person to enjoy life.

but the naive go on

The word *naive* is the Hebrew word *pethiy* which means simple or simplicity or naive. It has also been translated as too open-minded and foolish; a reckless impulsiveness that jumps before it examines. The naive person goes forward because it looks good. Right now things look rosy. They give no thought to the possibility that things could go wrong.

and are punished for it

How often have we seen people be punished because they did not adequately protect themselves? It is a shame that they are taken advantage of or that they bear a heavy price for not protecting themselves.

This is another argument against cohabiting without the societal commitment to a spouse called marriage. It will have the chance to go evil and without any protection or reason for the other person not to be evil.

March 23

PROVERBS 23:3
Do not desire his delicacies, for it is deceptive food

There are two fascinating directions that this proverb could refer to.

This could be an interesting study in nutrition and gluttony. Or this proverb could be a warning of the dangers of the plastic life of power, prestige, and fame.

do not desire his delicacies

The real warning comes against desiring the food of this ruler.

What is the food of the ruler? It could be the actual food of a rich, powerful leader. Or it could be a metaphor for what the ruler lives on; the air they breathe; the food they eat in terms of what they really use to sustain themselves.

In the one case it would be the actual food that should not be desired. In the other case it would be the arbitrary power that should not be desired.

In verse 29 of the previous chapter, God tells us that if you are a person of real skill, then leaders and high ranking people will find you. You will be doing your craft in front of men of real power and wealth. So the opening verses of Chapter 23 are the natural follow-up from that counsel. When you are in the presence of people of great wealth and power, don't develop a strong desire for their delicacies. Be prepared to want all the perks of their position but don't, as those benefits are not all they are cracked up to be. They are, in fact, deceptive.

Notice the flow of the first eight verses of Chapter 23 – they are about desiring the substance of the rich, powerful, and famous; not setting your sights on money and wealth and not eating any of the bread of the wicked person.

It would seem that the idea is to teach through analogies of food, eagles, and bread the life lessons which would make this proverb about arbitrary power, pomp and circumstance, and sycophantic attention.

If this is the case, then God is warning us that when your honed skill puts you in front of people with real power, don't allow yourself to begin to crave what they have. All of us would like to have arbitrary power, a great fuss made about everything we do, and people running around telling us that we are great and wise; but this is basically a lie. It fills you up, but it cannot really sustain life.

It is amazing how many are really pursuing these goals. Being able to tell people what to do; no questions asked; having everyone notice you and make a huge deal out of your presence; and gathering a group of people who only tell you, yes; do what you suggest; and act amazed at all you say and do. This, however, according to the Bible is not life but a lie and cannot sustain life. It is the fool in each of us that wants these goals.

If this proverb is about the actual food of powerful and wealthy people, then it is a warning not to let one's natural gluttony take over. A person of great wealth and power can have any and every type of food they want and usually they have an overabundance every meal. Many commentators have seen this proverb as a warning against gluttony. Put a knife to your throat. Actually force yourself to eat less than you think you can. Even though it all looks good and even though it is there for the taking, don't do it. Becoming addicted to food or drink pushes the focus of one's life to be completely upon this world. Do not be deceived; abundance of well-prepared food is a lie. As much food as you want is not the blessing that it seems. Food that costs a lot to enjoy is not the blessing that it seems.

for it is deceptive food

The word *deceptive* is the Hebrew word *kazab* which means untrue, false to reality, lie. It is regularly connected with vanity and emptiness. This is the word for falsehood.

If the issue in this proverb is really food, then God is pointing out that the food the ruler serves is a falsehood. Wealthy people serve food that is not good for you or too much of it like in Daniel's case where the king dined on rich and expensive foods that were bad for them and which Daniel refused. It is not reality. If you actually eat all that is available to you in the banquet room of a ruler, then you will be destroying yourself.

If the issue is actual food, then it is gluttony that is being warned against. Being in the presence of an abundance of food can make life seem to be only about satisfying physical needs. Jesus reminds the Devil that life is not about physical food alone but instead about the words that proceed out of the mouth of God.

In our day and age, gluttony is common place and obesity is an epidemic.

Is God talking about food at all or instead pointing us to what the ruler lives on? Is he trying to get us to realize that the power, prestige, respect, and deference that are the sustenance of the ruler are in truth deceptive? People do not really believe that you are worthy of all the subservience and respect they are giving you. They are acting this way because of the position you hold and the power you wield. Some people begin to believe their own press clippings and think that people are supposed to be this way to them all the time because of who they are, not the position they hold.

The positive lesson in this proverb – if food is a metaphor for power, wealth, and fame – is clearly that normal life of give-and-take relationships, hard work, anonymity, and opposition is real life and should be embraced fully instead of seeking to escape into a fairy tale of power, wealth, and prestige.

PROVERBS 24:3

By wisdom a house is built, and by understanding it is established; and by knowledge the rooms are filled with all precious and pleasant riches

Notice the thought connection between this proverb and the one before it. We are not to envy the gain of those with no scruples but to instead fill our lives with the precious and pleasant riches of wisdom. The evil use people and gain through violence; the wise fill their life with precious and pleasant riches – ones not available to those who pursue violence and immorality.

by wisdom a house is built

This is the theme of the whole book of Proverbs. The home is a metaphor for life. Building an adequate, wealthy, and enjoyable home is a symbol for building a wonderful life filled with great relationships, adequate treasure, and personal achievement. This two-verse couplet could be translated: *By wisdom a life is built and by understanding it is established; and by information and skill, good and positive activities and relationships are added.* So the question that this Proverb is asking is how do you build a life that is worth living? Also, realize that most houses were the site of the family business so this could also be the recipe for a successful business.

Wisdom is the ability to deny yourself the present pleasure to pursue the course that causes God and others to be winners. When I make sure that my family is a winner over my own purely selfish desires, then I am really setting up my life for some great success. When I am more focused on the customer winning than I am in turning a short-term profit, then I am building a really great company.

I must be focused on others winning as much, if not more, than my winning. In fact, I must choose the direction in which everyone wins and not just one group or the other. Wisdom is the Triple-Win.

The idea is that one cannot build a lasting future on selfishness, impulsiveness, and rebellion. Too many people in our day and age are trying to do this even though, from outward immediate appearances, they do not seem to be violating this principle. But they have locked themselves in credit card debt through compulsive (impulsive) spending. This desire to look good or have what they want now or not say the hard thing to a family member destroys the future that they are hoping to build. There is no lasting future built on foolishness (pride, deception, glitz, greed, impulsiveness).

and by understanding it is established

We need to constantly notice the relationships between things. There is a relationship between certain problems and their causes or contributing factors. Many of us do not want to admit that these connections exist. We don't want to admit that there is a connection to our growing weight and the ice cream, cookies, and fries that we enjoy eating; but there is a connection. We do not want to see that there is a connection between the amount of TV we watch and the level of boredom and lack of success we enjoy. We don't want to notice the connection between our temptations and certain items in our lives. If we are ever going to have a growing, stable life, we must always be aware of the relationship between things in our life. What will happen if I let this in my life? What will happen if I eliminate this from my life?

and by knowledge the rooms are filled

The word knowledge means both information and skills. One doesn't enjoy fullness in one's life unless there are developed skills that people will pay to receive or information that others do not have. This is the old adage: What do you do well? What do you have the potential of doing better than any other person near you? Do that and you will be better off than if you try and do a lot of things in a mediocre fashion. If you do not keep growing in your skill set or in your knowledge, the life you are leading will not be filled with the good things you would like.

In our day and age people keep looking for a job in which they do not have to keep growing or developing. Life does not work this way. All of life needs to be about growing and developing. More skills and more information – this is what actually brings in the wealth that allows the rooms to be filled.

Which one of these do you need to work on in your life?

Wisdom: Self-Denial and the Triple-Win

Understanding: Relationship between things

Knowledge: Information and skills

Learn to grow in each one

with all precious and pleasant riches

What are the precious and pleasant riches that wisdom and knowledge bring? While these certainly would include wealth, the primary focus of wisdom in the Scripture is strong relationships. It does not matter if your house is filled with every kind of possession imaginable if there are no relationships in your life of depth and meaning – a house filled with people you care about and care about you.

The older I get the more I realize that it is the relationships of life that give life its joy and meaning. Having an enjoyable relationship with my wife, deeply enjoying being with my kids and having them want to be with me, and enjoying friendships and mentoring relationships are what really give life its meaning and purpose. And most importantly of all, being close to God and having a back-and-forth relationship in which He is the delight of my soul and I please Him by my actions of faith.

Doesn't it change the focus of life when you realize that the goal of life is deep, joyful relationships – not money, fame, power, and glamour?

March 25

PROVERBS 25:3
As the heavens for height and the earth for depth, so the heart of kings is unsearchable

This is a very interesting proverb about leadership. It suggests that no one can know for certain what the soul of the leader will do for the soul is unsearchable. It is not predictable.

It could also suggest that any leader is capable of that which is shocking and unexpected – both for good and for bad. This is an interesting proverb about the depth of a person and especially the depth of a leader. We can believe we will know what a leader will say or do, but it is not a sure thing until we actually ask them. This suggests that there is much more than meets the eye when we are watching a leader lead. So often we buttonhole people whom we know at work or at church into a particular type of person and do not let them be the whole of the person that they really are.

Just as we have had astronomers searching and mapping the heavens, so we need to realize that there is much more to a leader than what meets the eye. Let them be more and try them in new directions. It may surprise you.

March 26

PROVERBS 26:3
A whip is for the horse, a bridle for the donkey, and a rod for the back of fools

The focus of this proverb is what brings about controlled positive behavior. The measures used with a horse, the measures used with a donkey, and the measures used with a fool are all harsh, constant, and demanding.

The clear teaching is that if a person is selfish, impulsive, and rebellious then constant, demanding, and even harsh constraints are the only way to bring out of the fool a positive and lasting set of behaviors. There is no easy way to deal with a person who has no self-discipline. This proverb is trying to cut away the sugarcoating and give the honest truth about dealing with a fool – as a son or daughter, as an employee, as a constituent, as anyone who is rightfully under your care and over whom you exercise oversight and direction.

Being upset with their behavior will not change their life; they need firm and even harsh, demanding, and constant direction to hopefully develop internal self-discipline over time. Some people, however, will never be self-motivated and need constant direction and boundaries.

The direction of this proverb is very difficult for our present culture to hear. Our culture has elevated choice and self-determination to the place of highest value. We can't tell or force anyone to do anything they don't want to do. We want to let everyone do what they want to do. This is, however, moral nonsense. Everyone cannot do what they want to do. Many times they have to do what is right even when they don't want to. This is the most difficult assignment for the fool. The fool has been on a constant journey of doing whatever he/she wants to do.

In order to build a great family, a great company, a great church, or a great community, everyone will have to do things that they don't want to do at times. Some people who are not given to restricting their own selfish impulses will need closer supervision and controls lest they detour into their own selfish ways again. It is important to help, supervise, direct, coach, and even control someone into doing the right thing.

This proverb is about the need for strong unbending controls to guide the fool back to a productive road. Realize that this is the role of the leader. Leadership is hard because you have to get people to sublimate their personal desires for the good of the team.

This would also imply that when you find an area of foolishness in your own life, that you not coddle yourself. Instead, you should be demanding, constant, and harsh for if there is a way for you to be selfish, impulsive, and rebellious in this area, then you will. And that tendency will move you away from the positive activities that you could be engaged in and send you down the path that leads to further trouble.

PROVERBS 27:3

A stone is heavy and the sand weighty, but the provocation of a fool is heavier than both of them

It is a dangerous thing to become a man of vexation. It leads to foolishness. And when a fool is vexed, it is always worse. When selfishness, impulsiveness, and rebelliousness get angry and allow that anger to motivate them to action, it is always a disaster.

We must turn our souls and our lives over to the Lord to live in the universe in which He is God and we are not; in which the laws that He has established reign rather than the laws which we would create.

The proverb states that this type of anger is heavier than stone or sand. It weighs down the person and the life. It will destroy you by keeping you from moving forward.

There will be many things that will happen to you that are against your plan and your convenience. Some will be from the direct hand of God overruling your desires and plans; others will be from the decisions and sin of others. But we must become people who submit our souls to the Lord to have Him right the wrongs, guide the journey, and redirect the way. Too often have we given into our selfish vexation and damaged others and ourselves in the process.

Oh God, give me a soul that will more quickly and easily surrender itself to your decisions and your universe. I have too often played the fool who is angry because everything did not go my way. It is you who are wise and all knowing. We, at best, see in a mirror dimly.

Remember, the goal when this life is over is not to have lots of God or memories of pleasure but to have a fully developed soul full of wisdom and love. In fact, true love is the height of wisdom.

March 28

PROVERBS 28:3
A poor man who oppresses the lowly is like a driving rain that leaves no food

poor

This is the Hebrew word *rus* which means poor, poverty; in many cases it means destitution – one who does not have the means to sustain life in its most basic level. There is food, water, and shelter that is missing from this person's life.

oppresses

This is the Hebrew word *asaq* which means to oppress, defraud, gain through deceit. This word carries the idea of an abuse of power and/or some form of fraud or deception in which the one party gains while the other party loses. This "I gain while you lose" form of getting ahead is what the Bible calls stealing. No matter how clever the person does it or how subtle it is, it is still stealing. If your gain is because of my loss, then it is stealing. It is oppression.

There is the intimation in this idea of the word *oppression* that when a person who is destitute moves into positions of authority over another and uses its gain at the lowly's expense, it is doubly bad for they have been betrayed by one of their own. And there is no benefit at all for having been driven or used. There is not even any profits for the poor person has squandered or consumed those. There is not even anyone to sue and gain just compensation.

lowly

This is the Hebrew word *dal* which means one who is low; those who for various reasons are knocked down. It could be physical, spiritual, emotional, mental, and/or financial reasons that have them at this point down and low; but it is this type of person whom the destitute person in the proverb comes and oppresses, comes and swindles.

These are the tragic stories that we constantly hear on the news. A person who is on the margins of life – elderly, poor, mentally challenged, physically handicapped – is the target of the person who swindles them. They are conned or defrauded of the one area that they had going for them. This is so tragic. This is so wrong.

Solomon's comparison is telling: *like a driving rain that leaves no food.* The literal translation is a driving rain that leaves no bread. The idea being that when the rains come and they are terrible to be out in and you are miserable, one can at least look forward to the wheat and other crops that will use this driving rain to grow. But when there are no seeds in the ground to turn the driving rain into some kind of profit, you are left having been driven and with nothing to show for it.

Solomon is pointing out that there is no good that comes from this type of conduct. There is no God allowing this because there is good coming down the road. This is just flat wrong and demands justice. It screams out for the perpetrators to be caught. It is true that God is so powerful that He can turn these incidents to become good things in the life of the person who loves Him (Romans 8:28). But this is not a good; it is a grievous evil. This is where Solomon is trying to train us, who will be leaders, to speak out against this; to demand justice to the perpetrators. It is not okay to just say that this is too bad; these people should be more careful. They were oppressed. If the leaders of a country or city or region are not willing to protect the rights of the lowly, then these completely unprofitable criminal acts will multiply and the society will become full of injustice.

Many people want to blame God. How could He let this happen? But He, through Solomon, is screaming back at us. How could you let this happen? We cannot allow the people who are at the margins to be killed, raped, conned, abused, etc. The strength of the society is shown on what it allows people to do to its vulnerable people: the elderly, the unborn, the minority, the children, the physically or mentally challenged.

This proverb is a lesson in justice and who is to blame for these travesties of righteousness. It is not God. It is the person who does this, and it is the society who does not prosecute this type of crime fully.

PROVERBS 29:3

A man who loves wisdom makes his father glad, but he who keeps company with harlots wastes his wealth

There are a number of things to notice here: the contrast between the two different objects of love; the results of the two different paths; the implied results of the two different loves which are not stated; the implications of harlotry; the contrast between two different objects of love.

Solomon is contrasting the results and the affection or pursuit of a young man's fancy. He can pursue the selfish impulses that inhabit every young man and spend time with harlots – women who will meet his sexual needs and turn him into more of a fool – a man unable to resist his selfish impulses. Or he can choose to love wisdom and thereby the application of knowledge and interpersonal skill to build strong and healthy relationships. The one builds selfish impulses and unhealthy relationships. The other builds a reservoir of information and healthy relationships. The selfish impulse looks like it is getting ahead at the beginning, but it falls behind to wisdom over the long haul. When deep, caring, and vibrant relationships are needed, wisdom is clearly the winner.

Solomon surprises us with the contrasts between the results of the various pathways. On the one hand there are parents who are glad and on the other is wasted wealth. These would not seem to be opposites. There is here a typical orientation to pleasing authority and demonstrating wisdom to those who have been down the road. In our present culture there is an orientation to peer pressure and peer approval that is destructive to young people. God wants to help us understand that the rewards in life – especially for young people – come from pleasing those who are older, not appearing cool to our peers. Consistently we have reinforced, as a culture, that which is destructive to young people. We have, in effect, praised people for orienting themselves to the fool's way. "Do the people who are your peers agree?" rather than "Are your parents pleased?"

One of the most consistent truths, very rarely violated, is that our parents want the best for us and want us to succeed. They have been down the road of life and know many of its potholes. They do not want us to make the same mistakes that they made. They truly want their children to succeed; even many times more than they want success for themselves. Our culture is teaching young people to ignore this source of wisdom and help and try and please their peers. This is a fool's errand.

Notice that Solomon is saying that when a young man lines up with the pursuit of wisdom, he will be pleasing to his parents. One could almost say the opposite also. If you want to take the fool's path or the one that will almost assuredly end in destruction and great damage to your life, then do things that displease your parents.

One of the things that I try and consistently impress upon my daughters is if you glance over your shoulder as you are about to make a decision and you see the glint of approval in my eye, this is almost always a wise decision. If you make a decision like I would make, then good things will happen to you. If, however, you make choices that you know I would not approve of or that I think are a waste of time or money, then you will be adding troubles to your life that don't need to be there.

I have watched young people consistently choose the rebel path from their parents' wisdom because they need to express their independence or they don't like their parents for some reason. This kind of thinking just destroys the potential and joy in the young person's life. Then they wonder how they got such a difficult life. Don't make this mistake. Would the decisions that you are about to make be consistent with a wise decision your parents would make? Yes, teens, it is possible for your parents to make foolish decisions also; you don't need to emulate those.

Notice the other result – the fool's pathway. It is a waste of wealth. This is so unexpected as a statement. We might expect Solomon to say that it will result in great emotional pain; that it will bring diseases; that it will produce a shallowness in your life; that it will drive a wedge with your parents; that it will cause you to miss God's best in your life; that it will bring God's punishment; and a thousand other things that are true.

Solomon rightly picks a negative consequence that will capture the attention of the young person who is being tempted by the lure of selfish impulses. He motivates the young person to avoid the fool's pathway with a fool's reasoning: don't waste your wealth. In other words, it pays to stay away from this impulse. He uses selfish impulses to motivate the person who is under the power of the fool's temptation. This may be a part of the answer to the statements that Solomon makes in 26:4,5: *answer a fool according to his folly.* If a person is following the lure of selfish impulses, they will not be motivated to change by altruistic reasons. They will be motivated by selfish consequences of the righteous way.

I am usually amused and saddened by the ways that people try and motivate others to give up their selfish ways. Don't do that, it will hurt me! How could you do that to us? Don't you know that you will offend God? If you do that you will be hurting lots of people! This type of reasoning makes no sense to the selfish person.

Solomon says you will be wasting your wealth. "REALLY?" replies the selfish person, "I better look into this." The selfish person understands selfish reasons.

The implied results of the two different loves are not stated. Because of what Solomon uses as the motivation to move in the direction of wisdom, it is possible to realize that there were things he could have said; things that we would have expected him to say that He did not that we can also learn from.

After Solomon says that the person who loves wisdom makes his father glad, we would expect him to say that the person who spends time with harlots makes his father and mother disheartened and grieving. This is a true statement that the selfish person does not understand.

Deep grief comes to the parents of those who choose the lascivious life. This is a warning to parents to parent the selfishness out of their children before they get old enough to make these kinds of choices. Yes, it is hard to parent constantly and consistently enough to cause your child to personally restrict their selfishness, but it must be done so that you can enjoy your family.

Unfortunately we live in a culture where parents do not like to live with the consequences of their parenting decisions. Parents can release their children to the schools, to the coaches, to the after-school programs, to the society at large and hope those people will train selfishness out of their children's lives; but it will not happen. The parents of selfish children receive emotional punches to the stomach year after year until the child repents of their selfishness. It is no fun to be the parent of a fool, so don't raise one. Raise children who do not always put themselves first. Raise children who can say no to themselves. Make sure that it is not just external forces that make your children stop. A high level of your parenting is to bring about a level of self-denial in your children. Just because they want it doesn't mean they should do it, say it, or get it. Can they say, "No, I don't really need it." "If I am going to achieve that, then I can't do this."

The implications of harlotry.

There needs to be a long discussion and understanding of harlotry. Solomon introduces the idea that harlots or women who sell or use their bodies to satisfy the desires of selfish men outside of marriage are promoting selfishness. They are a virus in the society because they encourage and fulfill the selfish pathway. While it may not be possible to completely eradicate this form of vice from any society, one should make it as inconvenient as possible. It is not helpful to the women, the man, or the whole of society.

Young ladies must be told that when they give into the selfish pressure of men, they do not help themselves but instead push themselves and this man further down the road of destruction. It is true that there will always be these types of people, but it doesn't have to be them. They can choose to get away from this lifestyle; they can choose to never go down that path. No matter what a man tells you, sexual relations outside of marriage is a destructive force for you and for him and for society.

March 30

PROVERBS 30:3
Neither have I learned wisdom, nor do I have the knowledge of the Holy One

These are the stylized ways of showing humility. Our culture has largely forgotten that it is not wise or righteous to brag about yourself and the people you know. In this proverb Agur is stating the obvious. He does not know all there is to know. He does not know all about God and His ways. While almost everyone would admit that, many in our day and age parade around like they know everything and understand God.

While this single verse is not the point of this section of the Proverbs, God's Word is always instructive even in its smallest sections. We need to have a way to acknowledge that we do not always know what to do. We need to acknowledge that there are a lot of things about God and why He lets certain things happen and other things not happen that we do not understand. We need to walk in daily humility, not as though we know it all.

How do you display to others that you are not a know-it-all? What phrase do you use to say, "I am still teachable." "There is a lot I still don't understand." This is how Agur says it, and it was breathed into by God so that we would see his humility.

I have found that it is important for me to say that I could be wrong or that people should feel free to disagree with me or that I would love to hear other people's point of view on a topic or if someone else has other insights then I would love to know them.

We must live with a level of humility that is on display. We must demonstrate that we do not think that we have arrived. It is crucial that we live this way and demonstrate this. Now many times we must demonstrate that we are teachable before we have actually embraced this truth. In other words, you must say that there is a lot you can learn, even when you do not believe that there is much that you can learn because your feelings of complete knowledge are always wrong. Find a way to say, live, and act in a humble way so that you do not have to apologize so much for your lack of knowledge and your proud, condescending attitude.

It is the wise person who is willing to admit that they will never know it all – even in their own area of expertise.

March 31

PROVERBS 31:3
Do not give your strength to women, or your ways to that which destroys kings

Remember that the first part of this proverb is written to those who would be leaders for God. It was written by a king who calls himself Lemuel which is "for God." He was a man who saw that God had called him to leadership and was recording the best advice he received as a child. It was from his mother and was either God-breathed from her or God-breathed in his recollection or God-breathed in the recording. But now it is inspired instructions for leadership.

Verse 3 is the opening command. It is negative. Don't get disqualified right out of the gate. Do not give your strength to women. Clearly this is a reference to not spending mental, emotional, physical, and spiritual energy on chasing or impressing women. It also seems to imply that the king who had a position of power should not be involved in the party scene and carousing just because he could. It is this dissipation of strength that is being outlawed. Too many great leaders with good ideas have not been able to control their appetites and have diminished, if not destroyed, the impact of their leadership for God.

When a person becomes a leader, they have offers open to them that are not open to more normal folks. These offers could be monetary, privileges, favors, social, sexual, or any number of desirable commodities. These are the ways which destroy kings.

If you are a leader for God, then you are to get about the business of leading for God. But, instead, the world system and the Devil would seek to distract you from the goal of accomplishing great things for God. If you are thinking about making sure that no one finds out what you did or how you can hang on to that pleasurable activity or gain a piece of the money you oversee for yourself, then you have succumbed to the temptation and cannot as effectively lead for God.

Notice that the proverb doesn't say that a leader cannot enjoy nice things and has to live like a monk. But instead they cannot give their ways to these pursuits. There are many wonderful things in this world that are not sinful or destructive. But if you begin to spend leadership time to planning how to pursue these things instead of what God has asked you to do, then it will begin to destroy your leadership.

Many Christian leaders do not reach the level of impact that they should because they fall victim to these temptations. The church in the Middle Ages suggested that these temptations would revolve around money, sex, and power. Watch these; don't give your strength to them. Give your strength to pleasing God with your leadership decisions.

April

April 1

PROVERBS 1:4
To give prudence to the naive, to the youth knowledge and discretion

to give prudence to the naive

prudence

The word translated *prudence* is the Hebrew word *arom* which has both a positive and negative meaning. When used negatively, it means a crafty schemer – one who plans out destructive, sinful things. When used positively, it means prudence. The English dictionary definition of the word prudence is a quality which allows a person to always choose the sensible path. This is not what the average person today thinks of when they hear the word prudence. The Hebrew word carries the idea of thoughtful planning to a good end with an ability to choose that good end. Perhaps the word should be translated: planning ahead or preparedness. It is the ability to realize that if I want this thing over there, then there are a number of steps that I have to take to get there.

It could be thought of as planning or goal-setting or preparation. In order to achieve anything in life, there is more planning than the naive is usually willing to realize. Things don't just come together at the last minute. Sometimes the plans take a decade to come together. In fact, one of the things about successful people is that they are always planning for the next ten or twenty years into the future. What education, investments, relationships, and experiences do you need this ten years to prepare you for the decade?

One of the greatest things that a young person could realize is – what kind of planning do we need to do this thing we want to do?

Recently my wife and I started putting a whole new level of prudence into our vacations, and the quality of the vacation has shot through the roof. We have started planning for a year or more for each trip we take. How much money will it take? What could we do? Where could we go? What is there to do at the various places? In fact as, I write this, I am enjoying a little trip with the family to Carmel, California, having ridden horses on the beach and kayaked in the ocean all because of prudence. Things go better with prudence.

We all like to be spontaneous and it can serve you well, but prudence or planning and goal-setting allows a much richer life. God prompted me when I was nineteen to lay out a basic plan for my life: what I wanted to accomplish, things I wanted to do, relationships I wanted to have, places to see, etc. That then allowed me to think through what kind of education I would need; when it might be appropriate to get married, have children, do various things. Through this general plan God has been able to guide me and prepare me to be more maximally useable for Him. I am more alert to opportunities and possibilities that are little pathways to accomplish much larger goals. I know what to look for and alert to information I might need later. The plan keeps developing and I try and update it every ten years. This process of prudence has suited me extremely well and given me a general map for my life as well as clarity about when to deviate and when not to. I am deeply enjoying life because of God's gracious direction in providence. When I turned fifty a few years ago, I updated it for the next twenty to fifty years – what I hope will be the most productive years of life.

I have noticed that the more impulsive I get, the less wise I get. Now spontaneity is wonderful within the boundaries of a good plan.

Take a few minutes at the beginning of the week to plan. Take a few minutes at the beginning of the day to plan. Take a day at the beginning of the year to plan. Look into the future and ask God, "What is possible?" Then begin planning how to get there.

naive

The quality of naiveté is simple-minded; taking things always at face value; only engaging in things that are right now in their pay-off;

being simplistic in your understanding or planning. It means only thinking about today or the section of the day that you are presently living in. "Are we having fun yet?" is the motto of these folks. It is all about the "right now." The Hebrew word *peti* comes from the idea of open or spacious. It is consistently translated simple or even foolish for the naive person is too open to the dangers and seductive allurements of the world.

In our day and age those who are open to the pressure of advertising are completely in debt. Those who are open to the suggestions of others get taken advantage of and lured into sin.

The one thing that the naive or simple person needs is a plan and the realization that not everyone or everything is as it seems. There are people who will take advantage of you. There are products and companies and groups that do not have your best at heart.

It is interesting that God wrote a book to make sure His people are not naïve, and yet many Christians have done this to their children by not training their children in the importance of prudence and by not helping them realize that there are selfish people out there who will use and abuse them. In fact, it is almost considered axiomatic that Christian kids will be naive about the ways of the world. The Scripture wants us to be as harmless as doves but as wise as serpents. We must learn to plan ahead and not be duped by the selfishness of others.

to the youth knowledge and discretion

youth

This is the Hebrew word *naar* which means boy or young maiden. It usually refers to a person who has not reached full maturity. In a girl it referred to a young maiden who was not married and, therefore, not into full adulthood. We would call this person the teenager.

knowledge

This is the Hebrew word *daat* which is knowledge, information, perception, skill. One of the things that young people need is information that they don't have and the development of skills that will allow them to live a good life. The proverb declares if young people will pay attention to the inspired words in this book, they will gain two things they desperately need: information about the way the world really is and skills that will allow them to develop a great life.

It is a shame when kids do not grow up in these two crucial areas. They need information about the real world, not the world of the pre-adult. They also need life skills: how to get along with people; what kind of people to avoid; what must be done to succeed at life. All these skills and much more are taught in this book.

discretion

This is the Hebrew word *mezimma* which means purpose, plot, goal, aim. It is used on a number of occasions for the goal or aim of a project. It does also carry with it the idea of planning or a plan. So in this way it is not that different from the word translated prudence. But its focus is more on the goal than the plan.

It seems clear that what Solomon is saying is that the two things that young people need desperately are information/skills and goals. Without these two things they will not have a successful life. They will instead, most likely, fall into the impulsive wanderings of a fool – selfish, impulsive, rebellious.

Don't fall into that trap. Gain the information that you need. Take the tests you need to take to discover what God-given talents, abilities, and gifts He has given you. Then chart a course to utilize those abilities.

An awful lot of trouble has come because a young person had no goal for the weekend or the summer or afternoon. Build this quality of being purpose-directed rather than just aimlessly wandering through life, waiting and hoping that something interesting or exciting will come along. Commit to good things. I know that some other good thing may come along, but more joy will be created by developing goals and plans than if you just sit and wait.

That means volunteer at the church or charitable organization. That means to sign up to work. That means to agree to go to a particular place even though something better might come up. There will always be a next time if it is a good thing.

April 2

PROVERBS 2:4
If you seek her as silver and search for her as for hidden treasures

Wisdom must be sought. It runs counter to our normal choices and is hidden from view by our own foolish tendencies. It begins to be more predictable once you have found it on a regular basis.

In this proverb, God tells us that we are needing to conduct a search of all the available options. One or a number of them represent wisdom. We must, however, lean hard into the search so that we will discern the proper direction.

What is interesting is that you will be searching for wisdom, but your will discerns the fear of the Lord first. These are the boundaries of God's moral law. There will probably be a number of fairly obvious and easy ways to accomplish the goals you want that involve cheating, anger, lying, etc. This is where you find the fear of the Lord. Do I really fear Him and believe that He has consequences for my actions, especially when I move beyond the boundaries of the Ten Commandments and God's moral law?

The Lord will give you wisdom, verse 2:5 says, when you have discerned the fear of the Lord first. Where are the boundaries? Our minds will find the deviant ways to accomplish our goals. But in seeking wisdom, we must reject these. If the goal is to be happily married, our fleshly nature will come up with the new mate, the affair, the alcoholic anesthesia that will make the possibility of a happy marriage look bright. You don't get a happy marriage that way; it just seems like you would. It is just that you have to cross significant moral boundaries to do that to your spouse. This is the direction of choice for many instead of putting in the work to make their present marriage work at a whole new level.

When you are facing a business decision and do not know how to achieve your goals, there will always be some scheme with the books that will come to mind that must be rejected or you will never find stable success or wisdom.

April 3

PROVERBS 3:4
So you will find favor and good repute in the sight of God and man

The reason why one should permanently tie love and truth to one's life is that it results in favorable relationship with God and mankind.

This is the ultimate "How to win friends and influence people" verse. In fact, this is the basis of all successful People Skill Courses. You are attempting to win favor with others when you learn people skills.

We are, because of our fallen nature, internally moved in a selfish direction. We think, "What do I want first?" Many never even consider what the other person wants or needs. The basis of all good People Skill Courses is trying to overcome our basic sin nature – which keeps us/self at the focal point of our lives. If we are to find favor with God and man, we must reorient our focus toward God and man. Notice that this is what verse 3 suggests. Do not let love and truth leave you.

No matter how selfish other people get, don't go selfish and self-focus on yourself. Keep the love of God flowing through you. You will not help anything by acting just like them.

If we stay self-focused, then it is not possible to be popular, well liked, respected, or enjoyed. No one wants to spend time around people who are always talking about themselves.

I have watched with a great deal of sadness as people in church have tried to make friends with people from a self-focused point of view. Trying to lure people into friendship – which is all about your stuff, your interests, your feelings, and your problems – will just not work. Learn what love really is – meeting needs, pursuing, pleasing.

If we learn to instinctively look to see what needs people have before we answer the question, "What do I want?" then there will be no end of favor and respect from others.

What are people's basic internal needs: a feeling of importance, to be heard, to be noticed, significance, security, acceptance. These and other basic internal needs are what we need to meet if we are to be experts at people skills.

Let me address another issue that comes up sometimes within Christian circles. The whole topic of whether we should, in any way, seek favor with man. Well this verse tells us how, so clearly it is not wrong to gain it. God wants us to know how to enjoy positive relationships with others. He does not want us to sin in order to gain them, but He does want us to know how to enjoy friends and relationships with all types of people. Too many Christians think it is spiritual to be a curmudgeon with an angry face and a condemning attitude. Not according to this verse.

April 4

PROVERBS 4:4
Then he taught me and said to me, "Let your heart hold fast my words; keep my commandments and live"

Solomon is remembering back when he was just a boy and how David, his father, would take him aside and talk with him about how to live and what to do in various situations. This makes a radically important impression in Solomon's life, and it is an important rite of passage for parents and children to participate in. It is the work of parenting.

To be a parent means to try and shepherd your children through the various choices that are out there so that they will have a great life. If they can avoid some of the mistakes that you made, they will be better off. If they can make the right choices that you made and that you would now make, they will have a much better life. Your children, however, are seeking to be independent and establish their own identity separate from you.

Notice Solomon's admonitions here in this proverb through his father's mouth: Let your heart hold fast my words; keep my commandments and live. You must begin to make decisions like I would make them or you will be embracing a life of death, needless pain, separation, and loneliness. Don't go down that road.

David's commandments, which were passed on to Solomon in these intimate encounters, were based on the Ten Commandments and the two great Commandments. This is why God could inspire and include Solomon's admonitions to us. It is absolutely imperative that you pass on to your children that fact that there is a way of life and a way of death in this life. One way pulsates with life through choosing to honor, respect, and cultivate other's ideas, needs, and interests. One is purely selfish, constantly asking the question, "What do I want?"

It is important that children realize that many times the right choice is counterintuitive. The way to really live is to get a little less of what you want and more of what everyone would want.

When David taught his son Solomon, he was carrying on an important function of fatherhood – teaching his children about life. Our culture has reduced fatherhood to a paycheck and a distant enforcer. God's role for fathers involves active relationships with their children and teaching life's lessons to them when they are ready to listen.

I recommend to parents and, especially, fathers that they set up a regular time to get together individually with their children. It should be the same time each week so that it is remembered. It should be with each child individually. Notice how Solomon says that David taught ME. He took time out of his busy schedule to spend time with ME and teach ME important things I need to know. Notice that there is a focus on interaction on important issues. As a child gets older, it is important that there is more listening and questions. A teenager needs to know that they have been listened to before they are willing to interact or hear what you have to say.

I recommend that you memorize the nine major relationships of life and be prepared to ask questions about how each of these is going in their life. If there are problems, questions, or difficulties, they will come out as you show specific interest in their life. Each week they may want to talk about a different relationship or the same relationship. Stay with the topic that they want to talk about. Be careful that you do not do all the talking and telling: How do you think you should handle it? or What do you think you could do?

As for those teens who are reading this, you have probably already made choices that have destroyed friendships or damaged grades or peace with your parents. It is important that you realize that your choices will largely determine the amount of peace you have in your life. That is why David drilled into Solomon, "Keep my commandments and live." If you do not keep God's commandments, then you will not have much life or peace. This is not a game where you can always proclaim that it is time to start over. This is life and the choices that you are making will create a life worth living or a hell on earth.

Ask yourself the question, "If I were to really do what my parents wanted me to do, what would it look like?"

PROVERBS 5:4
But in the end she is bitter as wormwood, sharp as a two edged sword

This is the part about adultery and lust that very few men take time to think about – the end. What kind of life do any of the parties end with? It is a dismal, guilty, diseased, alienated life. Adultery always promises to bring relationship intimacy and meet a deep need, but it doesn't. It is like drinking salt water; you are only more thirsty and it begins poisoning you.

The dire consequences of adultery need to be regularly repeated. It usually causes divorce; it siphons away financial resources; it distracts attention and focus on other crucial areas thereby reducing potential and success; it usually results in diseases – in some cases sterility; it results in the background radiation of guilt and a general angst; it offers a shortcut to intimacy but instead builds a pathway around true intimacy so it is never attained; it fractures friendships; it destroys the safety of the home for spouse and children; it often damages children, significantly limiting their potential; it often throws one or both parties into poverty; it weakens moral resolve in other areas of life; etc.

Some may dismiss these consequences as "not going to happen to me," but it is clear that these consequences cluster around those who commit adultery.

It is always wise when planning your life to picture where you want to be at the end of some part of the journey. How do you get there? Well, you have to take a serious look at what each pathway will entail.

There are limitations on the pathway of righteousness, but there is also great reward. There are limitations on the pathway of sin and there is a great consequence also.

Solomon says that the affair with an adulteress woman – while she may seem very exciting and enticing at the early stages of the affair –

will turn into a deeply bitter pill staining and souring your whole life. Don't go there.

bitter as wormwood

The Hebrew word for bitter is *mar* and the Hebrew word for wormwood is *laana*. The wormwood plant is known for its intense bitterness. It is referred to as hemlock in Amos 6:12 and in Revelation 8:10,11. It is represented as a star falling on the waters of the earth turning them poisonous. In Greece the people think of water with this plant in it as undrinkable.

Therefore, what Solomon is saying is that your whole life will be impacted by this act of adultery. It has a much greater impact than its actual size and duration would suggest.

I can remember talking with a woman who had grown tired of her marriage to a nice, contented, hard-working man. He still loved her, but she just wanted to experience the thrills and chills of life. She wanted to return the looks and attention of the men that noticed her. They came in for counseling and after talking to both of them at length about how to save their marriage, it became clear that she was not interested. I told her that in five or so years she would be used up and tired of the lifestyle that looked so appealing right now. She would forever break the heart of her husband and do untold damage to her two daughters. I remember telling her that there would be an awful price to pay, and she would pay a huge portion of it. She dismissed what I said, confident that her looks and her smarts would allow her to escape what I was saying. About four years later she moved back to the town where I pastored; she looked weathered and much older. I heard reports that she had been beaten by a number of the men she had taken up with. She moved back to town to be near her two girls whom she had abandoned. They wanted to have nothing to do with her. She was now stuck in a low-wage job with no husband and no prospect to trade on the looks she had used in the past.

The end of adultery is a difficult ride on a picket fence. The crop that you sowed with unfaithfulness will be reaped.

PROVERBS 6:4
Give no sleep to your eyes, nor slumber to your eyelids

This proverb is a word against the still common practice of being the guarantee for other's debts. Strictly speaking, this section means it is incredibly foolish to co-sign for a loan for others. It is ridiculously foolish to put your own goods at risk based on the behavior of others.

If you find yourself in this case, then go to the person who owes the debt and plead with them to repay the debt. Do not let yourself treat this as though it were nothing.

If one cannot secure a loan on the strength of their own pledges and work, then they are clearly a bad credit risk. And we do not help them by allowing them to borrow past their ability to pay back. We actually cripple them.

The appropriate response to the person who wants us to co-sign a loan for them is to look at our resources and see if we can spare the money. If we can and it seems especially helpful, then we should give it to them, telling them it is not a loan but a gift and the only repayment they must make is to someone else in need in the future.

Notice the unrelenting focus of this proverb's advice. Don't go to sleep; don't take a nap. In other words, do not procrastinate this problem. It will not go away. It is a serious problem. Your goods are at risk because of another's behavior. This is not good.

April 7

PROVERBS 7:4

Say to wisdom, "You are my sister," and call understanding your intimate friend

Notice that there are two separate items that a person needs to draw close to in this proverb – both wisdom and understanding.

Wisdom is the ability to choose the triple-win choice and to take the triple-win action: the one by which God is glorified, others are benefited, and you are profited. All three sighting mechanisms must be lined up, not just one or two.

Understanding is the connection between things. What happens to others if I do this? What happens in the future if I do this? What do others do if I do this? What happens in me spiritually, emotionally, mentally, physically if I do this?

Notice that the next proverb ties this need for wisdom and understanding to keeping a young man from pre-marital and extra-marital sexual activity. When one is under the pull and possibility of sexual involvement, one does not consider wisdom and understanding. It is imperative that one has thought through these types of scenarios before they come up. What will you do? How will you respond? How will you ensure that you do not go down that road? Why shouldn't you go down that road?

Too often, in our age, people just feel that if it is available then it is okay or they had no choice. No, they had a choice way before they got in that situation. They needed to embrace wisdom and understanding at a much earlier place like they want to embrace the illicit love now.

It is usually too late to think clearly when one is faced with the pull of temptation or with a willing paramour right in front of you. So the time to think about what you will do is now. The time to decide that you will not do this is now, not then.

This is the time to realize that there are permanent incurable diseases that come from this. That one of the reasons for infertility in women is premarital involvement and its disease involvements. That one will forever remember these involvements and they will have echoes into your future. That do you really want to be comparing your future spouse with this person? Do you really want this person to program how you will respond to intimacy? Those deep emotional wounds come from implicit promises that are not kept. That spiritual agreements and power are transferred in the act of intimacy; is this really the person that you want that to take place with? That lust tasted is hard, if not impossible, to satisfy and that ultimate sexual satisfaction does not come on the road of illicit romance and involvement. That this is a selfish act and will strengthen selfishness, not love, in both parties.

your sister... intimate friend

Solomon tells the young man to cling to wisdom and understanding. There is a suggestion that Solomon is saying something very unusual and involving a thought rhyme with the ideas that are coming. He may be saying, by using sister and intimate friend as the relationship connections, that he is encouraging an affair with wisdom and understanding rather than with this illicit individual. Solomon used very similar wording in the Song of Solomon 4:9,10 to describe his love for his fiancée.

It is entirely possible that Solomon is saying that before you get married, and even afterward, have an affair with wisdom and understanding. Make these two qualities of a wise life the means of deep satisfaction and pleasure. Don't try and find pleasure and satisfaction in the arms of a person who is not your lawful spouse. Find those pleasures in wisdom and understanding.

It is entirely consistent for Solomon to see – in wisdom and understanding – an endless source of joy, pleasure, and satisfaction. It is almost like he is saying to play a chess game with yourself about what happens if you do this and all the things that flow from that? And what happens if you do this and all the things that flow from that? Think through the various paths that your life can take. Be so enraptured with the possibilities and actions of wisdom that you are too busy to suck into the temporary pleasure of lust.

In other words, have your affair with wisdom and understanding rather than one with some loose individual who will destroy and disappoint. Wisdom and understanding do not disappoint but allow you to build a great life. Get real close with them.

Think through your life from all the various angles. Before you actually make a decision, think about it and look at all sides. Don't act impulsively or because of peer pressure. Will this decision still seem like a good one twenty years from now? Does this action actually move me towards my goals or away from it?

Since I have only girls in my home, let me say a word specifically to young women. I cannot tell you how many women have derailed their noble gifts and aspirations because they wanted to please a special boyfriend. Do not let a young man sidetrack what you know God is calling you to. The pressure of the moment and the "need" to have him like you should not be enough to throw away your future. Be strong. Do not give in. Even if the moment is passionate, do not sell yourself cheaply. If he is willing to make a permanent commitment to you through marriage, then you will think about whether he is the one and whether you are ready for that commitment and you will have other men you trust examine him also so that you are not fooled by a smooth talker. Sexual fulfillment requires a down payment upfront of lifetime commitment and examination by your physical and spiritual family. Anything less is a fool's choice.

Don't end up pregnant, diseased, or brokenhearted. Demand the down payment in full before any sexual involvement: lifetime commitment called marriage and examination by your physical and spiritual family.

PROVERBS 8:4
To you, O men, I call, and my voice is the sons of men

This is an often overlooked verse in the call of wisdom. It precedes a section where God, through Solomon, details what different people need to grasp to escape the folly of their lives. The naive need prudence; fools need wisdom; and everyone needs noble things, right things, truth, avoidance of wickedness, embrace of righteousness, understanding, knowledge, instruction. All of these are different and powerful in helping everyone sort out the way in which they should go.

This verse, however, is about a more specific attention-grabbing group of people who often miss wisdom's call as they rush off to business. Specifically, men. It is often true that men miss the subtleties of wisdom, understanding, skill, and nobility in the hurry to make a name for themselves. But the glories of riches, honor, and life are won using the subtleties of these very things.

Solomon stops just before he launches into the meat of the subject and says: Men, are you paying attention? Don't miss this, men. Don't be in such a hurry that you miss the things that will be required to be successful. The desire that you have to make a mark on the world is good, but it will make a far greater mark on you if you do not listen but learn what I am about to tell you.

The phrase *to the sons of men* is the balance statement which would include all children.

Do not miss that wisdom has a special call to men to slow down on their rush to make money and a name for themselves; to learn the subtleties of wisdom. It is hard to get young men, who are so sure of their talents and energy and direction, to embrace subtle issues of discernment and interaction. But it is crucial.

In applying this verse, ask yourself the question: Do you know the definition of the things wisdom wants to teach? If you do and how they work in the real world, you are ready. If you do not, then stop a while and listen to wisdom teach us.

- Prudence

- Wisdom

- Truth

- Wickedness

- Righteousness

- Perversion

- Understanding

- Knowledge

- Instruction

These terms should live with meaning from our study of Proverbs. If not, re-read the previous sections of Proverbs and learn what these words mean and how to live them out

PROVERBS 9:4

Whoever is naive, let him turn in here! To him who lacks understanding she says, Come eat of my food and drink of the wine I have mixed.

The naive see everything as much more simple than it really is, and they need to come to someone who has achieved what they want to achieve and ask them for the real truths that bring about that level of success.

This is truth whether it is the corporate executive of a large company or the successful housewife in a loving and enjoyable home or the successful pastor in a large church or the teenager enjoying good grades and popularity at school. Each of these successful enterprises involve far more than meets the eye. We are tempted to think that people are just lucky or it comes easy to them. No, it doesn't come easy to them; but they have learned to make it look easy.

The food they eat is varied and complex. They combine things that would not naturally be combined. The wine they have mixed. It is possible that the food they eat and the wine they mix are the different sources of information they receive and the skills they have acquired.

The key to understanding is perceiving how a choice or decision will affect everything before it happens. This takes lots of information, skill in choosing a path, and avoiding or steering around those consequences. Understanding is seeing relationships and reactions and implications – even two or three steps beyond where you are presently.

The person who is simple believes that championships are won by individuals with lots of talent but does not see the hours of practice, weight training, film work, and such that go into each championship team.

Naive or simple people seize on one characteristic of a winning program, organization, or team and think that is the full explanation of a group's success. They must be willing to be shaken out of their naiveté. They need to start chewing on some real food and drinking some strong, mixed drinks of the real information and skills required to build a winning program. Remember it is never as simple as it seems.

Just doing more of your simple formula for success will not get it done. There are hundreds of pastors who believe that if they just preach better, then hordes of people will come. There are hundreds of restaurant owners that believe that if they just had better cooking, they would have lots more customers. There are hundreds of companies that believe if they just made a better product, they would be successful. Each of these approaches is naïve; it is too simplistic. The development of a successful church is more than the sermon; the development of a successful restaurant is more than good cooking; the development of a good business is more than a good product. We have all seen successful churches that have lousy preachers, successful restaurants with lousy food (McDonald's), successful companies with lousy products.

The proverb screams "stop your folly" – selfish, simplistic ways that will not accomplish what you want. Start living in the real world with real complexity and lots of variables – especially people variables.

What follows in verse 9:7 and following is pure, distilled understanding. When you do this, you get this – watch for it. If you do that, you will get this – be aware of this.

This is one of the purest courses in real humanity that exists anywhere in the world.

- Correct a scoffer – results: dishonor for self
- Reprove a wicked person – results: insults thrown back
- Reprove a wise man – results love
- Instruct a wise man – results greater wisdom
- Teach a righteous man – results: increase his knowledge
- Give in to the strange woman – results death to relationships and eventually to self

PROVERBS 10:4
Poor is he who works with a negligent hand, but the hand of the diligent makes rich

poor is he who works with a negligent hand

The word *poor* is the word that refers to those who are destitute or have little or nothing. They have less than they really need. The principle here is that those who have less than they need have in some way been negligent. They had an opportunity to obtain what they needed, but at some point in the past they did not take advantage of that opportunity.

This clearly suggests that God has placed opportunity around us, and we are responsible for what we do with that opportunity. If we just expect others to provide for us, then we will be poor in some area that opportunity could have provided.

The word *negligent* is the Hebrew word *remiya* which is the word used for slackening, sloth, looseness. When something is needed to be tight, this is loose. When something is needed to be diligently pursued, this is just followed with a half heart. Go after the opportunity that God puts in your pathway. If we do not work hard on the opportunities that God has given us, then we will find that we are destitute and not having what we really need to enjoy and live a fulfilled life. Some people do not have what they need to live a fulfilled life because when opportunity came their way, they were too busy doing something else to be bothered by it or they pursued it with only a half heart.

Personal responsibility is essential if one is to build a wise life. There are opportunities around you every day. Take advantage of those opportunities. Now these opportunities for a blessed life come disguised as problems, hard work, or service; it is not gathering baskets of money. There is a process of turning your opportunity into something usable in your life.

While this proverb is clear, a balancing principle is also needed to understand the poor or destitute in any major city. The balance to this principle is this one: abundant food is in the fallow ground of the poor but injustice sweeps it away. There are opportunities that are given to everyone but the wickedness of some takes away that opportunity from those people. They never see that opportunity or are restricted from pursuing it.

but the hand of the diligent makes rich

The word *diligent* is *charuts* in the Hebrew and it is the word for sharp, decisive, diligent, and decision. This word is the key idea in this verse on the positive side. Diligent is contrasted with negligent. This word means one who is decisive and/or diligent. The translators chose to put the emphasis on the constant application of action and power, but the word also carries with it the idea of decisive, sharp, and clear actions that are unambiguous. Poor people are lazy procrastinators who do not take action; they do not continue to apply power to a situation over a long time. Their *modus operandi* is laid-back and tomorrow-oriented. The person who wants to have abundance must act constantly, consistently, and, at times, quickly. Solomon is telling us that we must be ready to take diligent and decisive action when opportunities come our way or they will be missed.

It will be interesting if we can play the tape of our lives and look back at the opportunities that we could have taken and how our lives would be different. The poor person misses most of these opportunities because they require work or decisive action. Don't let this be you. Develop the life which is diligent and decisive rather than the one that is always looking for the quick, easy score.

You may recognize your hand being negligent before you can see the opportunities that you are letting slip by. So ask yourself if you are becoming lazy; ask yourself if you are letting things be disorganized or incomplete too much.

April 11

PROVERBS 11:4
Riches do not profit in the day of wrath, but righteousness delivers from death

This is referring to the Day of Judgment – the time when God evaluates your life. Righteousness is not what you stayed away from but what you accomplished in terms of loving God or loving others.

Were you able to demonstrate your love for God through acts of faith? Too often people think of righteousness as negative things or what was not performed.

It is the righteousness of Christ that will deliver us from death on that day; the righteousness that comes from faith as Paul proves in Romans 3 and 4; the righteousness that only comes from obedience to the Word of God out of faith.

April 12

PROVERBS 12:4

An excellent wife is the crown of her husband, but she who shames him is like rottenness in his bones

This verse deals with a forgotten subject in today's Christianity – the conduct of wives and its effect on their husbands. There are actions of a wife that can mightily bless or curse her husband.

The word *excellent* is the Hebrew *hayil* which means mighty, powerful, able, virtuous. It has been translated *excellent* in the NASB. The word moves in the direction of virtue or moral mightiness – the actions of virtue and moral excellence that a wife can do to bring great honor and respect to the husband. If she searches for the positives in her husband and takes the morally high road in her interactions with people, this brings a whole new glow to his life.

We can understand the word excellent or virtuous also by seeing its results and contrasts in this verse.

The proverb is very interesting in that it intimates results and contrasts ideas that we would not.

crown of her husband

A wife's virtue causes a crown to be placed on her husband's life. Look at the possible implications or definitions of this crown on her husband's life: to potentially have more authority in his dealings with others, to carry a beauty and wonder not normally associated with that man, to adorn him.

These results would suggest that the word excellent or virtuous has to do with what she does to her husband directly and what she does to and for others.

shames him

One would not normally suggest that moral virtue is the opposite of shaming a person. But in this verse, this is the contrast. It means that Scripture feels that if a person is honest and trustworthy but shames others with their speech and conduct, then they are not a virtuous person.

Unfortunately, one of the regular habits of many wives is rehearsing all the bad, stupid, or ridiculous tendencies in their husbands. This expose' of his faults clearly comes under the title of shaming her husband, and it means he is viewed with suspicion by others. She has been sucked into the temptation to gossip and even slander. These are serious errors and undermine the type of marriage that she wants.

rottenness in his bones

This is an unseen disease. He remains largely unaware that his reputation and standing in the community is largely being corrupted by his wife's lack of virtue. She has crossed the line into gossip and slander. He pays the price through a diminished capacity to reach his full potential.

This means that virtue and moral excellence in a wife turns away from gossip and slander opportunities, especially when they involve intimate, negative details about her husband. It also means that a virtuous and morally excellent wife focuses on the positive, on building up her husband, on openly admiring her husband, and on steering clear of those who would engage in slam sessions on their husbands.

April 13

PROVERBS 13:4
The soul of the sluggard craves and gets nothing, but the soul of the diligent is made fat

There must be more than desires and dreams in your head. There must be plans and hard work. Too many people just want God to drop blessings down from the sky – often things that are purely materialistic. But God has given us the foolproof way of seeing if it is His will for us to have these things we desire: make plans to go after them but if getting to them requires that we violate God's righteous standards, then we will uncover that and hopefully abandon the pursuit.

Never just dream about things coming true. You must say: By what date could these things come true? What are the steps that allow this to happen?

It is amazing what can be accomplished when you actually set off in a direction with determination and a time frame. But on the other side, it is amazing how little is accomplished by just dreaming. We must answer the question: What does God want to accomplish through me in the next year? And then set about to move toward those goals.

What is soul fat?

Just as your body takes excess food and calories and turns it into fat stores that can be used later, so your soul has the ability to store excess goodness. But what are the calories and food of the soul? Relationships. Relational depth is soul fat. There are times when we need to convert those good feelings, memories, and connections into useable items for our life. It is always wonderful when they are there. It takes diligence to add to your relationships so that you actually can live off of those relationships later. Life is a complex web of relationships.

Each of these relationships needs food and water. Don't let your relationships starve or you will be left out in the cold.

Are you making sure that you are adding soul fat?

- Complimenting the people in each of your relationships

- Not criticizing, condemning, or complaining

- Smiling

- Adding value to their life

- Quickly apologizing for your mistakes and wrongs

April 14

PROVERBS 14:4

Where no oxen are, the manger is clean, but much revenue comes by the strength of the ox

This is a very interesting proverb because it states that simplicity is not the way to go. If one wants to grow something and increase a revenue stream, then one has to have things get more complicated. Oxen are messy, but they increase the ability to generate income.

There will always be those who, like Thoreau, will believe that the wisest path is to go back to nature and be simple and have no complexity at all. That does not work for all. In fact, it only works for a very few.

It is not ungodly to have the complexities of business and employees. In fact, it is wise; but if one allows that complexity to take one away from a walk with God and time with the family, then the complexity is not helpful. A growing business is supposed to provide for family, not rob one of time with the family.

Think about all that is involved in having an ox. There is feeding the ox, there is cleaning up after the ox, there is housing the ox, there are potential diseases, there is equipment to make the ox work effectively, and there is caring for the ox. All this happens when one wants to expand their business model. But there is great strength in the ox. By the way, this proverb would imply that one should make sure that the strength gained by the ox is many times greater than the strength expended to have the ox.

There is a clear need to move into staff and equipment and complexity and clutter and problems in order to grow a revenue stream that will sustain a family and others.

It is easy to handle yourself, but you must handle more than yourself and grow something if you are going to have a business that really goes anywhere.

April 15

PROVERBS 15:4

A soothing tongue is a tree of life, but perversion in it crushes the spirit

a soothing tongue

The word in Hebrew is actually a healing tongue. This could be one that you develop and use on other people or one that is used on you. Both are a source of life into people's lives. This type of tongue does not arise by happenstance but instead by choices about what to say and how to say it; about when to say something and whether to say something. We can all develop a healing tongue.

A healing tongue is one that promotes wholeness and growth and strength. This means that the person who would wield a healing tongue must ask the question, "How do I bring about health in the person I am speaking with? Is it by not speaking except to follow their train of thought? Is it by encouraging the positive strengths in this person's life? Is it by suggesting the need for change in an area in order to reach maximal potential? Is it by comforting and understanding where the other person is? Is it by being sympathetic with the other person's plight and situation? Is it by exhorting to specific action that will bring a person a new level of health or growth?" These are all appropriate actions of a healing tongue.

We must ask ourselves the question, "What can I say that will bring about the greatest amount of healing in this person's life?" Now there are some times when certain things need to be said, but I may not be the person to say them. So what I can say is a recommendation to go to a person who can say the more difficult thing. Many people can see the difficult thing that must be said, but only some people will be heard or accepted when it is said. Too many people want to be God to other people instead of just promoting health as much as possible.

but perversion in it crushes the spirit

The word *perversion* is the Hebrew word meaning *twisted*. This would suggest that the writer is contrasting the person who brings and promotes healing with the person who seems to promote healing but really has a different motive or purpose. The motive is twisted or not apparent at the first blush. When a person discovers that they have been flattered or positioned or manipulated, it will crush them.

Notice that there is no specific remedy for those who would use a perverse tongue on you in this proverb. This is more about the positive power of the healing tongue. The motivation to develop a healing tongue and be around those who have a healing tongue is great.

it is a tree of life

It gives some form of emotional and relational energy to have someone believe in you and root for you. On the other hand, it absolutely devastates a person to be played for the fool – to believe that you are loved, wanted, liked, etc., all the while you are really being used or even worse, despised. It is the twist in the use of the tongue that is like a dagger to the heart.

PROVERBS 16:4

The Lord has made everything for its own purpose. Even the
wicked for the day of evil.

There is much discussion about this verse and the idea that God made some people so that they could populate hell. This verse, however, does not say that.

It is best to understand the phrase "day of evil" as those times when consequences are meted out upon sinners – as in the case of the Assyrians and Babylonians attacking Israel.

This verse is a verse about purpose and use. Solomon is saying that God has a purpose for everything; and everything, including the wicked, will fulfill that purpose. God has a purpose for the wicked. But no one has to be wicked.

Why would God allow the wicked to continue and not destroy them immediately? Well, permitting a sinful, fallen world to exist to extract a small remnant of believers who would really love Him requires that parasites, scavengers, and even carnivores exist in the human realm as well as the biologic one.

The other truth that must be held in this regard is what Jesus states. It is inevitable that stumbling blocks come but woe to whom they come. There is free play in terms of who plays the scavenger or carnivore part. It may be inevitable that there is a stumbling block or wicked person, but it is not inevitable that I am one of them.

Once I make certain choices, then it is inevitable that I live out the purposes associated with those choices.

But, amazingly, our God is a God of mercy and will even allow our permanent choices to be redeemed through His mercy and grace given at the Cross of Christ. The path of wickedness can be escaped from through Jesus Christ.

This verse is pointing out the truth that God is not surprised by wickedness but instead is using it. Having permitted there to be a fallen, sinful world to exist, He must have consequences for it from within the organism itself.

I pray that my girls will throw themselves on the mercy of God in Jesus Christ and seek wisdom whereby they will not become a moral cockroach. It is a tragic thing – only seen in the moral realm – that the crowning achievement of God's creative energy can, through its own choice, become a moral maggot.

It is a truth that the path of wickedness changes a person's life; it also changes a person. It turns a person into something they were not originally meant to be but a something that God will use for His purposes in a twisted and fallen world.

I want the Lord to weigh my motives and my plans and direct me in the way of righteousness.

What is even more tragic is that in our day the culture is commending and encouraging and idolizing people who develop themselves into moral parasites and carnivores. The gangster, the hooker, the bully, the rebel, the liar, the thief, etc., are all glorified and promoted.

Many kids today want to pursue the path of wickedness because it is glorified. They are never told or shown what that path results in and what it does to the person who moves down that path.

You cannot escape God's boundaries; you cannot escape God's purposes. It is up to you which kind of life and which of His purposes you fulfill.

April 17

PROVERBS 17:4
An evildoer listens to wicked lips; a liar pays attention to a destructive tongue

What a person pays attention to tells a lot about what that person has going on inside.

an evildoer

This is the Hebrew word *ra* which means evil, badness, distress. Remember that in the book of Proverbs this is a person who does actions that clearly go beyond the Ten Commandments: other gods, cursing, rebellion, violence and murder, adultery, stealing, lying, plotting and scheming, the taking of other people's goods.

listens

This is the Hebrew word *qasab* which is to hear, be attentive to, heed, listen to. Paying close attention to or being obedient is part of the connotation of this word. It is not just that a person hears but that there is a high level of attentiveness paid.

wicked

This is the Hebrew word *awen* which means trouble, sorrow, idolatry, wickedness, iniquity. The basic idea seems to be trouble that moves toward or becomes wickedness. The word carries an idea of deception and planning to deceive in the evil or trouble it is involved with.

lips

This is the Hebrew word *sapa* which is lips, speech, language.

This proverb is designed to help us make decisions about who to become friends with, who to hire, who to begin a relationship with. If they are attentive to wickedness, then they are an evildoer. There is a connection between what a person pays a lot of attention to and what they are doing.

The second phrase in this proverb is not contrastive but a further illumination of the same truth.

liar

This is the Hebrew word *seqer* which is lie; that which is not true or designed to deceive.

pays attention

This is a standard Hebrew word *azan* which means listen or hear.

destructive

This is the Hebrew word *howa* which means calamity, disaster, destruction. Job refers to what happens to him using this word. The destruction that landed upon Job was howa.

tongue

This is the Hebrew word *lason*.

Putting this all together, Solomon is painting a picture of people who really enjoy listening to the details of evil. A person who lies enjoys listening to a person who destroys others with their words. It is a terrible thing to watch a person destroy another through their words, but it happens and the liar enjoys listening to this.

We often don't think that we need this advice, but we are all the time needing to make decisions about who we draw close to or begin relationships with. It is important to try and understand if this person is involved in evil. If they are, then they will make a destructive friend, hire, consultant, spouse, etc.

The other thing about this proverb is that it comes right after the declaration that God tests hearts. Will you give into the lower impulses that live within you? All of us are tempted to be interested or excited about the destruction of another. Bad news travels fast. If one pays too much attention to this mess, then one could become seduced into that lifestyle. How much evil, wickedness, and destruction are you listening to? The more you pay attention to that, the more it changes you in the hearing. It is hard enough to keep a positive attitude and servant's heart, let alone when you are surrounded mentally and emotionally by ideas and images of selfish and wicked people.

April 18

PROVERBS 18:4

The words of a man's mouth are deep waters; the fountain of wisdom is a bubbling brook

There are three pictures of the words that a person uses. They are deep waters; they are a fountain of wisdom; and they are a bubbling brook.

The way the second half of this proverb is translated is that it is a separate sentence, but it is not. It is just two more pictures of a man's words: a fountain of wisdom, a bubbling brook. In the NASB, the marginal reading shows this.

What is Solomon saying? He is pointing out that the person who is perceptive can learn a lot about a person from listening to them talk. What is really going on inside of the person will bubble out through their speech.

Unfortunately our culture has forgotten how to listen to others. We seem much more bent on waiting until there is a pause and speaking ourselves.

deep waters

The picture of deep waters suggests that there is much beyond the words themselves. There are motives, emotions, desires, fear, hopes, etc. If you listen to the people around you, they will uncover who they are in what they talk about and how they talk about it.

It is also true that you will give people an incredible gift if you listen to them intensely. All of us long for those people, that we respect and enjoy, to be fascinated with what we have to say. This means that you use the six aspects of good listening: eye contact, body lean, minimal encourages; and verbal following: paraphrasing, mirroring, summarizing, detachment, questions.

When a person cares enough to listen intently, using these means, they will discover a great wisdom about the person.

fountain of wisdom

This is the picture of a constant newness and freshness. The speech of a person – while it may sound the same with the same topics – there is a newness and freshness to what they are thinking. The words that they are using is a fountain bubbling up new water. It may be that they are fearful of new things which is what our modern advertising community wants to exploit. It may be that they are hopeful of attaining new heights which supplies energy to keep moving forward. It may be that they are able to see old truths in a new light which is how time heals many wounds.

Solomon is saying not to dismiss what a person is talking about just because the topic is the same. Listen for the new angle; the new information; the new emotion; the new insight.

a bubbling brook

This is a little bit of an unfortunate translation as the word means a river or torrent. It is something that pours forth or gushes forth. The kernel idea is something that has a lot of volume. Solomon seems to be saying that the words of a person can come rushing out at times, yelling wisdom about the person. There is the potential of lots of words from anyone if you hit the right topic or they are ready to talk.

One needs to ask: Why would this information be crucial to the development of a wise person? Answer: The wise person knows how to listen to others and listens beneath the surface. The wise person embraces the fact that there will never be a time when you know everything there is to know about a person. The wise person realizes that there is a torrent of information inside of this person that wants to come out or could come out at any time.

We need to be more fascinated by people – especially the people who are near to us. There is an appalling lack of curiosity in other people's souls. This is why our relationships are weak. Remember **LIFE IS RELATIONSHIPS**. If you don't have relationships, you don't have a life.

Go out today and listen with new vigor and insight.

PROVERBS 19:4

Wealth adds many friends, but a poor man is separated from his friend

wealth adds many friends

Every person who seeks anyone out, another person must see some benefit in the friendship. It is this benefit that is called wealth in this verse. Sometimes the wealth is social status; other times it is acceptance. Sometimes the wealth is wealth. Sometimes it is listening and attention.

If another person has no benefit for another person, there will be no friendship. This means that one must increase one's value to other people – through knowledge, skill, attitude, character, wisdom, etc. There is no such thing as a person who is worthless and cannot increase his/her value.

I do find people who have little value in the areas where others need them to be valuable, and they wonder why this person does not want to be their friend. There must be a perceived value in the friendship.

Ask yourself the question: Why would anyone want to be your friend? What is the value or benefit in it for them?

but a poor man is separated from his friend

If you do not bring value to the friendship, then you will eventually lose that friendship. If you are always taking and not giving, then you will not be pursued. It is the relational facts of life. You have to have value that you bring to the relationship.

There are many different elements of value that have nothing to do with money. Make sure that your life is full of these types of enriching treasures to share with others.

April 20

PROVERBS 20:4

The sluggard does not plow after the autumn, so he begs during the harvest and has nothing

The word *sluggard* is the standard Hebrew word for lazy or sluggish; one who is slow, enjoys ease and not work. This proverb is fascinating because it talks about the sluggard's unwillingness to do something a year ahead that causes him to have nothing to eat.

After harvest in the fall of the year, the farmers needed to plow under the remains of the harvest so that the winter would allow the nutrients to be put back into the soil. It was essential preparation for the next year's harvest for the farmer to till or plow under the remnants of this year's harvest. The lazy person sees this as too much work and waits to do it until he feels like it. It seems too far away and disconnected to eating next year. But because of his unwillingness to do essential things eleven months ahead, the harvest of the lazy person is less than is needed; and they have to ask for food when their weak harvest comes in.

This is a valuable lesson. Sometimes the key to your success is a small detail that you are willing to do which will not pay any dividends for months or even years. There is, at present, about a $20,000-$40,000 salary gap between those who graduate from college and those who have only a high school diploma. This means that four years of writing seemingly impractical papers and reading boring books translates into a $20,000-$40,000 a year difference in salary every year for forty years.

I am not saying that only those who go to college apply this principle. There are many long-range, diligence issues that increase a person's ability to have what they need to live. This applies to weight control, vacation planning, financial planning, extra certifications at work, community involvement, etc.

In the same way, diligence on a small opportunity allows a person to be ready to close a sale or invent a new product or receive a promotion. One cannot underestimate the importance of diligence. The lazy person is unwilling to work hard on things that don't have an immediate payoff. They keep telling themselves that if someone offered them a million dollars to do a particular chore, they would do it. But that is not how anyone gets a million dollars. One earns a living by doing the little things well and being rewarded for one's labor.

When someone who knows tells you that a certain detail needs to be done at a certain point to accomplish the final product months or years later, then don't shy away from that work.

I constantly tell my girls that the work you put in this ten-year period will pay off in the next ten-year period – whether that is junior high and high school grades allowing college entrance; whether that is college diligence allowing jobs; whether that is job performance allowing promotions, etc. In fact, right now I am investing lots of time, energy, money, and prayer in my relationships with my girls during this ten-year period so I have years of wonderful harvest of love and joy with them for the rest of our lives and on into eternity. Will the time be worth it? Yes. Will the sacrifice seem insignificant in twenty years? YES.

Don't be lazy; put the time into the right things and it will pay off.

What can you do today that will have a payoff in a year to five years?

Is there anything that I am avoiding doing because it doesn't seem to matter, but I know or have been told it is crucial to my future success?

April 21

PROVERBS 21:4
Haughty eyes and a proud heart, the lamp of the wicked is sin

This verse has a number of interesting angles. One, it states that the internal director for those who live outside the Ten Commandments box is that they feel they are superior to others and ultimately to God's rules and God. They are first in their life. It is the light unto their path. They put themselves first and what they want. "What would satisfy me; what would make me feel even more superior to others?" is one of their constant questions. It is their guiding light. This is what is meant by the lamp of the wicked is sin. Now sin is the violation of God's law, but its basic principle is selfishness. Sin always begins as selfishness. There is a place for self-interest, but sin at its heart is a "me-first" orientation. The world's literature even celebrates this "light" with books and ideas like "looking out for number one" or "what do you really want?" If we move forward with our own desires without any boundaries, we will surely harm others and end outside of God's law. This is why our guiding light cannot be selfishness, but it should be righteousness or God's wisdom.

Jesus uses this type of metaphor in the Sermon on the Mount when He says that the lamp of the body is the eye. If your eye be single then your whole body is full of light; but if the light that is in you is darkness, then your whole body will be darkness. Jesus is saying the same thing as the truth of this verse in Proverbs: if the guiding light of your life is selfishness and keeping yourself superior to others, then you will surely be guided by that light into trouble and difficulty. Your guiding light will guide you into a lousy life. But if, on the other side, your guiding light is love and humility and helping others and meeting their needs, it will guide you into a wonderful existence full of relationships and joy.

haughty eyes and a proud heart

When you think first about yourself and what will be the best advantage for yourself, you have haughty eyes and a proud heart. This "me first" orientation is what all of us have as our normal orientation, and we have to be rescued out of this by the Lord. We must be saved from our natural orientation to life. If our orientation is that we are first in our life, then we are placing ourselves in the higher place. This is the position of haughtiness that is the problem. We certainly do have rights and needs, but we must not pursue those at the expense of others or at all costs. Pride is an excessive self-focus. It can manifest itself through an overbearing braggadocious nature or it can manifest itself in a whiny, introverted cynical-ness which doesn't let anyone else have an opinion. A proud soul means that you have put yourself above the others around you.

What Solomon is saying is that if you allow selfishness to guide you, it will eventually lead you down a path that will be destructive and oppressive. It always does.

April 22

PROVERBS 22:4
The reward of humility and the fear of the Lord are riches,
honor, and life

the reward

We must never forget that there is a reward for living the way that God wants us to live. It pays to be righteous. We can often feel that the rewards and the payoff all go to the wicked, but nothing is further from the truth. They get the momentary pleasure of sin and the deep consequences of sin. We receive the continual feast of righteousness.

I believe that we too often do not speak enough about the way of joy in the Christian life. That what we have when we follow God's principles – they far outweigh what the world has, and we have no sorrow mixed in with it.

of humility

The ability to see your strengths and weaknesses with clarity. The willingness to let others shine and promote others. The ability to submit, to be a part of a bigger plan. These are elements within humility. To not have to be first and foremost. To not believe that you are the center of the universe or the most important person. It means to understand that you are a part, a piece of a much larger whole; an important part but not the whole. It means to willingly submit to God's plan and God's boundaries. God can use the humble vessel. He pours His grace through them. He, however, opposes the proud – those who do not acknowledge their personal dependence upon God and others. None of us are indispensable. God alone is God and we are not.

I believe that it is helpful to list and rehearse regularly those things that we need God to do for us and be for us. If that list is less than fifteen for any given day, we are probably too proud for God to pour His power through us. How do you need God to work in your life?

What do you need Him to do? What do you need Him to continue to do?

and the fear of the Lord

The fear of the Lord is the realization that walking contrary to the Almighty is foolish and fraught with danger. The fear of the Lord is being awestruck with the wonder and majesty of the Supreme Being. The fear of the Lord is offering worship to the Almighty and being caught in the power of His love and presence.

We do not speak enough about the fear of the Lord these days. The true believer is truly afraid to walk outside of the boundaries that God has fixed, knowing that God will bring consequences for each action. The true believer fears not fulfilling the directions of the Holy Spirit. He knows that God does not play games with His servants. He also knows that God can pass the blessing of obedience on to others if the servant is not ready to obey.

Both of these two conditions are attitudes of the mind and ways of thinking. If we are correct in our attitudes of the mind and the way we think, then our actions will be fine.

riches

These riches – which are the rewards of living God's way of life and thinking God's way about each choice – can be mental, emotional, spiritual, physical, and financial. It is only our impoverished, naturalistic worldview that wants to see these as monetary. Some of the greatest riches that can come to a person are those that are deeply emotional and spiritual; those that satisfy in the depth of your being in ways that mere piles of money and possessions can never satisfy.

God wants to pile up true riches in your life. He can only give them to you at the pace that you can handle them and not be destroyed by them. If you love Him, your pile of relational, emotional, spiritual, and monetary resources may accumulate slower because of His love for you and your inability to handle more without being destroyed by them.

honor

The Hebrew word is *kobed* which means great, honor, or weighty. The word literally means to be heavy or weighty and easily becomes the meaning of a great or weighty person. Therefore, honor is the weight or value of your life or being. When you follow God's prescription for a life worth living, you get something much more valuable than fame. You get value, honor, respect. It is the hidden moments of service that allow us to demonstrate whether God can invest high levels of value upon us. Everyone wants respect and admiration and value, but God allows it to rest upon those who walk with humility and a deep understanding of the Awesomeness of God.

What is interesting in our culture is that we are often trying to gain a small piece of honor in a quick way. We want to be noticed and have people think that we are important. We want fame or popularity or the place of pride. God is going after something much deeper and more significant. He says that He will reward you with honor, not the passing fancy of fame. Our imitation substitutes for honor come with snares and thorns.

life

God calls some to the martyr's life and that is a great privilege to be counted worthy to suffer for Christ's sake – even giving one's life. But the normal Christian life is the ability to exercise your vitality throughout your years and to not grow bitter in a pool of sorrow and guilt. As the following definition points out: Life is important; sin robs us of that life.

Life is the ability to exercise all one's vital power to the fullest; death is the opposite.

How often I have watched as those who have lived a life of carousing and wickedness cannot exercise their vital power to its fullest because they have permanently damaged their own life or a critical relationship in their life.

Each one of the next three proverbs (Proverbs 22:5,6,7) is about the long view of life. The long-term reward of humility and fearing the Lord is riches, honor, and life. The long-term view of the perverse and wicked is that they have an increasing amount of thorns and snares in their life. And the long-term view of raising children is that if you train your children to live right and consistent with whom they are, then they will not move away from it when they are older.

April 23

PROVERBS 23:4
Do not weary yourself to gain wealth, cease from your consideration of it

This is a crucial truth – the central aim of your life should not be to acquire money or possessions. Wealth, if God allows it to come to you, should be the by-product of doing what you were made to do. As you work diligently at the things you were wired to do, then the money you need to live will come. When people dedicate themselves to the pursuit of wealth apart from or over and above their skills and gifts, then they can expect that they will never be satisfied and that fulfillment in life will remain elusive

Do not weary yourself. This is a prohibition to stop going the extra mile for the attainment of monetary rewards. This is not a sufficient reason to wear oneself out. We should be working out of the gift, skill, and passion base that God has put within us. The money to live and satisfaction will come when we labor and strive out of this base and not out of a desire to heap up riches to our own gain. This proverb suggests that there will come into most of our lives the chance to go after wealth. There will be some offer to make us wealthy, but we will have to become weary to obtain it. For some that is that they must travel every week, missing their family or not even being able to start one.

For some the weariness comes in the form of twelve-to-fifteen hour days, six and seven days a week, where the job is the whole of one's life. For others the weariness will come in their soul for they have had to trade a clear conscience for money. They have money, but they had to break a law or do something unethical to obtain it. For still others, the weariness comes from disease for they pursued wealth through abusing their bodies sexually, physically, chemically, or relationally. Solomon is saying that there are shortcuts to wealth that will be offered but do not take them. Get rich slowly through hard work, diligence, and doing what you love. The shortcut is a dead end.

One of the things about wealth attainment is that it should be gradual and a part of what one is already doing. In our culture it has been called automatic building of wealth. Systematize the acquisition of wealth in an automatic way so that you do not even notice that you are building it. This would be by getting it saved without ever seeing it; setting up an automatic process that does not depend upon your discipline. You want to focus on the development of great relationships and hard work, not on whether your wealth is building. It should just do that automatically. Take between 10-20 percent of what you receive and set it aside automatically.

April 24

PROVERBS 24:4
And by knowledge the rooms are filled with all precious and pleasant riches

The word *knowledge* is the key to this continuation of the proverb. Knowledge is the Hebrew word *daath* which means information, perception, discernment, skill. This is the controlling idea for filling one's house with precious and pleasant riches. If one is going to fill one's life with true riches, then one is going to need information and skill. Too often we want to gain relational, material, emotional, and/or mental wealth without any effort or practice. Life does not work this way. We know from other parts of Scripture that relational wealth is the greatest treasure that one can have in life. Mark 12:30,31

Solomon is telling us that we come into the world without the information and abilities that we need to build a truly wealthy life. We must go after it. We need to understand what we are going after, and then we must admit that we need to learn. We need to see connections. We need to listen to people who have actually built a rich, relationally, wealthy life.

One of the first steps toward a wonderful life is to admit that you really don't know how to build one or you would already have built it. Jesus calls this being poor in spirit. The New Testament calls this humility. Solomon here calls this the need for knowledge, wisdom, and understanding.

Let me get specific:

Do you know and have you become skilled at the basic actions that are required to have a great marriage?

Do you know and have you become skilled at the basic actions that are required to have a great family?

Do you know and have you become skilled at the basic actions that are required to have a great walk with God?

Do you know and have you become skilled at the basic actions that are required to have a great career?

Do you know and have you become skilled at the basic actions that are required to have a great personal life?

Do you know and have you become skilled at the basic actions that are required to have great friendships?

Do you know and have you become skilled at the basic actions that are required to have a great financial portfolio?

Do you know and have you become skilled at the basic actions that are required to have a great community?

Do you know and have you become skilled at the basic actions that are required to have a great church?

Do you know and have you become skilled at the basic actions that are required to turn enemies into friends?

One of the tragic truths is that both Solomon and all of us have watched people fill their life with unpleasant riches and detestable riches. When your life is filled with bad relationships, guilt, shame, lack of generosity, hatred, stolen items, your life is filled; but it is not pleasant.

What is also important to realize is that the riches are not necessarily material ones. In fact, I believe that those are the specific kinds he is trying to get us to do some discerning about. All of us, at one time or another, have desired more stuff but those are not precious and pleasant riches.

The most precious and pleasant treasures that can fill a house are the people who love you and with whom you have a great relationship. It takes skill, perception, information, and ability to maintain a relationship with the people in your family. When the rooms are filled with loving family members, you have been skillful.

Now when one has material goods added to a base of great relationships, then it is called abundance. But I am aware, as you are, of many people who have lots of material wealth but a paltry amount of relationships. They cannot fill a house with the people who love them and they are really poor.

Realize that one of the things that you should focus on learning is how to get along with people. A solid course in people skills is one of the wisest investments you can make.

What good is it if you have a huge home but no one wants to come out of their rooms because they can't stand one another? If you have lots of money but your family despises you, then you are poor.

Ask yourself: What have I done this week that will increase the most valuable relationships in my life? It does matter if I relate to my wife using skill. It does matter if I interact with my children with knowledge and perception. I want my children to be able to trust me and know that I will listen to them.

What are the key skills for this type of room filling: eye contact, minimal encourages, listening, open-ended questions, time with the person, active paraphrasing and listening to them, asking them if you heard them correctly.

April 25

PROVERBS 25:4

Take away the dross from the silver, and there comes out a vessel for the smith

This is one of a string of leadership proverbs. It approaches the idea of leadership as a valuable gift that needs to be protected and nurtured. When we move into a position of leadership, we often allow more sin, selfishness, and temptations to be a part of our life. This is the opposite of what this proverb suggests.

It is the leaders who need to have the temptations removed from their life so that they can move the society forward.

The orientation of this Proverb is to take away the bad material – the dross – from the valuable silver. The word *dross* is the Hebrew word *sug* which means a moving back or what is removed from metal because it has no value. The clear idea is that when one becomes a leader, that which is not valuable will cling to them. This must be cleared away so that their leadership inclinations can shine.

What could this dross be? It could be temptation. It could be friendships that waste time or are counterproductive. It could be mundane, ungifted work. It could be activities that are of little or no value. It could be temptations and selfishness. Realize that when you want to move forward in wisdom or with the Lord, there will be these types of waiting dross that wants to keep you from making real progress with the Lord. These are the folding chairs tied to your backpack. These are storage units full of stuff you can't throw away. These are the things that you know that you need to move away from, but for many reasons you allow it or them to hang around and slow down your life.

Dross does not allow silver to be properly formed or molded. It compromises the malleability of the metal and allows cracks and flaws in the silver. So when people allow these waste relationships, these waste activities, these waste possessions to be a big part of their life, they are not able to be molded by the Lord. He wants to use you and is being held back to a low level of use because you can't handle the real assignments that He would like to use you on.

Honestly ask yourself to think of three things that hold you back from really listening to the Lord and being used in a greater way.

What is also interesting is that the silver needs help to get the dross away from it. The silver is not able to clear away that which clings to it. There is a need, in many cases, to have others help you pull the useless filler from your life. Be willing to seek that help; let people help you.

PROVERBS 26:4
Do not answer a fool according to his folly, or you will also be like him

Fools (the selfish, impulsive, rebellious) constantly want to embroil the diligent and productive in the quandaries of their life or thought. They can invent more problems with a plan than would ever actually appear in the plan. Remember the folly of the fool is when they are doing the impulsive, selfish, rebellious thing that strikes their fancy. In the midst of this they can see and even experience great difficulties and paradoxes. The answer is almost always – you shouldn't have been there in the first place. If you allow yourself to get sucked into the debate, then they have framed the issue and already won.

They get themselves into problems over whether to steal a drug, to save a life, or let a loved one starve. Problems, such as, should they abandon a mistress who would be destitute without them or return to fidelity with family; problems of living with the true expression of their feelings: sodomy or being sexually and emotionally unfulfilled their whole lives by remaining single or heterosexually married? Problems, such as, should I keep this unwanted baby and be miserable for twenty years, potentially destroying my marriage; or should I have the baby aborted and be able to focus on my spouse, myself, and my career? These conundrums often involve their emotions on the one side (which constantly change) and the inflexible rules and laws of righteousness on the other. Fools are impulsive and oriented toward themselves so their ideas and emotions and happiness trump any societal, familial, or revealed righteousness.

Much of the Hollywood productions these days seek to raise the fool's point of view as a profound paradox. They muck around in wickedness and find dilemmas that are real but could have been avoided by being moral at a much earlier place. The answer to dealing with the fool's dilemma is always the same: do the righteous thing, even if it costs you personally. The only way to get out of the mess you have made is to do the right thing – righteousness as defined by God. This, in the book of Proverbs, would be that which is inside of the moral boundaries of the Ten Commandments.

After having counseled dozens and dozens of these "hard" cases, I just try and get them to cut to the chase: do the right thing. I will not play the game of "What should I do?" with them. By the way, the right thing almost always involves personal pain for this person. That is the way you can tell a person has sincerely repented and the power of God is at work in their life. If they are willing to do something that is clearly not selfish, God is at work. Until they are willing to do that, then there is little hope.

Notice the dictum *do not answer... according to his folly*. Do not get sucked into the discussion of the selfish actions and the discussion from the fool's point of view. But, instead, ask questions that cut to the chase of the selfishness or moral degeneracy. The goal of your discussion and questions with the fool is that they would not be able to maintain that they are wise, knowledgeable, and handling life well.

April 27

PROVERBS 27:4

Wrath is fierce and anger is a flood, but who can stand before jealousy

This is a comparison proverb to get us to take notice of the volatility of jealousy. We are most often drawn to notice anger and wrath as inappropriate reactions, but there are hundreds of other emotional reactions that can come from us. Solomon is trying to warn us that even though wrath and anger seem like big landmines to stay away from, do not underestimate the power of jealousy. *The reason that jealousy needs to be noticed is that men especially can be tempted into flirting and side relationships that will make the key people in their life jealous. There is this idea that jealousy will fade with time, but it is not true. When a person is betrayed by another, they have a deep and long-lasting reaction that they will never get over completely. Solomon is warning us: don't make the people in our life jealous; they will not get over it.*

Wrath is the word *hema* which means white hot or hot displeasure. The word *anger* is the Hebrew word *ap* which means nostril, face, or anger. Each of these two first emotions is very strong and makes people move in various directions. But when compared to jealousy, these are nothing. Jealousy is the emotion of protected faithfulness violated or threatened with violation. *Jealousy* is the word *qina* which means zeal, jealous, ardor. It is an emotion that is extremely strong and attaches passiveness to a person or object even though the person or object might not reciprocate.

One further word must be said in a day and age of computer porn. Men do not see that their involvement in pornography has anything to do with their wives, but it does. To your wife your consumption of porn is a form of flirtation and mental adultery. To her she has been tried and found wanting. Your porn involvement develops jealousy which is something that will deeply damage your marriage. It may even destroy it. You may think that your viewing porn on the computer is not a relationship, but your wife knows different and she feels that difference – even if at one time she once watched it with you. Those images are her competition. She cannot measure up and she knows it. Even those women in real life cannot measure up with what they are made up to look like. The women in the pictures are not real. The time and attention and pleasure you derive from porn speaks deep into your wife's soul about your priority on her. Do not awaken the monster of jealousy in any of its forms – even pornography. I wrote a book to help men turn away from porn, lust, and sexual temptation called **Mission Possible: Winning the Battle over Temptation**. If you are moving in the wrong direction in this area, men or women, I would strongly suggest that you get help so that you do not cross a crucial line and awaken the monster of jealousy.

PROVERBS 28:4
Those who forsake the law praise the wicked, but those who keep the law strive with them

This proverb is about the constant struggle in a fallen world to maintain order and moral boundaries. People are not naturally good; they are naturally sinful. Therefore they will try and push against the boundaries of decency and morality that God has told us to enforce.

If Christian people do nothing in their society, then the forces of wickedness will have their way and destroy the society by pushing the boundaries of decency until wrong is right and right is blamed for the ills of society.

Those who forsake the law praise the wicked

There are those who are in the midst of forsaking the boundaries of the moral law of God. Their forsaking of God's limits on behavior is marked outwardly by praise for those who live outside the boundaries of God.

Remember the wicked are those who live outside the Ten Commandments. There are three types of sin in the Bible. First, sins of omission: where a person should have done something but did not; this is called missing the mark; not living up to God's standard. Second, trespass sins: where a person does what God says not to do but then stops and moves back into moral living. But the third type of sin in the Bible is wickedness: where a person moves out into open defiance of God by constantly doing what God says is wrong. This could be lying, stealing, murder, adultery, coveting, false religion, contempt for all authority. A person is biblically defined as wicked when he/she lives outside the boundaries of the Ten Commandments.

In our culture we only define people who murder or rape children or multiple people as wicked. But that is not God's definition.

Our society is being given over almost completely to the experiments of the wicked because those who are righteous forsook the law. We are reaping the kind of society that comes when those who want the freedom to be wicked move into the positions of power. In less than forty years our culture has learned to praise people for committing forms of murder; we have learned to encourage a lack of sexual self-control and come to embrace adulterous perversion that will spread disease, depression, and shorten life spans. We have learned to tolerate and even encourage rebellion against parents and authority. We have come to tolerate, embrace, and encourage – through advertising, debt, and gambling – coveting on a scale seldom seen in the history of the world. Numerous other examples of wickedness becoming the norm abound in our society.

The first step in reclaiming the country is not a protest march but Christians who live within God's moral boundaries themselves. If you are committing adultery, stop and practice purity. If you have murdered through abortion, repent and promote life. If you envy everyone else, stop and give thanks for the blessings God has given you. If you are stealing at work, return the items and work hard to make your company profitable. If you swear and curse, stop and learn to say positive things about others instead. There is a powerful testimony awaiting those who will begin living within basic moral boundaries.

Now are we bound by the law as a way of salvation? No, we use the Ten Commandments as an outer limit. We really strive to cooperate with the Holy Spirit to produce in our lives the fruit of the spirit: Love, Joy, Peace, Patience, Kindness, Goodness, Meekness, Faithfulness, Self-Control.

but those who keep the law strive with them

It must be clear that there will always be people who want to live past the boundaries of God's moral law. When they do, there must be a group of people who strive with them to protect and defend the society against the wicked. If the wicked triumph in pushing the boundaries of morality to the ridiculous levels they want, then the society will begin to consume itself until utter destruction.

It is not possible for righteous people to sit by and watch the wicked drag a whole society into ruin without saying and doing something. Remember, the wicked are those who want to live outside the boundaries of the Ten Commandments.

God will raise up champions to fight against each of the groups that seek to violate His law. Righteous people must join the fight and resist the work of the devil in the world system.

Ask yourself if there are particular issues of encroaching wickedness that God is prompting you about and what you can do to get involved to stand for righteousness. Write a letter, join a group, pray more specifically, place a call, give money to help, volunteer time, etc. Remember if the righteous do not strive with those who would destroy morality, there will be no peaceful society to live in.

This proverb states that if we are not willing to strive with the wicked, then we have an area where we also forsake the law. For if we kept it, we would fight against the wicked. We would point out the consequences of immorality.

It is interesting that the word *strive* is used rather than put down or destroy. The righteous will not always win in their struggle against wickedness, but the striving must be present or wickedness will just destroy a whole society by eliminating peace, safety, security, and prosperity. It is the responsibility of the righteous to shine the light of truth into the actions of those who are wicked and thereby strive or meddle or conflict with them. Slowing them down and allowing others to see what is taking place – do we really want this to take place? Shouldn't this be stopped?

April 29

PROVERBS 29:4

The king gives stability to the land by justice, but a man who takes bribes overthrows it

A leader is one who brings consistency and harmony to the area that he leads; it is not okay to have a constant revolution. It is justice or predictable patterns of behavior that bring reward and predictable patterns of behavior that bring punishment that cause or allow stability to arise. When a leader, in his leadership, allows for back doors to fairness, then the whole of the leader's goals and accomplishments are thrown into doubt.

Justice is a very sure, moral thing – an action to stop those who would violate God's moral law: the Ten Commandments. There must be a box to operate in; it must be consistent; and it must be consistently enforced. The rule of law is the best friend of a real leader.

There is an interesting direction that this proverb takes if one sees it as a lesson in leadership. The word stability is the word standing. It could mean stability, significance, or endurance. The word justice is the Hebrew word *misphat* which is the word for judgment as well as justice. It could deal with the decisions of the leader as much as the moral character of the leader. The idea of land is that which is ruled by the leader.

This proverb could be saying that the leader gives endurance or even significance to his company, family, and civic organization by the type of decisions that he makes. If he allows his decision making to be influenced by bribes, then all the stability that he thought he had is gone.

This principle is true in business or politics or family. When a leader allows his decision to be influenced by whether he will get or keep getting favors because of it, then the organization that he is leading will crumble. We see this with political leaders who become corrupt through money flowing to them. We see this through civic organizations and people receiving favors to allow certain people to be involved. We see this in families when affairs begin or credit cards are hidden.

When you make decisions as a leader, you need to make the best decision for everyone – not one influenced by whether your pockets will continue to be lined.

April 30

PROVERBS 30:4
Who has ascended into heaven and descended?
Who has gathered the wind in His fists?
Who has wrapped the waters in His garment?
Who has established all the ends of the earth?
What is His name or His son's name?
Surely you know.

This proverb is a series of questions designed to produce a growing awareness in the person reading and meditating upon these words that there is a world beyond this one, and there is a being dwelling there who wears this universe like a garment. This being we call God has a personal name. He has given that name to the Jewish people.

The idea of this proverb is to remind us of the fact that we are locked in a four-plus dimensional universe which we cannot escape, and that there is an outer world outside our planet and outside our universe that we were meant to have access to and in which our real life is waiting. It is this outer world – the Bible calls eternity – where God dwells. It is God alone who dwells in this outer world outside the limited wonders of this universe. We cannot go there without His help, and no one from this place has ever gone there and come back to tell us about it.

But thankfully someone from there has come here to tell us about it before He returned. Never forget that God so loved the world – this world – that He sent His only begotten Son to be the atoning sacrifice for our sins and betrayals of His trust.

May

May 1

PROVERBS 1:5
A wise man will hear and increase in learning, a man of understanding will acquire wise counsel

The message in this verse is that the person who is already recognized as a person who makes right choices and does not selfishly hew to his own way can gain enormous value from reading and absorbing the information in these divinely inspired passages.

There are experiences and observations and situations that are beyond what any one person can have experienced. These truths and insights can make a person more ready for whatever life throws at us.

There is another interesting point made in the first phrase of this fifth verse. If you are wise, then reading the Proverbs will make you wiser; but if you do not get anything out of the Proverbs, then you are not as wise as you suppose. No matter how wise you are or suppose yourself to be, there is always another level or series of insights waiting for you in this God-breathed book.

May 2

PROVERBS 2:5
Then you will discern the fear of the Lord and discover the knowledge of God

It is absolutely crucial in the gaining of knowledge that this information not be cut off from knowledge of God – that He is a Holy God and that He keeps track of all the things that we do and that He will call a man into judgment for everything that he has ever done, said, or thought.

When information is divorced from an understanding of God and His nature and the eventual eternal evaluation, then it becomes perverted and twisted and can be used to destroy instead of to aid mankind.

Remember that what you are searching for is wisdom and understanding, not information and power. Too often we think that these concepts are synonymous. They are not. To be wise means, at times, that you give up power. At times it means that you do not gain intimate or detailed knowledge of certain things.

The fear of the Lord is a crucial concept to a righteous life. It is associated in the New Testament with the knowledge of God's review of your life when you die.

2 Corinthians 5:10 - *For we must all appear before the judgment seat of Christ, so that each one may be recompensed for his deeds in the body, according to what he has done, whether good or bad.*

1 Corinthians 5:5 - *Therefore do not go on passing judgment before the time, but wait until the Lord comes who will both bring to light the things hidden in the darkness and disclose the motives of men's hearts; and then each man's praise will come to him from God.*

There is a subtle suggestion that you do not have accurate knowledge of God until your knowledge includes fear of Him. He is a fearful being with all power and all knowledge. We are sinful and disgraced and rebellious against the Holy God who set us here.

I am deeply concerned that people have invented a conception of God that has removed all the fear. They have a tame God of their own invention. What a shock that they will see not that God is their pet willing to bend to their wishes but Holy, awesome, and bending time, space, and eternity to His own wishes. He demands my allegiance and submission just by the power of His being, and yet He asks for it as though it is not His to demand.

The ethic of both the Old and New Testament is love God and love your neighbor. Are you doing anything positive in your life to change the life of those around you or are you living a purely selfish life? Is the record of your life going to show that you were selfish to the core even when you seemed to be loving or that you are willing to be transformed by the message of God's love and forgiveness?

May 3

PROVERBS 3:5
Trust in the Lord with all your heart and do not lean on your own understanding

The word *trust* is the Hebrew word *batah* which is translated in the Septuagint by the word hope rather than the word *believe in*. The idea here seems to be that one must put one's hope completely in God's ability to resolve the issues of life. You trust in Him and do not worry or fret things that are beyond your control.

A number of years ago I was putting my daughter to sleep and she absolutely insisted that I lie down next to her. She was frightened and could not go to sleep or calm down. When I lay down next to her, she checked to see that I was there and then rolled on to her side and within a minute or two was sound asleep. She had confidence that if Dad was next to her and watching over her, then everything was okay and she was safe. Her total confidence in me and my ability to handle anything that might come was amazing. I realized as I lay there watching her that this is the type of trust that I must have in the Lord. I must rest in His ability to handle everything in my world. As long as He is near to me, I am okay. My responsibility is just to do what He says just as my daughter's responsibility was to do what I said.

When she began to doubt and lean on her own understanding, then she saw monsters under the bed and heard sounds of mice running in the closet and shadows crossing the room. These things from her own understanding were so disturbing that she was not able to sleep. But she trusted in me then, and she knew that she was safe because I would not let anything happen to her.

In the same way, when I lean on my own understanding, I invent all kinds of things that can derail a bright future – things that I can't handle. But if I just make sure that I do what God wants and submit my choices to Him, then I can have confidence in the future and know

He will work it out. My job is to throw myself into the box that He has put me in and put my full confidence in His ability to change boxes and what comes into the box.

May 4

PROVERBS 4:5
Acquire wisdom!
Acquire understanding!
Do not forget nor turn away from the words of my mouth.

This is the first commandment that David gave to Solomon. After a lengthy build-up in the beginning of Proverbs 4 about the wonder of being taught by the father and the importance of remembering what dad taught, this is actually what dad taught.

How to make the triple-win choice within the boundaries of God's morality and how things are related to one another – especially those things that seem unrelated.

acquire

This is the word purchase, buy, or gain in some way. Since this is a command, it means that the idea must be to procure wisdom that you don't have. You must be willing to listen to the advice of others. More than that, you must be willing to pay for wise counsel to help you avoid the pitfalls of others. Since the opposite of wisdom is foolishness which leads to wickedness, we can assume that Solomon is being taught about how to live a righteous life and how to make decisions in which every righteous person and God wins through the things you decide. It is easy to do the impulsive thing and to be tempted to do the wicked thing. But we must realize that it is wisdom that truly wins the day, and you do not always have it in yourself. Trusting yourself alone for your decisions is a good recipe for disaster. There is a need to purchase or gain by sacrifice, if necessary, the best course of action.

wisdom

Wisdom is the ability to discern the best course of action in any given situation which will result in a win for God's glory, a win for others, and a win for yourself. The wisdom of the ancients was regularly capsulated in pithy sayings called proverbs or riddles so that they could be more easily remembered. These sayings were meant to inform you of directions to go when these directions were counterintuitive. The instructions of the wisdom literature was the collected wisdom of the ages by those who had lived both good and bad and in the case of the biblical wisdom literature, it was inspired by God. Thus this God-breathed set of counterintuitive guides were to keep you from making the same mistakes that 90% of the population makes because it seems right to them.

David was saying to Solomon, his son, that you must always be on the lookout for practical knowledge that truly works. We would almost call these the slogans of life and the bits of truth that make life work. I believe David is saying that these practical bits of knowledge that make life work are everywhere, and we must collect these so that we will know what to do when the time comes. They must fit the triple-win parameters, but they themselves are lessons that we need to make life work. Let me give you some examples:

- Always put God first

- Never have the first argument with your wife

- Put your wife on a pedestal

- A penny saved is a penny earned

- A team can accomplish more than a talented individual

- God can do more with your 90% than we can with a 100%

- Set goals and go after them

- Cease striving after wealth

Some of these sayings are Scripture and some are things we pick up from parents, mentors, teachers, and others. We must make sure that they are true, and we must hang on to them so that they will guide us when we don't know what decision to make. We can then pull out these bits of wisdom from our memory bank and apply them to the triple-win grid and the current situation and see if they fit.

Jesus gives us a helpful corrective about these bits of wisdom. Not all of the slogans of wisdom that we have rattling around in our brains are actually wisdom. They may, in fact, be the opposite of wisdom. Jesus says, "If the light that is in you is darkness, how great is the darkness." In other words, if every time you dip inside yourself for a bit of wisdom to help you in a certain situation and the wisdom that you pull up is actually wrong, then you are going further afield when you do what you think is wise. Let me give you some examples.

- Let's say that you are playing a game and you wonder which move to make. Up pops the slogan "Winning isn't everything; it's the only thing." You let that idea guide you to be ruthless in some game so that you can win, but you lose the respect of the people you are playing with.

- Let's say that you are in your 20's and you are at a party and there is an attractive young lady who seems to be interested in you. You are not all that interested in her, and you do not see a long-term future with her at all. You dig into your bag of wisdom and up pops, "You only go around once in life, so go for the gusto" This tells you to fake interest in the young lady at the party because you don't want her interest to be wasted.

There are hundreds of these little bits of bad wisdom floating around in every culture. They turn us aside from righteousness and the blessings of God.

One of the things that we have to make sure that we gather is actual wisdom and not pithy slogans from our culture that are actually bad advice.

The other thing that David told Solomon was that he should acquire understanding or insight. This is the Hebrew word bin. The word means to discern between and to grasp the connections. I am amazed at the number of times people miss the obvious connections between things and then are baffled why they have problems.

Let me give you a few examples:

- There is a connection between what you eat and what you look like and weigh. All kinds of people do not see the connections between the amount of food they are consuming and the way they look, feel, and perform. There are only a few people who can eat everything and not gain weight. These people have different connections and problems, but we want to make them the norm.

- There is an absolute connection between what we say to people and whether we are close friends and they like us. But I watch people say the rudest things to their spouse, their children, their colleagues and expect to have a good relationship with these people. I watch people treat clients, customers, and strangers with kinder words and better manners than the people closest to them. The people closest to you should receive the kindest words from you.

It is entirely possible that David is saying to Solomon to memorize these pithy sayings in which is contained the collected wisdom of our civilization and culture and those of other cultures. For this is clearly what Solomon did. He collected the wisdom literature, committed it to memory, and even himself wrote and spoke thousands of proverbs – some of which were inspired by God.

David, the father of Solomon and the prophet of God, was telling Solomon that one does not have to learn by experience; one can grow beyond his peers – and even the leaders – by committing to memory the counterintuitive directives of life.

May 5

PROVERBS 5:5
Her feet go down to death, her steps take hold of Sheol

Solomon says delicately, but clearly, that spending time with an adulterous person is a sure way to shorten your lifespan. You will be dead much quicker than you would have if you had not been sexually unfaithful.

It is amazing that people are trying to be quiet about the real danger of sexually transmitted diseases. These are real problems that really will destroy you and that is not even dealing with divorce, financial ruin, reputation, and violence.

The following is a partial list of the various sexually transmitted diseases. Some of these will kill you. Some will leave you sterile, some produce great pain, some cause cervical cancer, some allow for a higher infection rate of HIV/AIDS. Do not be a fool and give into the prompting of temptation.

- Bacterial Vaginosis (BV)
- Chlamydia
- Genital Herpes
- Gonorrhea
- Hepatitis B
- HIV/AIDS
- Human Papillomavirus (HPV)
- Pubic Lice
- Syphilis
- Trichomoniasis
- Pelvic inflammatory disease (PID)

In Solomon's time the various diseases and their differences and biological footprint would have been unknown. But because of his powers of observation, he and most were aware that playing around with a morally loose man or woman would cause you to get sick and potentially to die.

He is saying that no matter how strong the impulses are, don't do it because it will change your life.

What is also nice is that Solomon does not become vulgar in his depiction of the whole process of adultery. Those who commit adultery want to glorify the details of the sinful act. Those who want to get a real picture of adultery look at the whole life.

May 6

PROVERBS 6:5
Deliver yourself like a gazelle from the hunter's hand and like a bird from the hand of the fowler

This is the application of this whole section on making pledges, going surety, or even getting into debt. Just like a gazelle who had been caught would struggle with all its life to become free, so should the person who is in this unwise position.

You need to fight like your life depends on it to be free from the debt of this loan. This also means work hard; show that you want out of this arrangement. You may not realize it, but this is a life-and-death struggle. If you get on the wrong side of the credit struggle, it will destroy you.

One Christian financial guru suggests that a person get a second job until the debt is paid off. He takes the admonition of verse 4 seriously. Give no sleep to your eyes. His thinking is that until you are free of the debt, emergency measures are needed. Deliver pizza, sell something – with a guaranteed paycheck that can get the debt snowball rolling in the right direction.

PROVERBS 7:5

That they may keep you from an adulteress, from the foreigner who flatters with her words

The word *foreigner* is the Hebrew word *nokri* which means that which is foreign or strange. The word translated *adulteress* is the Hebrew word *zur* which is stranger. This is clearly a reference to the practice of allowing foreign women to ply their trade as prostitutes within a Jewish city. It also would suggest that everyone except the person you are to marry is strange or a foreigner to you.

Many times young people in a search for love will take any kind of love just to have some comfort. This is unfortunately a misguided action and only results in difficulty and pain. The proverb here reminds us yet again that wisdom and understanding will keep you from the person who is foreign to you. Seek the Lord and His choices for you

The idea of a strange man or woman has considerable potency for singles. I have asked men and women whether they feel that the person they are presently dating is really the right person for them. Countless numbers will say no; they are just right for right now. In other words, this is a person they are putting up with so they can get some love and companionship while they are waiting for Mr. or Ms. Right. Often this Mr. or Ms. Right now becomes their life companion because they did not use wisdom and understanding to distance themselves from a person who was not really the right mate for them.

May 8

PROVERBS 8:5
O naive ones, understand prudence; and, O fools understand wisdom

The idea of prudence is very important. Many people do not have it or the desire to get it.

The English dictionary lists these ideas for the word:
1. the ability to govern and discipline oneself by the use of reason
2. sagacity or shrewdness in the management of affairs
3. skill and good judgment in the use of resources

The simple need to understand how to plan well and execute the various phases of a plan. It won't go as simple as we think it should; it will be complex.

If you are one of those simple people who does not understand that the shortest distance between two people is not always a straight line, then you need to grasp the words of the proverbs. Don't keep being so simple. If you keep saying, why can't people just or why can't this thing or that thing happen...Things are more complex than just one simple reaction triggering another simple reaction. There are multiple people and multiple reactions plus events outside of people's control.

These are the definitions for the word *provident* that prudent comes from:
1. making provision for the future: prudent
2. archaic: marked by foresight: prudent

To summarize these two ideas: To be prudent is to be ruled by reason rather than emotion and to see the present decisions and actions in light of their future consequences.

These sentences suggest prudence:

I shouldn't do this because it will probably lead to this or that.

I should do this because it will put me in a position to do this in the future

I want so much for my girls to be able to tie their present decisions and actions to the future that they will live in. It is absolutely true that we are creating the future that we live in.

God has given us great latitude within the boundaries of His will to create our own lives.

To be simplistic, naive, and impulsive and refuse to see how our actions affect the future is like taking our future in our hands and destroying it.

May 9

PROVERBS 9:5
Come, eat of my food and drink of the wine I have mixed

Wisdom does have an agenda. It wants more people to enjoy the fruits of wise choices. It does not try and hoard what it knows. In fact, wisdom is trying to get the message out. It is just that many are not interested in long-term gain. Many are only interested in short-term pleasure and fulfilling their selfish desires at the moment.

This proverb continues the banquet analogy with food being the substitute for wisdom. The food of wisdom looks different than the food of fools. One is filled with selfish delights; the other is filled with deep and abiding joy. They look different. One is pastry and immediate sugar highs; the other is vegetables and fruits and whole grains for stable health.

come eat of my food

Wisdom is doing a recruiting job for people to mentor. If you are not passing on your leadership secrets, then you are not being wise.

The picture of wisdom being food is that wisdom brings nourishment. Wisdom is what the soul feeds on – a long-term plan to build a successful family, a good marriage, a satisfying career, and a deep relationship with God. It is the nourishment of wisdom that feeds the pursuit of real life. This is not the quick-fix of sin and selfishness.

The obvious questions arise: Have you been feasting on wisdom's nourishment or the folly of selfishness? Do you have a reasonable plan to have a better marriage in five years than you have today? Do you have a workable plan to have a great family that you are working and that has worked elsewhere? Are you planning your career in such a way that you have a constantly renewing sense of purpose and satisfaction? Is there a growing amount of resources so that you can smooth out more of the difficulties and storms of life?

drink of the wine I have mixed

Notice that the wine is mixed. This means that the alcoholic content was cut, not strengthened. This analogy continues with the drink being healthful. In that day and age, diluted wine was much better for the stomach than straight cistern water. This was the way to decrease your exposure to disease and quiet your stomach. This wine was not designed to get a person drunk but instead to satisfy thirst in a healthful manner. Wisdom and understanding are like that. They may not be flashy, but they get the job done. And over time there is a significant difference between the results that flow from wisdom and what flows from folly.

Let the slower satisfaction of the nourishment of wisdom and understanding minister to you rather than seeking the thrill ride and consequences of selfishness.

May 10

PROVERBS 10:5

He who gathers in summer is a son who acts wisely, but he who sleeps in harvest is a son who acts shamefully

This proverb reminds us of a crucial truth: there is a time to act. When that time comes, then you should act. It is possible to wait too long; to do too much planning; to keep putting off to the future the opportunities that are here right now.

I was just reading a report that a high percentage of people who retire thought they would have had more, but they just never got around to saving. It was summer while they were working and now that it is time to live off of what they harvested, it is gone.

This principle is true in relationships. There are times when one can connect; when it is summer in that relationship – whether it is romance or parenting or friendships or networking. One has to seize the day when it is harvest time. Our culture has warned people so much to look before they leap that many never leap. In many of the cases, every week it is summer in some aspect of your life. Don't sleep during the moment. Be assertive and try and get the benefits out of that moment. It is better to have tried and failed than not to have tried at all. By far the vast majority of people let opportunities with God, in their marriage, with their family, monetarily, vocationally, with friends slip by them.

Take stock this week of the opportunities that God has given you to make significant strides in some area of life. At any given time it is summer and time to act in that area of our life. Spend the time harvesting when it is appropriate. There will always be reasons why you can't or shouldn't. There will always be a little less certainty than we would like; but if there is an opening, probe and see if it will open more. If there is a chance to do something good and harvest a great personal and public good, then go after it.

The proverbs talks a lot about planning and seeking counsel, but it also wants us to move when the time is right. When it is harvest time, act with strong and consistent strokes. Remember that it is relationships that you are trying to build up. It is relationships that are the goal of life – a relationship with God and relationships in the other major areas of life. The two great commandments are love God and your neighbor as yourself. It is also important to say that one should not strengthen one relationship at the expense of all others.

Remember, harvesting is not just physical blessing – it is relational connection. The richest person is the one who has the deepest relationships across the relational spectrum.

In what area should you be harvesting this week?

What is holding you back from harvesting in that relationship at a new clip?

May 11

PROVERBS 11:5

The righteousness of the blameless will smooth his way, but the wicked will fall by his own wickedness

This is a contrasting proverb designed to show the stark difference that choices make. There is a multiplying effect with good and bad choices. Every good choice opens up more good choices and the blessings that result from good choices. Every bad choice results in more bad choices that were not available before the bad choice was made, and then the consequences of that bad choice come along also. So there is at least a four-fold multiplying effect for every choice.

Let me spell it out this way. If I choose the right choice then, first, I gain the blessings of that good choice; second, I have new good choices available to me; third, I do not have the consequences of the bad choice I could have made; fourth, I do not have new bad choices available to me.

the righteousness of the blameless will smooth his way

There are results from choosing wisely. All of us believe that, but we need to be reminded of that from time to time because at times it seems that the wicked get all the good stuff. But this is not true. Their way is hard and full of difficulty.

The word righteousness *sedeq* means conformity to an ethical or moral standard. What is that moral or ethical standard in the Scriptures? It is the Ten Commandments. So if you make choices to stay within the boundaries of the Ten Commandments, then you have made choices to be righteous.

Let's just review what these are...

- You shall have no other gods before Me
- You shall not make for yourself any idols
- You shall not take the name of the Lord your God in vain
- Remember the Sabbath Day to keep it holy
- Honor you Father and your Mother
- You shall not murder
- You shall not commit adultery
- You shall not steal
- You shall not bear false witness against your neighbor
- You shall not covet your neighbor's goods

These ten mark the edge of acceptable behavior. They each also point to a much deeper, ethical behavior. Instead of playing around the edge of what is allowed, we want to please God by being in the center of His will. Let's take a look at the hoped-for opposite behavior that each commandment implies.

- You shall love the Lord your God with all you heart, soul, mind, and strength.
- Understand and contemplate the wonder, infinity, and transcendence of God and never reduce Him to something in this world.
- Let your actions match your words and become a testimony of the integrity of a person who walks with God. Do what you say you will do.
- Live a balanced life full of work, worship, rest, and relationships.
- Add value to everyone around you, especially authorities who keep watch over you.

- Develop a flexibility in the face of life and opposition that does not strike back or seethe, instead looking for a new option in the face of the reality of the situation.

- Work hard to build abundance that you can generously share with others. Be honest in your dealings with others.

- Enjoy the blessings and relationships that you already possess, maximizing their contribution to your life.

This verse claims that when we make choices to stay within the boundaries of the Ten Commandments, our lives will smooth out and not have many of the obstacles, difficulties, and problems of those who live outside of these moral boundaries.

the wicked will fall by his own wickedness

We need to hear that wicked choices bring difficulty. Unfortunately the TV, movies, and magazines hide the difficulties of those who live outside of God's boundaries. We see mob bosses who don't have problems. We see sexually promiscuous men and women who never get diseases or are deeply lonely or have multiple alimony payments or emotionally break down under the weight of their broken relationships. We see thieves who live in rich houses and never get arrested or have to deal with unsavory characters or get cheated themselves. We see envious people who always get what they want instead of destroying what they are after in the lives of others and their own life in the process of pursing the great prize they must have. We see foul-mouthed hero types whose verbal filth does not limit job opportunities, earning potential, relationships, or team cohesiveness. All these unreal images are constantly driven into the minds of our children and ourselves until we really believe that there are not consequences to wickedness.

Do not believe that; limit your exposure to these lies and remember that wickedness brings consequences: spiritually, emotionally, mentally, physically, relationally, and in a whole host of ways beyond this.

It is important to say, at this point, that this verse points out that it is not God who curses the wicked; it is their own wickedness. Their own choices bring consequences. Many people will scream at God and ask, "Why are you against me?" I believe that He answers, "I am not against you; you are against yourself. Repent and come to me that you may live and enjoy My blessings."

Too many people want to continue to make the choices that they have been making and that they are comfortable with and get a different result. It won't happen.

What trips up those who make bad choices? The bad choices that they make.

May 12

PROVERBS 12:5
The thoughts of the righteous are just, but the counsels of the wicked are deceitful

The word *thoughts* is the Hebrew word *hissabon* which means ideas, new thoughts. It largely has to do with using the mind to create something new.

The word translated *just* in this passage is *mispat* which means justice, judgment, ordinance. It carries with it the idea of practical application of right, holy, and good. It is also often used of a governmental function in which decisions must be rendered or judging between people or between competing interests.

Clearly this proverb tells us what the various kinds of people think about.

The righteous people think about how to make sure that the right decisions are made. How new ways of doing the right thing can be invented. How to make sure that that which is right is done rather than what is wrong. How to make sure that injustice does not win.

What is interesting is that this tells us about what righteous people think about; how more righteousness can be spread. The things that wicked people think about are deceptive.

The word translated *deceit* in this verse is the word *mirma* in the Hebrew which means deceit, treachery, fraud, swindle. It is used of a plan in which someone is clearly being defrauded or stolen from in a deceptive or secretive way. In other words, how to get away with something so that nobody even knows that something has been done. This is different from stealing in that the person or organization is to never know that anything was done. It is hidden.

What do you spend your time thinking about: How to make sure that your boss doesn't find out what you are doing? How to make sure that your spouse is not aware of how you are spending your time? How to hide your income from the IRS?

The question in this proverb is what do you spend your time thinking about or planning. This will tell you whether you are becoming a wicked person and/or whether you are interacting with a wicked or a righteous person.

All of us can move from thinking about promoting righteous things to hiding wicked activities. Emphasize the former and you will become a more righteous person.

One of the troubles in our world is that we do not have a clear picture of what righteousness is all about. One needs to think about two things: what is right and relationships. To promote righteousness one needs to promote that which is right for people. If you were to begin to think more righteously, you would begin to think about how you could draw closer to God and please Him. You would begin to think about how you could strengthen your marriage. You would spend some time thinking about how to connect with your family – parents, children, relatives, etc. You would think about how to promote positive and helpful interaction with people at church. You would think about making the workplace a more relationally positive place with less back-stabbing and gossip. You would spend time thinking about how to promote peace, safety, and security in the community and country. What we have to realize is that when people promote positive interaction between people, they are performing a righteous act. Righteousness involves people and what is done to people.

If you are not careful, you can find yourself thinking about how to become deceitful rather than how to promote righteousness. It is easy to fall into thinking only about yourself and how to promote your interests.

May 13

PROVERBS 13:5
A righteous man hates falsehood, but a wicked man acts disgustingly and shamefully

righteous

This is the Hebrew word *saddiq* which means just, lawful, righteous. It means conforming to an ethical or moral standard. It would be, in this case, that the person stays within the boundaries of the Ten Commandments and performs the positive demands which are in most cases the opposite of the Ten Commandments. This was the righteous person in the Old Testament.

It must be added that even in the Old Testament it was clear that no one did this perfectly enough to earn their way into God's favor. That is why there was a sacrificial system which atoned for their sins or lack of righteousness.

falsehood

This is the word *seqer* which means lie or falsehood; that which is not true or is a fraud. This would include the breaking of a promise and deceit.

hates

This is the word *sinah* which means hatred, disgust. It is a strong emotional reaction of opposition and disgust towards something to be avoided and despised; something that is altogether unappealing.

Solomon is telling us something very valuable when he describes the behavior of the person who is righteous because in our day we have strayed so far from righteousness, we are not used to a virtuous person when we see one. God tells us, through Solomon, that the righteous person will have a natural aversion or emotional reaction to fraud, deceit, lying. They will not be able to easily go along with it or hear about it without a reaction. They will not participate in it.

This insight is important as we constantly have to evaluate people we meet or intend to hire or want to become deeper friends with. Solomon proposes a test: what is their reaction to lying, falsehood, or deceit.

Another application of this insight is to gauge your reaction to deceit, fraud, lies. Have you participated in these things? Do you regularly deceive people? How do you react when people tell of practical jokes they pulled on people? What is your reaction when someone says that they deceived a person in business?

If this is no big deal or if it is a part of life or a part of business, then you need to come to grips with the fact that you do not understand righteous living or Christ-like living. It most likely means that you have not allowed God to work on your speech patterns so that they are positive and encouraging. It may mean that your goals are off and that money, fame, and power are still too much what you are after instead of the glory of God. Don't be fooled; righteous people do not like being in the presence of lying.

but a wicked man acts disgustingly and shamefully

Wickedness is the Hebrew word *rasa* which means those who continually do wrong; those who live outside the boundaries of the Ten Commandments. Remember that it is possible to violate one of the commandments and then admit that it was wrong and get back inside the moral boundaries. But the wicked person is the one who no longer recognizes the commandment as a boundary they will abide by; in this case, specifically, they no longer respect the 9th Commandment: *Thou shalt not bear false witness against thy neighbor.*

But it is also true that wickedness or living beyond God's moral boundary structure embraces falsehood and lying. They think nothing of deceiving people to get what they want. I know a number of people who would not want to admit that they are wicked because they would say that they generally tell the truth, but they would not have any difficulty deceiving someone to get what they want. This is wickedness. If you are not willing to stop your behavior because of God's boundaries, then God defines this as wickedness. If you are willing to lie to your husband or wife to get some item or activity you want; if you are willing to lie to your boss or a customer to get what you want; if you are willing to lie to your parents or your teachers to get what you want – then you have sinned and allowed selfishness to win. Repent and thank God for the forgiveness that is in Jesus Christ's death on the cross. Be willing to not get what you want so that God will get glory.

May 14

PROVERBS 14:5
A trustworthy witness will not lie, but a false witness utters lies

This is another in a whole series of bits of wisdom that seem to be business wisdom. Notice the verse above this one about oxen or multiplied effect with equipment and personnel. Also notice the one after this which involves a scoffer and then a fool in the verse after that. Solomon is trying to school the young, the young at heart, the naive, and those who have not learned yet.

A person who is trustworthy will not lie even if it is to their advantage. So if you want to find if a person is trustworthy, ask the question: Do they lie to save their own skin or benefit their position? The implication is to hire the trustworthy person and do not hire the false witness.

This proverb is an understanding proverb. It is trying to help you build a connection between things that you might not normally make: lying and lack of faithfulness; truth and steady faithfulness. These are linked, Solomon says.

One of the obvious personal applications is: Are you trustworthy? Most people would say "yes." But this proverb asks the question: Do you lie to save yourself or to enrich yourself? If you do, then there is also a trustworthy issue. If a person cannot be trusted to make personal sacrifice for the truth, then there is not enough of a commitment to truth.

May 15

PROVERBS 15:5
A fool rejects his father's discipline, but he who regards reproof is sensible

a fool rejects his father's discipline

The first part of the verse could be viewed with an "even this he won't do." They will not even pay attention when someone who deeply loves them and is committed to their success tries and corrects them. They see it as messing with the life they want to lead. How tragic that some people will not be corrected. They want to do what they want; they want to think that they are the captain of their own ship regardless of what it costs them.

but he who regards reproof is sensible

The word *regards* is the Hebrew word *samar* which is keep, guard, observe, give heed to. One of the consistent things about the life of fools is that they are unwilling to notice when they are being spanked by their own choices. There are all kinds of reproofs in life: there are ones that come from authority where they correct us; there are ones that come through our finances – usually lack of money or debt; there are ones that come through friends – sometimes moving away from us; there are reproofs from driving – as in accidents that are our fault; there are reproofs from our career – such as not getting the promotion; there are reproofs from marriage – often tension or fights with our spouse; there are reproofs from our children – such as their rebellion or a lack of anything to talk about with them. Reproofs are ways that God is trying to get our attention. He is saying what you are currently doing is not working; change. This is not the right way to act, speak, think, or go so go a different way. But the fool blames everybody else except themselves. They are completely oblivious that they might be the source of many of their problems.

PROVERBS 16:5

Everyone who is proud in heart is an abomination to the Lord; assuredly, he will not be unpunished

The proverb in the original Hebrew starts: Abominable to the Lord is the person who is proud in their heart. The emphasis is on how terrible this issue of pride is.

We do not think of pride in our day as that big of a thing. In fact, in many cases we like the idea of pride and think it is good.

The word *pride* is the Hebrew word *gaboah* which means high, exalted, superior, higher. The idea is that people see themselves and act in a way as to suggest that they are higher, better, or superior to another person.

Our culture is full of this thinking: My errand is more important than yours so I should go first in line, in the door, on the freeway... What I am thinking about is more important than what you are saying, so I will listen long enough only to change the subject to what I want to talk about. What I like should be first and central – that is why I do not want to watch a T.V. program that I don't really like. I don't want to go to a show, play, game, event that you like but I don't. My judgment of you is true and right, therefore, I will tell everyone what I think of you.

God says, repeatedly, that pride is a hateful thing. It is very important that we develop humility or we will find ourselves fighting God. We may think it is the Devil, but it will be God going after the pride in our lives.

What would our lives look like if we actually valued the other person as much as we valued ourselves? How would we drive, talk, act, serve, give?

The person who does not repent of pride, the proverb says, will be chastised for this violation of God's basic rule of peace between people.

In fact, God says that He will shoot arrows against those who persist in pride. He will be against them.

Even though you may have a position of importance, you are still not better than that person. Do not allow your heart to be lifted up inside, secretly telling yourself that "I am better than others" because of what you have done or who you are, etc.

I read a bumper sticker the other day that summed up this pride: *God loves you, but He loves me more!!!*

Don't get caught in this.

Work hard; be everything you can be. But stay humble.

PROVERBS 17:5

He who mocks the poor taunts his Maker; He who rejoices at calamity will not go unpunished

The word *mock* means to deride, to ridicule, to treat with contempt. When we are arrogant and look down our noses about the station in life of others and somehow feel that because we are in a different station we are better, we are challenging and taunting God's wisdom.

In the United States we have embraced that idea that no one need remain poor and, therefore, their financial condition is their own responsibility while the idea of personal responsibility is a biblical idea and a needed theme in every culture – personal responsibility as the reason, cause, and solution to poverty. However is not true and does not take into account the cultural values that one is immersed in; nor the relative justice or injustice around the person; nor opportunities for advancement and the needed mental, physical, and emotional skills needed to take advantage of them. God does, in some cases, put a person in a circumstance in which they will not be able to make much money, but that person should not be derided or mocked or insulted or put down because they have little money.

May 18

PROVERBS 18:5

To show partiality to the wicked is not good, nor to thrust aside the righteous in judgment

This seems so obvious as a statement. But there are numerous pressures that would make you want to violate this axiom in the midst of life.

partiality

This is the Hebrew word *nasa* and it opens the sentence in Hebrew for emphasis. It means to forgive or carry or bear the burden of. It has the idea that a favor is being done for this person. Thus the translation *partiality*. The idea is that one should not do special favors for wicked people.

Solomon is saying that you and I will be tempted to do special favors for those who live beyond the boundaries of the Ten Commandments. It may be that we think that this will cause them to like us, respect us, or turn and begin living inside God's boundaries. None of these things will work. These are people who have chosen to pursue selfishness past God's and society's limits. They are all about themselves. They will accept your favor as further evidence that people recognize that they should be favored over other people.

When you are in a place of decision, make a fair, clear, and righteous decision when it comes to those who live outside of God's boundaries. Only the realities of God's Universe will convince them that the world does not revolve around them. The ultimate day of reckoning is coming, but you can shine little shards of light into their life through unbiased, impartial, and righteous decisions.

wicked

This is the Hebrew word *rasa* which means wickedness. In the book of Proverbs – and really in the Old Testament – this is the person who has decided to live without remorse outside of God's moral boundaries as spelled out in the Ten Commandments. Remember there are three types of transgression of God's law. There are the sins of omission – something that you should have done but you did not. There are sins of commission or trespass – something that you should not have done but you did. Then there is wickedness or iniquity – this is where you do not attempt to hide or come back within the boundaries of righteousness; you just continue violating God's standard as a matter of course. Examples would be you continue stealing, you continue committing adultery, you continue killing, etc.

nor to thrust aside the righteous in judgment

thrust aside

This is from the Hebrew root *nata* which means to stretch out or turn aside. It means that a righteous person has come to the right person for a decision; but that authority person has decided to delay, defer, or deny the righteous person's claim for some reason. Don't do this. If a person has a righteous claim, then grant it no matter what the political climate is at the time. There are all kinds of reasons why a decision may be unpopular and one would want to delay or deny a righteous decision. It often seems like if one could just put this decision off, it would help a situation. Solomon is saying to be careful of this temptation. Face the tough decisions when they need to be faced within the normal accepted parameters. There will just be tough decisions that will make you unpopular. But making the right tough decisions now will put you in the place to make other tough decisions later.

There will always be difficult decisions to make. But often they are clear when the emotion and or political dimension is stripped out of them. Do not push aside a righteous person's just decision because of a political, emotional, or social issue that does not change this righteous person's claim.

May 19

PROVERBS 19:5

A false witness will not go unpunished, and he who tells lies will not escape

Everybody lies – it's no big deal – is what many people think in our culture. This is not true. God, through Solomon, wants to point out the consequences of lying and breaking the 9th commandment. There are not enough reminders of the dangers of lying.

witness

The word *witness* is the Hebrew word *ed*. It comes from the root word which means to repeat, return, or do again. The idea seems to clearly have grown into the word of a firsthand witness to actual events that you repeat or verbally return to again.

In the case of OT law, the witness to a capital crime had to be the first person throwing the stone to begin the capital punishment process. Deuteronomy 17:7; Acts 7:58.

false

This is the Hebrew word *seqer* which is the word for lie or lying or deceptive. When a person is a deceptive witness, he/she is testifying to the truth of something that did not happen or did not happen that way. This person is distorting the actual truth of a situation to their own favor or to deflect blame coming their way. There are five forms of this lying witness. The Cruel lie motivated by getting back at another; the Cowardly lie motivated by a desire to escape blame or punishment; the Conceited lie motivated by the desire to appear more important and significant than one really is; the Calculated lie motivated by greed or selfish desires; the Convenient lie which is motivated by laziness and the desire to escape work.

unpunished

This is the Hebrew word *naqi* which means clear, free, innocent, acquitted. The truth stated in this proverb is that the person who moves through life solemnly telling people that which is not true is going to be caught in lies and will have significant consequences for this behavior.

Many times people do not remember that the meaning in life comes from their relationships. Life is relationships and all the meaning and significance that I derive from life comes from my relationships. If your relationships are built on lies – or you try and live in the midst of lies – then depth of relationships will be greatly damaged.

Think about what happens when you find out that someone has been lying to you. They don't like you; they weren't where they said; they really perceive you differently than they said; they have had an affair; they did steal from you. All these things break trust and destroy joy, meaning, significance, and connection between people. You destroy yourself when you lie.

escape

This is the Hebrew word *malat* which means be delivered, escape, saved. The liars always believe that one more lie will deliver them; one more lie will allow them to escape the punishment. It is not true. There will eventually be a day of reckoning, and liars will not escape. Even if there is a temporal escape, it will be without your relationships. Eventually the more you lie, the more alone you become as more and more people realize that they cannot trust you.

Solomon is trying to help the person who has found lying as the new wonder key that unlocks pleasures and avoids punishments in their life. Solomon reminds you this key will get you into a lot more trouble than it gets you out of, and it will lead to a level of aloneness and misery that you should avoid at all costs. Tell the truth.

If you have a habit of lying, you need to begin to memorize Scripture and repeat it over and over again during the day to rebuild the pathways of truth in your soul. Tell the truth.

May 20

PROVERBS 20:5
A plan in the heart of man is like deep water, but a man of understanding draws it out

a plan in the heart of man is like deep water

The word *plan* is the Hebrew word *etsah* meaning counsel, purpose, plan. This phrase could be understood in two ways based upon the meaning of that word. The NASB translates it as plan. If this is correct, then the verse means that when a man is planning his future or dreaming about what he would like to do, he keeps it hidden and it is deep in his soul. It is then the one with great understanding who brings it to the surface and gets the person talking about his dreams and plans and hopes; sometimes even shocking the person who has these dreams down deep in his heart.

If the word is understood as purpose then the meaning is much deeper. It is that each person has a purpose for which they were put on the earth. They were given skills, talents, gifts, experiences, opportunities, social standing, and certain parents all for the purpose of fulfilling that purpose. All of these things point to the purpose of the person. Many times the persons themselves cannot see what it suggests that they should do. They are too close to themselves to see how all the things work together to show what God wants them to do. They may still be fixated on a childhood dream which they have no skills to pursue. It is the man of understanding who is able to draw it out and show how the various threads of their life make a particular picture.

but a man of understanding draws it out

The word translated *understanding* is the Hebrew word *tabuwnah*. This word means to understand or have insight. It comes from the physical idea of between. It carries with it the idea that this facility of intelligence sees relationships between things that others do not see.

The one who has insight or understanding sees how things are connected or how they should be connected. In this case, it would mean in the first understanding of the text that the person who has understanding sees the relationships between various actions and various comments and begins to piece together what the plan in the heart is. They anticipate, therefore, the next move and ask about it or confront the person if the plan is different than their own or is evil.

Under the second understanding of the verse, the person of understanding sees the relationships between all the things that God has allowed a person to experience – the gifts that they possess and the opportunities that they have been given – and is able to draw out the purpose of God for their life. Is it not true that we need others to see our lives from an objective position that is not possible for us? That trusted person then helps us figure out what we are to do with what God has given us. Too often we end up pining away over the fact that we did not get to do something that we were not meant to do. Get about the business that you were meant to do. God has not made a mistake when you were born, and He is prepared to use all the experiences that you have had to glorify Him and give you a real future of significance. Stop wishing that you could have been a singer or President or rich or taller or athletically gifted in some area. You are gifted in the area that you were supposed to be gifted. Let a man or woman of understanding help you see how it fits together.

The man or woman of understanding is the key focus of this verse. It is they who are seeing the relationships and drawing crucial insights. It would seem obvious that one would want to become a person of understanding and see relationships between seemingly disconnected things. It would also seem to be obvious that we would want some people of understanding in our lives; people who can connect the dots in the pictures of our lives when we just can't get perspective. Become one of these kinds of people and let these kinds of people in your life.

I will say that the persons of understanding in my life have, at times, said some hard things about what God is doing – things that I do not always want to hear but usually know is true when I hear it. Do not drive these wonderful people who have insight into your life away but instead collect more of them to help you as you follow in the Lord's path for you.

PROVERBS 21:5

The plans of the diligent lead surely to advantage, but everyone who is hasty comes surely to poverty

There are six key words in this passage: plans; diligent; advantage; everyone; hasty; poverty

plans

This is the Hebrew word *machashebeth* which is the idea of thinking and creating of new ideas. In this case it is translated as planning or the creating of a pathway for life that has not been accomplished yet.

Now what is interesting is that this creative thinking about the future is being done by a particular kind of person: the diligent. Creative planning done by others will not be as productive. Creative planning done by the fool is problematic. Creative planning done by the proud will lead to a fall. Creative planning done by a scorner will tear down another.

Let's reflect on this for a moment. The new ideas that you come up with will be the major source of advantage you have. So write them down and begin working towards initiating action to make them happen. Nothing will happen if you do nothing about them. If you have an idea for a new book, start writing. If you have an idea about a new product, start making it. If you have an idea for a new way to do something at work, then write it out and turn it in. It is only the flow of new ideas that you pay attention to that will bring you advantage. The new ideas that you ignore are gone.

diligent

The word *diligent* is the Hebrew word *charuts*. The basic root idea is to cut, to sharpen, or to decide. The translators felt the word diligent carried the meaning best in this context. It, however, might be even closer to translate the word *decisive*. The idea is that execution of all these new ideas will take place. These are not new ideas in the mind of a sloth. These are not new ideas in the mind of an evil person. This is a person who decisively will set about evaluating and accomplishing the new ideas that they have. It is the action and the decisiveness that causes the new ideas in this person's mind to come to an advantage.

Now the proverb is not suggesting that some people have the decisiveness gene or temperament and others do not. In fact, the idea is that everyone should develop this diligent decisiveness. It is not beyond your grasp. Start making some decisions and put them into practice – little ones at first until you get the hang of it. We read constantly about someone who was morbidly obese who began to make small decisive actions steps and now is a completely different person. We read about those who are sick of their poverty and welfare status and condition and begin making small but significant action steps and change their situation.

advantage

This is the Hebrew word for more than – *motar*. Interestingly enough, the proverb doesn't suggest that the advantage or more than that is gained is exactly what the diligent person was planning. It is, instead, clear that the person who is decisively diligent about executing their new ideas comes up eventually with situations and ideas that are to their advantage and to a more-than solution. There are more than opportunities out there for everyone, but they must be pursued with diligence and decisiveness. Stop being lazy – launch out into a new opportunity and be alert for the more than directions that will come up when you are on the path.

everyone

The word *everyone* is interesting in this context because one would almost expect a particular type of foolish person to be named here. But, instead, Solomon writes that anyone and everyone who becomes hasty will end up in poverty. In this sense the proverb takes an unexpected turn. He has just told us about a particular person's ability to find the advantageous situation. Then he talks about everyone's opportunity to find the disadvantageous situation. Clearly he is screaming at us under the inspiration of God: BE DILIGENT – DON'T BE HASTY.

hasty

This is the Hebrew word *'uts* which means hurry, haste, urge, to be pressed, to be narrow. The idea is that a person is allowing something to press in upon them and push them forward in a quicker than normal manner. It may be an internal urge or an external urge. It may be some other person or a perceived calendar issue. But the overall issue is that a person is being moved forward at the above-normal rate. It is this quicker rate that causes the problems and develops the bad decisions and actions that lead to poverty.

Let's reflect on this for a moment. When you are being pressed to drive fast, ask why and slow down and be late. When a sales person is pressing for a decision, walk away; good purchases aren't rushed. When some internal want is driving you to spend money you don't have, stop and spend a day thinking and praying. God is saying to us: nothing good comes from hurried decisions, hurried actions, and hurried words. Think through what you are deciding, think through what you are doing, think through what you are going to say. As a balance to careful deliberation, remember it is the new ideas of the decisively diligent that will lead to advantage. Somewhere between hurry and laziness is executing new ideas diligently. Find that place and it will surely lead to advantage.

poverty

The Hebrew word *machor* means lacking or in need of. It is, in this context, translated poverty. But look at what is really being said. If you are hasty, then you will create a situation in which you will begin lacking something or become in need of something. In other words, in your hurry to accomplish one thing, you miss another thing you were supposed to see or you create a deficit in another area. It is the hurry – the press of some urge – that creates a lacking in some area. The hurry makes you out of balance, creating a deficit that will leave you exposed and depleted. That saying "the faster I go, the more behind I get" is appropriate.

PROVERBS 22:5

Train up a child in the way he should go, even when he is old he will not depart from it.

There are two ideas that should be explored in this verse:

One, that each child has a way that suits them – according to their way is how the original reads. Each child in your family has a pathway that is unique to them. They have been given certain gifts, talents, and abilities that direct them for God's glory in a specific direction. It is that direction that the parents must be sensitive to. God is counting on the parents to watch for the signs of an aptitude and gifting in a particular area. It is not okay to just send them down the path that you went down. What is their path?

Two, that each child must make sure that their path stays within the boundaries of righteousness. The place to learn how to live in a moral sense is with parents. Right and wrong; good and evil; and even good, better, and best is something that parents must instill. The verses that precede this verse and form the odd type of context that Proverbs contains are verses about the reward of humility and the fear of the Lord are riches, honor, and life. Thorns and snares are in the way of the perverse; he who guards himself will be far from them. It is incumbent upon the parents that they show their children how to be humble and how to live in the fear of the Lord. It is absolutely crucial that parents also show their children the thorns and the snares that are in the way of the twisted – those who live outside the boundaries of the Ten Commandments. Their lives are filled with lies, rape, anger, and insecurity. This type of training is a part of the parents' responsibility.

The other day when our family went to a local swap meet, we had a window on the life of all kinds of people – especially the thorns and snares that are in the path of the perverse. The number of people who were living out a life of trying to get by on the crumbs of sin was amazing. They were bottom feeding. I want my girls to understand that if you embrace that life, you get those consequences; or if you embrace a person like that, you get that life.

God has so richly blessed me and my family. We have been spiritually blessed with a sense of God's presence and guidance. We have been mentally blessed by great schools and monies to send our girls to good schools. We have been emotionally blessed by having peace in our home and an I-want-to-be-here atmosphere. We have been blessed physically by health and an absence of catastrophes. I desperately want my children to understand how to live in the fear of the Lord and live in the bounty of His love. He is a great and awesome God who has saved us from our sins and asks us to live life a certain way within a broad and wonderful plan. It is not narrow and confining but deep and exciting. It does not have the deep sorrow of those who live in iniquity outside the boundaries of the Ten Commandments.

May 23

PROVERBS 23:5

When you set your eyes on it, it is gone. For wealth certainly makes itself wings like an eagle that flies toward the heavens.

This is an interesting and important proverb that suggests what we want money to do, it will not do. And we must use money for some other purpose.

The LXX (Septuagint) version of this verse says, "If you place your vision or direction towards wealth you will have no light in your life. For it equips itself with the wings of an eagle and turns back or flies out of the house of the one who sets it before them or makes it their goal."

Money, wealth, and possessions are always on the move. You may want to hoard them, but they are moving through your life. They are not a static commodity. You cannot keep them – either in this life or in death. This is the point that this proverb is trying to say. Don't make the acquisition of money the goal of your life.

You must decide that you will use it as it flows through your life. It is your use of money as it moves through your life that should be your concern. If your use of money is selfish, then you have not taken advantage of the power of this resource. I am amazed at how many people are trying to capture money and make a big pile of it, yet all the while they do not use money to deepen the relationships in their life. Money is a tool, when used properly, that can deepen and expand your relationships. When it becomes the goal of your life, then it makes itself the wings of an eagle and flies away.

It is not wrong to have a savings and to try and build up a decent retirement. That is not the point of this proverb. The point is that money flows through your life and rather than making the collection of money the goal of your life, make the appropriate use of money one of the abiding principles of your life.

There is another perspective on this proverb that also bears development. Wealth – the allusive target of many people – is always on the move. Just when you think that you have enough to call yourself wealthy, you need a little bit more. The goal keeps moving. As a person collects more and more wealth, there are always people with more of it. It seems that whatever numerical amount of wealth that you might fix upon as that which will make you rich, it is never enough and you discover when you get to that number that "being wealthy" has moved.

May 24

PROVERBS 24:5
A wise man is strong, and a man of knowledge increases power

The wise man cannot be tipped over through temptation or through greed. He is strong because his focus is upon helping those around him to win.

The person who is temptable is weak. He can be easily knocked over. The person who can deny his own interests in the interest of God's glory and other's blessings is indeed a strong person.

and a man of knowledge increases power

If one adds to this ability to deny self and look for the best for others and God – this ability that the proverb calls knowledge – then the level of personal power for the individual goes up incredibly. The idea of knowledge is information and skills. This is an additive verse. Start with the base of wisdom and then add to it a person of information and skill and one has an unbeatable combination.

Can you deny yourself long enough to pursue a better choice – one in which more people win?

Are you working on more information that you don't currently have and are you developing your skills to a higher level so that you are a more valuable person?

The man of knowledge is always looking for more power – ways of exercising leverage in various ways: physical power, emotional power, spiritual power, mental power, leadership power, organizational power. These are just a few of the different ways that power may be increased. Are you growing in these ways and in the use of these different kinds of power?

Many times we want to stop trying to grow once we become adults. This is tragic. There is no age limit on this proverb. Knowledgeable people keep looking for ways to bring more impact.

PROVERBS 25:5

Take away the wicked before the king, and his throne will be established in righteousness

This verse proves that environment does impact everyone – even the righteous leader. If you are constantly surrounded by those who live outside of God's moral boundary structures, then you will begin giving in to those wider moral boundary ideas. If, however, there are not people who are lying, stealing, coveting, committing adultery, and being physically violent with others around you, then you will not be influenced to excuse these kinds of things or participate in these things.

When we are raising our children this is why we should make sure that the environment that surrounds our children does not baptize them in evil. Instead, they should be incubated in righteousness and not be pulled toward wickedness. While we cannot protect our children from all exposure to evil and sin, it is unwise to allow them to live in the midst of that which is wicked constantly. The danger is that even in good Christian homes, children can have daily access to wickedness through television, computers, internet, video games, etc.

Notice that this is about the leader. The leader cannot afford to build an entourage that is wicked or the good that his leadership could do will never take place.

May 26

PROVERBS 26:5
Answer a fool as his folly deserves, that he not be wise in his own eyes

This proverb is so powerful in its advice dealing with someone who is right in the midst of being selfish. Some have seen this proverb as almost a contradiction to the immediately preceding proverb:

Proverbs 26:4 - *Do not answer a fool according to his folly, or you will also be like him.* But these are actually complementary discussions of how to deal with a person who is being selfish, rebellious, impulsive, egotistical, etc.

Notice that verse 4 says do not answer a fool according to his folly or from inside his folly. Do not allow the conundrums and paradoxes that grow within the midst of selfish actions to frame how you answer. I have regularly had people come and see me about how to fix a problem they are having and then have them tell me that certain solutions wouldn't work for them. Usually the ones that won't work for them involve repentance and abandonment of sin. Sin and selfishness create all kinds of quandaries. Do not get sucked into their universe of limited choices but instead retain the right to do what verse 5 says: answer a fool as his selfish and sinful actions deserve.

The answer that a fool deserves is one that points back to righteousness, morality, and self-sacrifice. Let me give you a few examples of the difficulties that face the person who chooses the fool's path. I have been asked what to do when you can't pay the house payments or put food on the table because not enough people have bought illegal drugs that month (they had been living off of their ability to sell illegal drugs). I have been asked what to do to heal a couple's marriage and keep income coming in because the husband had been making money by selling nude pictures of his wife on the Internet. I have been asked how to get a wife to take her husband back into the marriage and also allow him to move his mistress into a back bedroom. I have been asked how to be close to God and still keep partying.

Remember, from within their universe of choices, they don't see the way out. They need to be told how sinful and selfish their choices have been and that only if they begin choosing wisely and with righteousness can they escape this type of difficulty.

People will be selfish and will make selfish choices; it is these choices that put them in situations that there seems no way out. There is always a way out. Do the right thing. Look at the final section of this verse.

that he not be wise in his own eyes

Most really selfish people believe that they are very clever and have found a way to beat the system. They just bump into these difficulties which they can't answer. Realize that they need a different answer than their question is framed to give. They need the answer of repentance in some form. They have to change their mind about the selfish lifestyle they have been living. Do not allow them to continue with the notion that they are very clever.

The rebellious teen thinks they are clever because someone is funding their lifestyle.

The unfaithful spouse thinks they are being clever because they do not see all the things they will lose by this behavior.

The embezzling employee thinks they are being clever because they do not realize that they will get caught and face great shame.

The gossip thinks they are being clever because they always have a story to tell but do not realize that people don't want to draw close to them and will starve them from deep relationships.

If right now, as you read this devotional, you are dealing with a person who is clearly being morally foolish by their selfish, impulsive, rebellious, and arrogant behavior, realize that you must speak truth into this person's life. If you feed the thinking that this person is really clever, they will never ever get on the right pathway.

If you are being morally foolish, then listen. You are not being clever; you have not found the cheat sheet to life. Selfishness, pride, and rebellion will get you into deep trouble. Stop, repent, turn toward God and righteous living. Even if it costs significantly. Do the right thing.

May 27

PROVERBS 27:5
Better is open rebuke than love that is concealed

This is an amazing proverb because it compares two different things and values open rebuke over concealed love. This is amazing. It will take some digging to understand how the thinking works here.

The word *love* is the Hebrew word *abaha* which is the word love. It is the word used in the second great commandment: *Thou shalt love thy neighbor as thyself.* It would fit this idea of love as meeting needs, pursuing, and pleasing.

The word *concealed* is the word *satar* which means to hide or to conceal.

This proverb is saying that an open rebuke is of more value than someone who has a desire to meet your need, pursue you, or praise you but never actually does anything about it.

We often misinterpret this and other proverbs that involve love because our current definition of love is about a feeling that we feel towards another person. But neither in the Old Testament nor the New Testament do we see love as a reactive feeling but rather an action that you perform. It is meeting the real needs of the other person, pursuing them, or pleasing them. Love is what you do, not what is done to you. In our culture we have labeled the feeling we have when our needs meet as love. Therefore we are on the constant search for others who will meet our needs because we want the feeling. But that is not biblical love; it is the result of biblical love.

May 28

PROVERBS 28:5
Evil men do not understand justice, but those who seek the Lord understand all things

evil men

The biblical definition of evil men is those who live outside of the moral boundaries of God. They have thumbed their nose at God to the point that they live in open rebellion to His standards of life. Life outside the Ten Commandments is an evil life, God declares. A righteous life is only possible inside of His standards. Then it must be a life of faith and trust in Him. For the evil person, life waits outside of God's moral law. Magic, Idols, Fortune Telling, Swearing, Cursing, Workaholism, Evolution, Rebellion, Independence, Anger, Intimidation, Violence, Abortion, Adultery, Sodomy, Stealing, Corruption, Kick-backs, Lying, Fraud, Legal Technicalities, Greed, Gambling, Divorce, etc. – all of these are where the evil person finds their life. It is where they will lose their life also for this way of life does not work long term.

understand

The word *understand* is the Hebrew word *ben* which is to comprehend, to contemplate, to distinguish, knowledge that which is better than mere data, the ability to distinguish the connection between information.

justice

This is truly a key word in this proverb. If one does not understand the meaning and relation of this word, then it is not possible to grasp the thinking and power of this proverb. The word justice, *mishapt*, is both governmental and personal in its meaning. It most often has connection to that which is decided by a king or leader and has the official stamp of judgment. This is the idea of a leader dispensing that which is right; a decision which is made irrespective of individuals and political bias but that which does the best for everyone and conforms most closely to God's law.

This word also means that which conforms to what is right – the thinking of and execution of that which is right.

It is clear that evil man does not understand either of these two senses of the word. They do not comprehend governmental decisions that do not favor them. They are completely dumbfounded to understand leadership that wants everyone to win. The consistent characteristic of evil men is that they have honed their selfishness to a high degree and pursue it with no moral stops.

It is also clear that evil men do not understand the thinking of the righteous; the contemplation of moral boundaries over which a person should not go; the consideration of others and whether they will win in a decision.

One of the points of this proverb is that evil men will never agree that justice was a good decision. They will never agree that a governmental decision that takes away from them could ever be the right thing to do. They cannot wrap their thinking around something bigger than themselves, so they can't see how their own perspective could ever be trumped by God or by others. So if you want those who live outside of the boundaries of the Ten Commandments to agree with a decision that is righteous, they will never be able to do it. Their perspective is one of pure confirmed selfishness.

seek the Lord

The Hebrew word *baqash* has the meaning of earnestly seeking something. This is a perseverant search until the object is found. It is not looking with the hopes of finding. Neither is it looking for something while doing other things. This is intensified, focused search.

The proverb before us declares that something in just the focused search for the Lord allows the person to begin comprehending why things happen. Connections between events and people begin to be clear. One begins to be stripped of their selfish perspective and can see the world for what is really happening. There is an ability to see the purpose and point of the Lord.

Notice that it is not just justice that is comprehended by the one seeking the Lord – but all things.

Now this will not make any sense to most people – especially those who are evil – but it makes perfect sense to those who are also following hard after the Lord.

It is the single-minded pursuit of the Lord that begins to give right perspective. The single-minded pursuit of selfishness – especially across crucial moral boundaries – brings clouded reasoning and an inability to perceive the connections between events and people.

PROVERBS 29:5
A man who flatters his neighbor is spreading a net for his steps

This proverb is meant to be a warning. When you get in the presence of someone who is always praising you for things that are not true or overblowing your positive qualities, then there is a catch coming.

Flattery is the Hebrew word *halaq* which means smooth. It is always negative when used in connection with speaking. It is making smooth one's speech to puff up others or oneself. It originally had the idea of making metal smooth. This idea carries over and refers to using the tongue to smooth over any rough spots and paint yourself or another as much better than you/they are.

The question in this proverb is who is the net being spread for? Is it the one who flatters who is spreading a net for himself, or is the one who flatters spreading a net for the person they are flattering? I would take the view that the one who flatters is spreading a net for the person who is being flattered. This is a warning. There is always a catch when someone is treating you in this way. There is a difference between focusing on the positive and flattery. Flattery is over the top or has no basis in truth. Beware of those who treat you this way; there is a net being spread. You are trying to be trapped.

When salesmen do this, they want a sale. When politicians do this, they want your votes or money. When con men do this, they want to swindle you out of money, property, or valuables.

May 30

PROVERBS 30:5
Every word of God is tested; He is a shield to those who take refuge in Him

The word *tested* is the word *sarap* which means smelt, refine, test. This means that God's Word has been purified and refined. One can have confidence in it. God has filtered out impurities in His Word. If someone was going to write something wrong in the Scriptures, then God made sure that did not get written. Some of my favorite passages in the Scriptures are where the author of a particular book says, "I wanted to write about... but I couldn't" or" I would like to tell you about this or that but I have to tell you about this other thing." I believe that is evidence of God's superintending hand keeping error out of the Scriptures.

Now there are areas where the Scriptures speak clearly and it is out of line with our culture. When the culture or value system of a particular people is out of line with the Scripture, it is the culture that is off and not the Scriptures. We can have confidence that God's Word is not wrong. It gives us a super-righteous position. Examples would be when our culture tells us that beauty or sexual aggressiveness in women is extremely desirable; and yet the proverbs say that beauty can be deceitful, but wisdom is more desirable in a wife. When our culture says that unborn children are not really human and can be discarded if they are an inconvenience, the Scriptures say that the unborn child is a fully valuable human life as when John the Baptist and Jesus in the womb were aware of each other's presence. When our culture says that money is the ultimate value and anything you can do to get it is okay; but the Scriptures say that the love of money is the root of all sorts of evil, and one should cease striving after wealth for certainly it makes itself wings. Also, the Scriptures say that the ultimate goals in all of life are relational goals not monetary goals.

We need to have ultimate confidence in the Scriptures to speak into our culture and help us put the values right.

He is a shield to those who take refuge in Him

This is a great verse because it says that when you do what the Scriptures tell you, you are then entering into a deeper relationship with God and seeking refuge in God from the destructive forces in the world around you.

God and His Word, when applied, are shields. They protect people from many of the consequences of wrong choices. The Scriptures have a self- limiting direction in their commands. They tell us when to stop doing something; when an action you might take goes too far. The Scriptures ask us to change our behavior and to be fully behind the protection of God. It also tells us that if we don't modify our behavior, we will be sticking out from behind the shield of God and could be hit by the flying shrapnel of the world we live in.

I am amazed at how often we do not want to limit our behavior in the ways that the Scriptures suggest because it runs counter to the cultural values that we have learned even though it is obvious that if we limited our actions in a particular way, we would limit our exposure to dangerous or difficult consequences.

God is stating a powerful fact that we need to pay attention to. Get behind His shield through living a life of applying the Scriptures and you will avoid many of the problems others experience. Our culture says that we should pursue fame, get-rich-quick schemes, sexual conquest, material possessions, power, freedom to do whatever you want. And yet the Scriptures tell us that these things do not produce what you think they produce. They are not shortcuts to the life you want but to a boatload of troubles. What you are really searching for is different and takes a different path to achieve.

May 31

PROVERBS 31:5
For they will drink and forget what is decreed and pervert the rights of all the afflicted

This whole first part of the Proverb 31 section implies and reinforces the godly calling to leadership. If God has equipped you and called you to be a leader, then there is much good that you can do. Do not squander your ability to influence people on influencing them for selfish purposes or influencing others so that you can enjoy selfish pursuits.

The world needs leaders who will push back the darkness of sin and depravity. Not everyone is a leader. Not everyone has the ability to move others, organize groups of people for maximum effectiveness, initiate new projects and ideas. Those who do must use these abilities and gifts for the common good. It is a high calling to have been given the gifts of leadership. Use them wisely.

drink

This is the Hebrew word *shathah* which means to drink. It does not specify alcohol, but the verse above this clearly refers to wine and strong drink.

One is not to use their position of leadership to indulge their desires or fantasies. The leader bears a responsibility to all those who come under their leadership or are affected by their leadership. Do not waste your gift of leadership by following alcohol or drugs or parties.

forget

This is the Hebrew word *shakach* which means to forget. It is a shame when the gifts of leadership to make a difference in the lives of those who are powerless to initiate or improve their situation is squandered by alcohol. How many significant leaders have had their level of leadership blunted by drink. One of the foremost was Ulysses S. Grant who was a great general but became a drunken, ineffective, and corrupt politician as President. There have been many others down through history.

pervert

This is the Hebrew word *shanah* which means to change, to alter, to disguise, the idea of turning or altering the intended purpose of something so that it does something else or appears in a different way.

The great danger is that the leader has the power to do this. Because of his or her ability to initiate and to get people to follow, they can cause people to embrace something that is not right; something that is a perversion of their interests. Leaders must look at what they do with a higher level of scrutiny because what they do will have a much greater ripple effect than others.

rights

The Hebrew word is *din* which means judgment or decision or justice. The idea is that under the influence of drink, a leader can use their power to diminish justice or oppress those whom they should support.

It is not just drink that can cause this kind of twisting of the right decision. Sometimes it comes because of money or prestige or favors or some other perks. The leader must remain free from this kind of corruption.

afflicted

This word is two words in the Hebrew *ben* and *oni* which means sons of affliction. The idea is that there are people who have no leadership power; they are pushed around and shoved down. The person with godly leadership makes sure that they do not get abused or used any more.

If, however, the leader gets wrapped up in their own personal world of pain or disappointment, they can turn to drink. The leader has a higher calling than this. This proverb says: accept your high calling and do not coddle or misdirect yourself because you have great things to accomplish and people who are counting on you.

June

PROVERBS 1:6
To understand a proverb, a figure, the words of the wise and their riddles

Solomon begins this first chapter by explaining what the whole of the book is for. If someone will pay attention to the comparisons, the riddles, and the ideas that are mentioned here in the book of Proverbs, they will become wise and avoid lots of the problems of normal life.

to understand

The Hebrew word translated *to understand* is the word *bin*. It means to perceive, to embrace the information contained in what was said or the situation; but it also means that one grasps the connections between things. If a person is going to be wise, they must see that things are connected to each other. Solomon has included over 700 observations about human nature in these proverbs. Each one of the proverbs is pregnant with meaning in all kinds of directions. Solomon wants us to look beneath the surface and see all the ways that a particular proverb could apply to your life. He wants us to know that there are levels of meaning in each proverb. Don't just read a proverb – seek to understand its core idea and watch as that core idea connects to all different parts of your life.

These are not just Solomon's observations on life. They are also God's approved observations on life. Solomon made many observations on life that we do not have a record of, but these that are included in Scripture are the ones that God wanted us to have because they were the truth at a deep level. The fact that they are in the Scriptures speaks to the inspiration that God breathed into them. These human relationship principles have stood the test of time because they were penned by the wisest person who ever lived, and they were approved as accurate by the superintending Holy Spirit. Long before there were any people skill books, there were Solomon's insights on how to deal with people recorded in the book of Proverbs. We can have confidence that the insight that is shared in a particular proverb is true on many levels. And we can have confidence that spending the time to dig out the meaning and application for our lives is worth it on relational, spiritual, emotional, and mental levels.

I find myself going back to the proverbs again and again. I see new application and new depth in these timeless proverbs just as Solomon and God knew that I would. Seek to understand the complexity and simplicity of the comparisons, the riddles, and the ideas that are recorded here. The thoughts in this book are designed to be helpful ways of taking these insights into your daily interactions with people. I do find that the more that I can see my people interactions and relationships through the lenses of the proverbs, the more wise I look to others.

a proverb

The Hebrew word that is translated *proverb* here in this verse is the word *masal*. It can mean anything from a short pithy saying to an extended story. Jesus used the extended form when He was teaching His parables in the New Testament. He encased deep truth in a simple story. People could enjoy the story but ignore the point. They could enjoy the story and get the point. They could enjoy the story, get the point, and keep pushing for the deeper applications of the story for themselves. The same is true for the proverbs that are recorded here by Solomon. The insights that Solomon packs into the phrases and comparisons that he uses are weightier than most people skill platitudes. These are suitcases out of which we can pull truths and projects that don't seem to fit in such a few words.

When you are praying over the proverbs and God seems to highlight a particular proverb for you that day or in a particular situation, spend the time to unpack that proverb and grasp its connection with your situation. Sometimes I have spent an hour working through how a particular proverb could be connected to my situation. One time, recently, I thought I had unpacked why God had highlighted a particular proverb to me after three hours only to find that six hours later in the middle of the night a whole new perspective on that proverb and my life opened up.

a figure

The Hebrew word for *figure* is the word *melisah*. It means an elusive saying or a figure or a proverb. It often is associated with scorn or satire which suggests that this was a way of saying something that made you see an issue from a completely different angle. In our day this could be comparing the fact that Americans spend ten times more on cosmetics than they do on mental health. This is shown in the book of Proverbs where Solomon hyperbolizes a comparison: "It is better to live in a desert land than with a contentious woman." "It is better to be unknown and have a servant than to be well known but be a self-promoter."

As you read through the proverbs you will read of Solomon making crazy comparisons or crazy statements to jolt you into realizing a truth. God is goading us through Solomon's figure of speech to notice a deeper truth. Dig for understanding and how this truth relates to life. Each proverb or figure relates to real life and can help us be wise, avoid a foolish decision, deal with a foolish person, and chart a course of decisions that will develop a great life. But too often the big things of life are hidden by our culture, and we just blindly move forward making the same decisions as all of the people around us. This results in the same consequences as everybody else. What we really need to look at is whether we should choose some different choice because it really does make more sense if we just stop and look at it.

Wise people do not throw their pearls around for everyone to misuse or misappropriate. Wise people hide their wisdom in riddles and mysteries so that their insights will only be revealed to the person who looks with intensity or pursues the truth with tenacity. In the book of Proverbs you will find a wealth of people knowledge. There are sixty-three different types of fools that are described with the appropriate responses to them. You will find the eight friends of wisdom and how to use them to find wisdom and a great life. You will find some of the most amazing leadership advice so you can accomplish the purposes that God put in you. I often find myself asking God, through the book of Proverbs, how to handle a leadership situation I am facing by looking at every verse that talks about the king. I often prayerfully ask God to guide me through working with a person who is driving me sideways because of a particular trait. I will look up their version of foolishness (arrogance, anger, laziness, sexuality, violence, etc.) and pay special attention to what Solomon says to do with this kind of person.

PROVERBS 2:6

For the Lord gives wisdom. From His mouth comes knowledge and understanding.

What is interesting in this proverb is that while you search for wisdom, it is the Lord who eventually gives it to you. It would seem that in at least some cases, if not many, you cannot connect the dots to wisdom using only your rational faculty or you would not need to search so hard and the Lord would not have to give it.

Those who care about God and seek to please Him are interested in not just what direction makes sense and will bring the prosperity or goal they seek, but they are interested in what does the Lord want. It is this level of wisdom that needs to be given to you. It does not always make the most sense of all the options available to you. It is just clear what He wants you to do.

Notice that He gives it to you. It comes from Him. It will often make perfect sense in retrospect, but there is no way for us to know what He knows. He is outside the time domain and understands everything that will possibly happen down any time tangent. If something looks like the wise thing to do but He knows something that will happen in six months that we can never know, then we need His choice not just ours. If He knows that we will encounter a person who will present an irresistible temptation to us at some point down a particular path, then we need to avoid that path. We need His wisdom. If He knows that all types of support and help and encouragement will be available about three months from now going down a particular path, then while it does not make the "best" sense at the time, it is the path to go down. If He sees that we need to learn certain qualities and those will only be learned going down path Y instead of the more popular or immediately successful path Z, then we need His wisdom not just the sum total of our own.

June 3

PROVERBS 3:6
In all your ways acknowledge Him and He will make your paths straight

This verse is very interesting in that it tells us things we would not expect. There is truth hidden behind the plain-looking words here. The word *acknowledge* is not: let people know about...or pray a little prayer to... a little tip of the hat or cross of yourself....to acknowledge God in each aspect of your life. Instead the word is the word *to know* and suggests intimate knowledge of God and is suggested in each of the avenues of your life in order for the promise to kick in. In every arena, in every situation, in every relationship the believer is to be intimately aware of and related to God. Clearly this carries with it the idea that you are interacting and reacting in these arenas as God would.

It is this relational connection to God and understanding of His desired reaction or action that allows Him to so readily make your path straight. This is not guidance through the difficulties of life; this is road building and throwing obstacles and difficulties out of the way. God is actively at work for you, making your pathways through life less complicated. Boy, don't I need this. I gain this incredible blessing by having a deeper relationship with God.

God says that He blessed Cyrus and made his paths straight so that He would be in a situation to release the captive Israelites at the appointed time. This idea of the Lord making a person's path straight is a clear acknowledgement of the fact that the world is a much more complex place than one person can control. There are things and actions that are completely beyond the control of the individual that must come together in order for that person to live and enjoy the blessed life. One of the ideas is that it would be wise to be intimately acquainted with the road-builder of life who controls everything and can smooth the way for you. We will never know on this side of heaven – and maybe not there – how many obstacles and difficulties the Lord threw out of the way. It will be interesting to see the unedited tape of what the Lord was doing behind the scenes to give us the life we lived. Jeremiah 10:23 says it is not in a man to direct His steps. Jeremiah realized that there were forces way beyond himself that controlled how he lived his life – all kinds of forces.

June 4

PROVERBS 4:6

Do not forsake her, and she will guard you; love her, and she will watch over you

This proverb takes the collective actions, statements, and choices of wisdom and groups them together as if they were a person. This collective wisdom is then seen as a woman. Solomon is trying to get us to realize that like a spouse, there are two specific actions that we can take toward wisdom that will be very positive and beneficial to our life. In a sense he is saying that we should act like we are married to this collective body of wisdom, and that we want a growing relationship with her.

There are two actions we must take, and there are two benefits that will come from the growing relationship with wisdom.

The first action is to stay faithful or not to forsake her. *Forsake* is the Hebrew word *azab* which means to depart, to abandon, to lose. Wisdom is not to be something that we date occasionally, but the greatest benefit will come to our lives if we make a permanent commitment to go after the triple-win solution all the time. To, in a sense, say "I will make sure wisdom is pleased with my choices and actions." In the same way that a great marriage has two people who really seek to please each other in how they act and how they live, so with wisdom. Business marriages ask the question what do I want to do or what will she/he allow me to get away with. This kind of thinking sees the other person as a restrictor on your life instead of one of the center energizers of your life.

Great marriages do not try and get away with selfishness that their spouse will allow; they try and please their spouse and find their connection to joy and pleasure through their spouse.

Too many people treat wisdom as an occasional date. This time I will date wisdom and make a wise choice, but I want my freedom to be selfish anytime I want. This type of thinking is what Solomon is trying to rule out. In one sense Solomon is saying, "Before you ever get married to a person, get married to wisdom!!" And do not cheat on her.

The benefit of staying faithful to wisdom is that she will guard you. The word guard means exercise great care over. It is this idea that is a mirror image of the marital relationship that seems to be in view here. The benefit of faithfulness is greater connection and attention from wisdom. There is an idea here – and in other places in Proverbs and in the Old Testament – that wisdom has a cumulative effect in which a safe zone is built around you where some level of the accumulating problems of life and civilization, in general, will not reach you. The idea is that if you consistently make the wise choice which promotes the good for God, others, and yourself, you will have strong allies and people who will want you to succeed. The sum total of the wisdom that you have done over time will rise up and protect you. This is not true if you only occasionally date wisdom. In other words, if you occasionally do a wise thing but do not adopt a wise lifestyle, you will not see this cumulative "force field" of wisdom protecting you.

love her, and she will watch over you

This is a second action and benefit, but it is really a mirror image of the first. Solomon is not just saying, "Stay committed to wisdom and don't be unfaithful." He is saying, "Find your joy in serving wisdom. Go after wisdom as the center of your life. Seek to please wisdom with your choices and actions."

Great marriages are produced when both parties think through the decisions they are about to make and/or actions they are about to do and ask themselves: Will this please my spouse? Will this meet the needs of my spouse? Does this allow me to connect more closely to my spouse? Regular marriages and okay marriages do not have this focus.

It is this kind of thinking that Solomon is asking us to engage in with wisdom. It is like looking over at this person called wisdom and seeing if she would be pleased before you make a decision. Would she be delighted with what you are about to do?

When you act selfishly and, therefore, foolishly, you are being unfaithful to wisdom and trampling on the growing relationship with wisdom.

The Hebrew word translated *watch over* is the word *nasar* which means watch, guard, keep. It is very similar to the word guard from the first part of this proverb. The idea is that when a strong relationship is built between wisdom and the individual – wisdom as a growing accumulation in the individual's life attends to the person, interacts with the individual, and keeps them out of trouble. Wisdom provides a buffer around them so that trouble does not reach them.

I see one type of this result regularly in the news. A shooting occurs at a nightclub – if the person had not been at the night club, they would not have been shot. There is an altercation at a bar or other undesirable place – if they had not been at that place, it would not have occurred. There is usually a choice to be selfish or foolish at some earlier point that got them to the place where harm could come to them. Now it is not that the wise person sits in a locked, protected room all the time; but their thoughts are oriented to wisdom, to pleasing others, to pleasing God, and not just themselves. The places they go and the things that they do are different.

PROVERBS 5:6
*She does not ponder the path of life; her ways are unstable,
she does not know it*

These truths are spoken about the adulterous woman but are also true of every person who gives themselves to a form of selfishness. They have stopped pondering the path of life. Where does it end up? What is the point of life? Why am I here? What contribution am I supposed to make? Their whole focus is what they want and the particular form of foolishness that they have embraced.

ponder

This is the Hebrew word *palas* which means to weigh, balance, or make level. Clearly the translators wanted to bring out the idea of thinking and contemplation. This idea is a part of this word, but there is also the idea of action which brings balance. This woman does not balance her life. She knows that what she is doing, by committing adultery, is bringing an instability to her life. It leans her life over so that it cannot sustain itself. One cannot sustain a life in which unfaithfulness is involved. It is fundamentally unbalanced. It is like riding a car on just two wheels. This word carries the idea that this woman's life is not balanced, sustainable, level, and she likes it that way – careening from one impulsive encounter to the other and following one lustful impulse after another.

This word also suggests that there is a balance to life: a way that it is supposed to operate for long-term survival. There is supposed to be balance in the path of life. It cannot all be passion. It cannot all be sadness. It cannot all be war. It cannot all be love. As Ecclesiastes says, *there is a time for each thing under the sun...* This person who commits adultery runs after the feelings that come from lust, passion, and romance. Those are meant to be enjoyed within a long-term, committed relationship between a man and a woman called marriage.

path of life

This Hebrew phrase is more than the sum of its parts. It seems to refer to at least three ideas: One, the general way that a person should live their life; a trail marked by the boundaries of the Ten Commandments. Second, the specific destiny, good works, and plan that each individual is to do with their life. Third, the pathway that connects a person to the life that is in God. Psalm 139:24; Matthew 7:14; Psalm 16:11.

God is life. He is the source of life, and He knows the path we need to take to obtain a constant flow of life towards us. He talks about a path which you should not get off of. He talks about a balance which you should not put too much on one side or the other. In our day and age and in our culture, people have the idea that they should be able to do anything that they want to do. If I want to do it, then it is okay. They do not think about a small, narrow path that they should stay on, refusing to be drawn off that path to a phony better time.

Solomon is trying to get us to see inside the world of the person who follows their lusts. They don't see the big picture of life. They have given over control of their life to the impulses they feel. They do not think through what will happen if they commit unfaithfulness. They do not run out the consequences of their decisions. Later they are shocked by the diseases, divorce, loneliness, destruction, and lack of fulfillment that is all over their life.

There is a path that your life should take in order to maximize the gifts, talents, abilities, and dreams you have. That path is a moral path. That path leads to humility before God. That path includes impulse control and refusal to stray from God's righteous boundaries.

unstable

This is the Hebrew word *nua* which means to shake, stagger, quiver, totter, swing to and fro, etc. She is at the mercy of the latest impulse that comes her way. There is no firmness of purpose. There are no commitments that she will not do. This is the kind of person who regularly says, "It seemed like the right thing to do at the time."

The stability that Solomon does not see in this woman is what is supplied by the Ten Commandments. I will not do this or that. I can do lots of things within these boundaries, but I will not do that. This level of stability is what we need in business, in government, in the home, in Hollywood, in schools, etc. Now we have all types of people who will do what is expedient for them rather than steadfastly do what is best for the common good.

If you are willing to do just about anything that strikes you as interesting, pleasurable, or profitable, then you are unstable. In fact a great question for people is, "What won't you do?"

she does not know it

This is the most tragic part of this person's life. She is living her life based upon impulses and feelings and temptations. She has no sense that her life is out of balance or headed for trouble. She is headed for trouble and is not aware of it. It is like the person who is talking on their cell phone while driving and is headed right into another car but is too distracted by the phone.

She will be completely blindsided by the eventual breakup, by the diseases, by the lonely feelings, by the financial consequences, by the alienation of her husband's affections, by the disconnect of spiritual power and life, by the swirling emotional tornado that will come as this affair progresses and ends, by the impact of her affair in her children, by the change in her reputation, by the ease of the next affair, by other temptations that will come calling, by the need to dull the pain that is coming, by the guilt she will feel, by the stain on her soul.

There are a number of lessons here in this verse. Do not repeat the folly of this woman by being unfaithful. Do not embrace a form of selfishness which blinds you to the whole of life. Make sure that you are balancing and pondering your life. Are you fulfilling the unique calling and mission that God has given you or have you thrown it away pursuing some pleasure or pain-avoidance technique? If you are sitting in a pile of consequences from your own choices, then it is time to humble yourself before God and repent. Cry out to Him to forgive you and give you a new perspective and an ability to not give into the impulses and temptations around you.

June 6

PROVERBS 6:6
Go to the ant O Sluggard, observe her ways and be wise

The sluggard is the habitually lazy person who does not put out maximum energy.

One of the dangers of foolishness is that "I will only try when I feel like it or when I want to."

This quickly becomes "I will not put out when it is needed" which becomes "I cannot put out maximum effort when others are counting on me."

The sluggard becomes a sluggard by a slow easy-choice process.

It is important to do your best even when you don't feel like it so that when your best is really needed, you will be able to give it.

The sluggard ends up in poverty while hoping for instant riches.

They need to watch those who work hard. They need to be around people who work hard. They need to be in a context in which the minimum is still a lot. This is the only way to speed up a person with sluggard tendencies.

Do not give in to the tendencies of laziness. The television is a big help to sluggishness. Also, it is true that attitude is the key to combating sluggishness. A willing attitude to try what those in authority tell me keeps sluggishness from more deeply affecting my life.

I find that I must fight the tendency to be sluggish. It is not enough to just be active and busy. Sluggishness is also when you spend time doing what is not the most productive use of your time; it is just the easiest or most convenient at that moment.

June 7

PROVERBS 7:6
For at the window of my house I looked out through my lattice

This simple statement reminds us of so much about sin. Notice that Solomon was looking out of the lattice of his house. His house would have been one of the biggest houses of the city. It would have been on one of the highest points of the city - God's house being the highest and then the king's house. He could literally look out over the whole city just as his father David had done when he spied Solomon's mother, Bathsheba, taking a bath on the roof which led to their adultery, Uriah's murder, and David's eventual marriage of Bathsheba, the baby's death, and then Solomon's birth.

Solomon could see the whole city through his lattice which meant that the young man could not see him. Solomon probably knew who the man was and that he did not belong in that part of the city and that the woman who came to see him was not his wife. There is always someone watching. Sin seems private and hidden, but there are people who are watching. God is watching and someone else is aware.

What you are doing will come out. We have blinders on when we are in the pursuit of sin which makes it seem as though our sin is more private than it is. I know a man who was having an affair that he thought no one could know about. He was proud of how he had deceived everyone, and yet it became known and his denials and deception just broke trust to a deeper level. Realize that your sin will find you out.

Solomon is introducing a real life story to describe the deceptiveness of sin and the naiveté of the sinner. He goes on in this section to describe the actions, words, and even thoughts of adulterer and adulteress. He also does something that few do in these kinds of detailed descriptions of the course of sin. He gives the consequences of following this course of action in verses 23, 26, and 27.

PROVERBS 8:6
Listen, for I will speak noble things; and the opening of my lips will reveal right things

Solomon is trying to get the reader to pay attention and not just read. "Listen!" he shouts, "I am about to give you pearls of truth that few have heard." The danger is that you won't know what to do with this information and will not treat it with the dignity and value it deserves.

I will speak of noble things

The word *noble* is the Hebrew word *nagad* which means to place a previously unknown matter or unknowable matter right in front of a person. It can mean telling the solution or proof to bring something to light; to make it visible. The idea here seems to be that wisdom is hidden from the naive and the fool and the average person. God, through Solomon, is going to begin sharing this hidden knowledge with us. We just need to be prepared for the information. Too often we miss the profundity of wisdom, mistaking it for a solution that is too hard or too remote or too simple for us.

One of the key ideas is that wisdom – when it is revealed – is that wisdom was hidden and not initially obvious or a contemplated solution. It is high, hidden. The translators of the NASB used the word noble to infer that it is different and higher and more sublime than the information and solutions that are regularly suggested in the marketplace of ideas.

When a problem or a difficulty is brought up, the typical solutions are bantered about and can be collected rather easily and often. But then there is wisdom: it is the solution that is stunningly helpful; it is unusual; it is right in a much higher way. It does not promote self as the justification for its actions. It promotes God and the common good as well as the individual's well-being. It is high and noble and hidden from most people as they pursue the self-first solution.

When you are looking for the way out of your troubles, do you take the selfish solutions and its many variants or do you wait until wisdom speaks? Wisdom will speak if you listen. It will speak of a noble solution that honors God, promotes the value and worth of others – especially others directly affected by this problem – and it will over the long haul build your reputation and value.

the opening of my lips will reveal right things

The Hebrew word *meysha* at its root means to go straight and direct rather than the crooked or twisting way. In the moral and ethical realm it, therefore, means to go straight according to God's law and not to twist or pervert the rules of conduct that God has handed down; to not use myself or my actions in ways that God clearly did not intend. We do not talk about this "natural" or obvious rightness to what one should do, but it used to be called the natural law because morality obviously fit within that which nature allowed. Going against nature was a perversion of it.

One could rightly talk about the unnaturalness of premarital or extramarital sexual relations because it gave rise to sexually-transmitted diseases. Our physical bodies were not designed to handle more than one partner. The spread of disease was the result of the twisting or perverting of God's natural or right order. The same and even more could be said about the homosexual sins as these were a further twisting of obvious natural order. Murder was an obvious violation of the natural order because it produced death – an argument gone horribly too far. A discussion is supposed to produce cooperation, not death. Stealing is another twisting of the natural order – the goods of one person being abrogated to another without work and at great loss to the owner. To gain money or goods in the right way requires that all parties be pleased with the transaction. If one is displeased or feels defrauded, then the transaction has been perverted. Each of the

Ten Commandments had a clear understanding in this natural law. It was natural to stay within its boundaries. Each violation was a form of selfishness and twisting what was clearly right in this natural order. We have abandoned this form of simple and profound wisdom because we as a culture want to do what we want to do. We see God's laws as too restrictive. Our culture has basically said: What Jesus says in the parable; we don't want this king to rule over us. We push the limits of what is acceptable and then wonder why we have the diseases and heartbreak and depression and crime that are throughout our culture. Until we get back to a basic understanding of what is right, it will be difficult – if not impossible – to dwell together in peace and safety.

I was on an airplane the other day talking with a 22-year old computer whiz kid who had never talked with someone who advocated abstaining from premarital sex until marriage. He was fascinated by my logic and morals and said repeatedly that he had never heard this line of reasoning before. "You mean to say that you think that I should abstain from going to bed with a woman until I get married to her?" he exclaimed! I had a fascinating discussion with him about the naturalness of godly morals and the selfishness that is in every heart. It was stunning to me that here was a college-educated and brilliant young man who had never encountered a cogent person make the case for premarital abstinence.

Until we are willing to listen to wisdom, our culture will continue on this twisted and broken path and our way of life will collapse. It cannot be sustained if it is not righteous. It is undoubtedly true that our culture will collapse if it does not repent of its immoral ways, but it is also true that each of us as individuals do not have to be a part of that collapse. We can choose to listen to wisdom and follow the right things that wisdom speaks, even if it is against the common wisdom of the office or the streets.

Follow God. It is worth it. Listen to His wisdom. I have read the last chapter... HE WINS.

June 9

PROVERBS 9:6
Forsake your folly and live, and proceed in the way of understanding

Those who are simple and do not know how to handle a particular problem or accomplish a particular goal often hold onto the wrong things or act impulsively because they are unable to understand how things really work.

The words *forsake your folly and live* is really let go of your selfishness, impulsiveness, and rebelliousness in certain areas and you will find the solution; the goals that you are looking for coming to you. Realize that there is a relationship between what you want and what you must do that right now in your selfishness you are blocking yourself from accomplishing.

Another clear point can be made from these verses. One can never really live when one is operating out of a selfish mindset. It is cooperation, compromise, interaction, togetherness, etc., that will produce the life we really want. People so often want other people to like them and do things for them, but they try and get them to do this by force or seduction rather than voluntarily through wisdom and good will.

One could make an interesting case that biblically it is selfishness (folly) that keeps us from the abundant life God created us to enjoy. What is it that you want? If you are not enjoying the bounty of the Lord, it is selfishness that is keeping you from embracing it – either yours or others.

Forsake your folly and live is a command. Live away from selfishness. It may seem like it is in the direction of what I want to the exclusion of others, but that is really the way of death and separation. What is the type of selfishness that you are most prone to embrace? Pride, Impulsiveness, Anger, Rebellion, Mocking, Lasciviousness, Lying, Gluttony, etc. Forsake that type of folly and learn to live. It is this type of selfishness that clings to you like a wet T-shirt that must be abandoned.

Realize that if you can't find the way of wisdom when facing a decision, it is because you are still clinging to folly and your own brand of selfishness. All of us have ways in which we win and the others around us lose. These are our folly. We must be willing to strike out in new directions and find those actions that produce wins for all. What is the choice or action that the most people in my life win along with my win? What is the pathway which will allow God to be exalted and me to prosper and others to benefit? That is the pathway of wisdom.

June 10

PROVERBS 10:6

Blessings are on the head of the righteous, but the mouth of the wicked conceals violence

It is worth it to live life God's way. It sometimes seems like the people who break God's rules have all the fun, but this is not the case. In this proverb Solomon gives us a reminder of what happens when we live God's way to the fullest.

The word *righteous* is the Hebrew word *sedeq* which means justice, righteous, conformity to a standard or norm. It is best to understand this as staying within the boundaries of the Ten Commandments and not just staying away from the violations of the standards but doing the opposite – really living out the life of faith. Blessings are actual spiritual, emotional, mental, physical, and material progress in life – additions and pleasures and encouragements. These are waiting for the people who will understand what God wants and move toward them. Being a righteous person meant that one would live out the meaning of the Ten Commandments by going in the opposite direction of the negative ones and doing the intent of the positive ones. For instance, it is not enough to not steal; one must work hard to produce a valuable product or service so that they can have abundance to share with others. The opposite of stealing is generous abundance. It is not enough to not murder; one must look for those whom God wants you to love by meeting their needs. It is not enough to not covet other people's possessions; one must embrace their lot in life with a deep level of contentment. It is not enough to not bear false witness; one must speak truth and blessings into the lives of others.

PROVERBS 11:6

The righteousness of the upright will deliver them, but the treacherous will be caught by their own greed

This is another in this series of proverbs that reminds us what righteousness fully-embraced in a person's life is able to do.

Notice that Solomon separates righteousness from the person who acts righteously. He acts as though it is a separate entity. It is your righteousness that will speak to you. It will deliver you. It will smooth your way.

Basically he is saying that righteousness – when embraced as a lifestyle – does generate its own power in your life. It steers you around many problems and protects you from those that come to destroy you.

It is actually extremely realistic in its portrayal of problems coming to the righteous person. Too many other religious epics seem to suggest that the truly righteous person is excused of all problems. Notice that God gives it to the believer straight: You will have problems – even if you are righteous – but you will be shown a way out of the problem. It is the process of agonizing for a solution that is guaranteed. God will send, through righteousness, a solution to the dilemma.

Now it is often thought that it is outside of strict righteousness that deliverance is to be found. But this is not so. When a person asks themselves what is the truly God-honoring right thing to do, they come up with a way that will deliver themselves from unseen troubles and a proper solution.

but the treacherous will be caught by their own greed

It is the desire more for selfish gain that does not allow the treacherous person to escape from the scam. The con man always gets the sucker to make a little illegal money before he moves for the big score. It is the greed of the person that draws them into the trap.

Be careful and do not be sucked into something that is just a little on the sly or just barely illegal. If the product or service does not really help people or it is illegal to do it, then one should move away from it no matter how lucrative it is.

PROVERBS 12:6
The words of the wicked lie in wait for blood, but the mouth of the upright will deliver them

words

This is the Hebrew word *dabar* which means words or speech or speaking. The idea here is that Solomon says that the intent of the person who is wicked is for someone to lose, to be hurt. One of the characteristics of wickedness is that this person gains through the loss of others. It is the win-lose way of negotiating and living.

Remember that the wicked person – according to the Old Testament – is one who lives outside of the Ten Commandments as a way of life. Lying is okay if it gets you what you want; stealing is okay as long as you get what you want; intimidation, physical violence – even murder – is okay as long as you get what you want; pretending to worship other gods is okay as long as you get what you want; sexual unfaithfulness is okay as long as you get what you want; planning and plotting how to take other people's possessions is okay as long as you win; open rebellion against authority is okay as long as you are living the life you really want. All of these are the components of a wicked life.

This is why Solomon says that underneath the speech of the wicked person is a motive for them to win and you to lose. In their mind there is no looking for the win-win; they only focus on gain through other's loss.

The wicked use words to their advantage to get what they want; there are no boundaries to how they use words. They use them to serve their purposes and do harm to their opponents and others who have what they want.

Notice how carefully God says that the righteous person needs to be with what they say. The wicked person is trying to trip you up through their words or using your words. The righteous person will be delivered through their constant focus on what is right and good for everyone.

The righteous person will not participate in the schemes of the wicked. As soon as it becomes apparent that a plan is designed to rob others of their gains or possessions, then the righteous person is out. It doesn't matter how much the profit is or how easy it is or that someone else will just get the profit or gain. It matters that the gain comes by making other people hurt or wounded or lose.

When you are with a person, what do their words tell you as you read between the lines? Are they out for themselves? Are they twisting their words so that they profit while others lose? Is it clear that their intent is to hurt another or make them lose? This is a signal that you are dealing with a wicked person even though they may be a relative or close friend or respected person. If their words belie a waiting for blood, then the person is beyond the boundary of acceptable behavior in God's eyes. They are living a wicked life in some area or areas of their life.

You need to be extra careful with what you say and make sure you are looking for the triple-win. Does what you want to do really benefit the other person as well as you?

PROVERBS 13:6
Righteousness guards the one whose way is blameless, but wickedness subverts the sinner

The word *righteousness* is the word *sedeq* which originally meant to be straight and then became to conform to the standard or norm. In other words, to be righteous means to do things God's right way; to line up with God's norm. When one does things the way God would want them done, then they have performed righteously.

The word *guard* is the Hebrew word *nasar* which means to watch over, to protect. Notice that one's righteous acts are said to take an active role in watching over or protecting one's life and lifestyle. When one has the habit of doing things the way God would want them done, then those tendencies keep a person from many of the troubles that would come upon those who skirt the edges of what is ethical or legal.

This is the idea that presenting an unethical or illegal opportunity to a person who has consistently acted righteously will not entice them to act. In fact, it is this principle that is used in many sting operations. If a clearly illegal act is presented to a righteous person, they will not act. Therefore the police are in their rights to offer an illegal action for it is not a strong temptation to righteous people.

Your past history of righteousness protects you from being involved in wickedness. There are many business opportunities and individual actions which we need to steer clear of or we will be caught in a web of trouble.

but wickedness subverts the sinner

The idea in this phrase is that going beyond the boundaries of the Ten Commandments in order to accomplish something you want will dig tunnels under your path which will eventually cause the whole thing to collapse. It may look like you are getting ahead, but eventually it will come crashing down – in this life and definitely in the life to come.

I think of the person who cheats to save on their taxes and then learns to cheat in other things. At some point they will be caught or key relationships will be destroyed. The smooth road to success you thought you were taking will collapse, and it will end up in a place you don't want to be.

Each of the commandments marks the boundaries of selfish actions that should not be taken to advance your own cause. Remember the reason is that wickedness seems like progress, but it has rotten timbers over the difficulties in life that will fall eventually.

- Commandment number 1: Do not use magic, other religions, occult, or secret societies to advance your wealth, position, prestige, reputation, romantic leverage.

- Commandment number 2: Do not give reverence to other gods, idols, or spirit powers to advance your wealth, position, prestige, reputation, romantic leverage.

- Commandment number 3: Do not use curses, oaths, or swearing to try and advance your wealth, position, prestige, reputation, romantic leverage.

- Commandment number 4: Do not refuse to take time to worship God so as to advance your wealth, position, prestige, reputation, romantic leverage.

- Commandment number 5: Do not rebel from God-given authorities or lead in such a way as it would be impossible for those you lead to value you in order to advance your wealth, position, prestige, reputation, romantic leverage.

- Commandment number 6: Do not devalue others verbally, emotionally, mentally, physically, or through open violence and intimidation so as to advance your wealth, position, prestige, reputation, romantic leverage.

- Commandment number 7: Do not promote sensuality and sexual unfaithfulness so as to advance your wealth, position, prestige, reputation, romantic leverage.

- Commandment number 8: Do not defraud, devalue, or remove other people's property so as to advance your wealth, position, prestige, reputation, romantic leverage.

- Commandment number 9: Do not gossip, slander, lie, testify falsely, or speak that which is untrue with the view to advancing your wealth, position, prestige, reputation, romantic leverage.

- Commandment number 10: Do not fixate upon taking the possessions, relationships, employees, or homes of others as though that will be the ultimate way to advance your wealth, position, prestige, reputation, romantic leverage.

June 14

PROVERBS 14:6

*A scoffer seeks wisdom and finds none, but knowledge is
easy to one who has understanding*

As in anyone's life there comes times when the scoffer does not
know what to do. They are at a crossroads and desperately want to
know which choice is the right choice. But their negative, mocking
perspective keeps the wise choice from being perceived. They see it as
too simplistic, impossible, and it will never turn around and benefit
them. They are literally blinded to the truth because they have had the
mocking, scoffing tone. They cannot see the Triple-Win choice as a
viable winning strategy. It looks like a sure losing play to them.

scoffer

This is the critic's way of life. The Bible makes a direct link
between pride and the scoffer. In fact James 4:6 *God is opposed to the
proud but gives grace to the humble* is a repeat of Proverbs 3:34 in which
the word *proud* is the word *scoffer*. It is the height of arrogance to always
point out what is wrong with something or someone. When you put
yourself in the position of being the critic of something, then you put
yourself in the position of being superior over that thing. Often it is
those who cannot do it themselves who become critics.

It is so easy to see the negative-attacking style of the scoffer as
sophisticated and intelligent, but it really robs these people of the
ability to find wisdom when they need it. They are so used to seeing
everything wrong with things that they invent negative outcomes for
the wise course which prevent them from taking it. In other words,
when they see the wise course that would put God, others, and then
themselves, they are prevented from choosing this course of action
because they can see too many potential problems and too many ways
that this course of action could go wrong. They cannot factor in the
goodness and grace of God or the good side of people. So they count

on negative consequences and bad reactions from others and generally get them.

Finding the negative and bad possibilities and seeing the glass as half-full can become a way of life. It is a dark-cloud perspective and will color your whole view of life and eventually rob you of the ability to perceive wisdom.

Scoffers are like a leech that sucks away the energy and joy of a positive project. Every project worth doing will have problems, but these become reasons not to continue the project – to the scoffer.

- **Proverbs 1:22** - *Scoffers delight themselves in scoffing.* It is one thing to notice potential problems and concerns but to retain a positive outlook on life and most projects. But it is another thing to take delight in finding the negative and bad. It can become a delight in scoffing and criticalness. This becomes a whole lifestyle in which the scoffer usually feels that they are superior to everyone else because they can see all the problems – even ones that aren't there. These people have less friends because who wants a critic around all the time. Their whole life takes a negative cast. They begin to believe that they are better than others. It is often the case that if they get into this way of life enough, everything they do begins to involve seeing the wrong with something. Eventually they may lose the ability to be negative, skeptical, and condescending about everything. They also will not be able to be positive or empowering about anything.

- **Proverbs 3:34** - God scoffs at the scoffers. He finds a lot negative and is critical about their arrogant, critical, and negative way of life.

- **Proverbs 19:25** - The scoffer must be severely punished for their critical, negative ways in order to keep the naive from thinking their sophomoric questions and critical negative assessment of everything they are involved with is a wise and righteous way of life.

- **Proverbs 21:24** - Proud, Haughty, Scoffer are his names. The scoffer is the most common form of pride. I can only place myself above you and criticize what you are doing or have done.

- **Proverbs 22:10** - Get rid of the scoffer and contention, strife and discord will stop. These people can just see the negative perspective and create gossip, hard feelings, and rumors over even the simplest things.

- **Proverbs 24:9** - says that the scoffer is an abomination to all men.

- **Psalms 1:1** - Do not become involved in this way of life.

PROVERBS 15:6
Great wealth is in the house of the righteous, but trouble is in the income of the wicked

great wealth is in the house of the righteous

The word *wealth* is the Hebrew word *hosen* which means treasure, wealth, strength. It is important to note that not all righteous people are wealthy in material possessions, but they do have treasure.

There are all kinds of wealth in the house of the righteous: Relational wealth; Intellectual wealth; Material wealth; Wealth of good will; Political wealth; Spiritual Wealth; Emotional Wealth.

One of the key things that righteous people enjoy is relational wealth. Because their orientation is to serve others, there are strong bonds of love and care built between people. Never discount the enormous wealth of great relationships with family and friends. It is the strength of these relationships, along with God, that really make life worth living.

When one is truly righteous and wise, then they build rather than spend selfishly. They have treasure to give and do not move at impulse to spend whatever comes in.

trouble is in the income of the wicked

Remember that the basic definition of wickedness in the Proverbs is that which is outside of the Ten Commandments: another god, idolatry, cursing or oaths of allegiance to another god, refusal to have reverent rest, rebellion against God-given authority, murder and hatred, adultery and lasciviousness, stealing, false statements, deceptions and lies; covetousness of others' goods.

When I gain through going outside the moral boundaries of the Ten Commandments, then I trouble my house. That type of fortune will haunt me until I have no taste for the supposed good life it will buy. We cannot be undiscerning about where our wealth is coming from. It does matter where it comes from and whether it had to make a trip to the immoral side of the street to get into our pocket. The world is more than just a materialistic composite; our actions and reactions and creations have metaphysical components to them.

PROVERBS 16:6

By lovingkindness and truth iniquity is atoned for, and by the fear of the Lord one keeps away from evil

What should you do when you sin?

How do you get people to really forgive you?

How can you get people to really forget what you did?

This proverb gives insight into the two things that are required if others are really going to forgive you. You must be truthful about what you did and consistently loving towards those you offended.

Too many people want to put their offense behind them without ever really admitting that they did it. Whether you have offended God or others, there is a level of confession that is needed to get the slate started anew.

The word *truth* in the Hebrew is the word *omnam* which means truly or truth or faithful or with certainty. In this verse it would seem to carry to ideas that are a part of moving past iniquity and having people not define you by that sin. First the idea of truth or what actually happened – that needs to be declared and then a judgment on whether it was right or wrong. When one does something to offend another, there was a place where they made a choice to do something wrong. It is that choice point that needs to be exposed. "I chose to _____ and that was wrong." Until one can see the choice point and understand it from a moral point of view, then one does not understand the offense. *"God, I was wrong when I did this or that. It was wrong and I ask you to apply the blood of Christ to my sin. Remind me as I approach that point so that I would not sin against you again."*

The second idea in this word translated truth is faithfulness. If a person has offended God or another and they declare their desire to change and not offend in the same way, then they must truly repent and move off in a new direction. They must demonstrate that they will not offend in that way again. Often the person offended has to watch you come to the place where you could offend and actually see you turn away a few times before they will really be able to relax and forgive you. It is your faithfulness to the new road that brings a complete covering for sin. Many people are not really ready to forgive you for a deep offense until they see that you are not like that anymore.

Theologically the only reason why we can have forgiveness of our sins is because of what Jesus Christ did on the cross. He was willing to be our sin bearer. Now interestingly enough it was His lovingkindness and faithfulness that secured for us the sacrifice for our sins. This is the foundation of and reason for any forgiveness we receive.

We need to act like Jesus and act with lovingkindness and faithfulness to show people that our belief in the Savior has made a real difference in our lives.

The word for *lovingkindness* is the Hebrew word *hesed*. This is the word for love, lovingkindness, mercy, goodness. You must demonstrate lovingkindness to those you have offended if they are ever to really forgive you and move past the scar you have left in their life. This is difficult and seems harsh, but if you have truly repented of what you did, then lovingkindness toward the offended party would seem reasonable.

I have talked with a number of people who say: Why can't they just get over it? They always seem to hold it over my head? The answer is that the scar is very deep and affected them significantly. Therefore your change must last and your lovingkindness must overshadow the scar.

The word love is an action word which I have understood means to meet needs, to pursue, and to please. I have loved a person when I have met their needs, pursued them, or pleased them. It is these actions done over time that will atone for sin that I have committed in another person's life.

It is important to say that it is almost impossible to be in relationship with another person and not offend them. We cannot expect fallen people not to do offensive things. We can, however, make sure that we meet their needs and pursue them and please them and in that way swallow our sins with our love. Relationships have ups and downs, but they all go better with lovingkindness.

The word *hesed* has recently been translated *loyalty* as though the major element of one's love for God in the Old Testament was loyalty to the covenant that God brought the people. This, however, obscures the love for the God of the covenant. Most significantly Jesus understands the word to be love not loyalty. I believe that the best translation of the word *hesed* is the older translation of lovingkindness.

The type of sin which is being discussed here is iniquity which is moving outside of the boundaries of the Ten Commandments and living there. This is much more serious than trespass sins which is going outside of God's boundaries and getting back. Iniquity is disregarding God's right to tell you what to do and living in sin for some period of time. The question in this proverb is how do you have people forgive you when you have openly rebelled against God's moral boundaries and lived in sin causing deep scars and offense. The answer is that one must truthfully confess and begin a process of faithfully living a life of lovingkindness.

Do not expect people to just "forgive" because they are supposed to. Demonstrate a repentant heart through truth and faithfulness. In this way you will begin healing the scars that you caused.

June 17

PROVERBS 17:6
Grandchildren are the crown of old men, and the glory of sons is their fathers

The word *grandchildren* is the Hebrew word *ben* which could mean son or grandchildren or any descendant. In this case the translators of the NASB have used the term grandchildren because of the term old men in the proverb. The idea is not necessarily that it is the children of your children that cause you to have a crown but your children and your children's children. Remember, it was not very common that one would live long enough to see their grandchildren.

Realize that Proverbs is always trying to get people to see value and to not be fooled by the way that the world wants you to live. With that in mind, I think it may be best to see this proverb as a warning shot across the bow of career-oriented men.

Solomon is saying that when you get old, it is not your position or the pile of money or anything like that that will be the crowning achievement of your life; but instead it will be your children, so don't neglect them. Don't try and build your life around your position or your business or your hobby, etc. – ignoring your children. For when you get old, it will be your children and how they are living and whether they want to have anything to do with you that will determine whether you think life has been good to you.

Notice that he uses the word *crown* – the Hebrew word is *atara* which means crown or wreath or designation of honor and importance. In other words, I am important because of the relationship of my children and what they have achieved.

This whole section of the Proverbs is about the value of relationships – **LIFE IS RELATIONSHIPS** and it is so common to miss the real point of life. Look, he says, you have this amazing set up:

When you are old all you will want is to have a relationship with your children and grandchildren; and when your kids are growing up, all they want to do is brag about their fathers. Don't be so busy doing this world's stuff that you miss connecting. Unfortunately this is what happens all the time. When the kids are the most interested in their dads, he is too busy making a name for himself in the world. When he is most interested in them, they are too busy or bitter at him to take the time for him.

God, through Solomon's insightful perspective, is trying to get us to be wise and make choices that deepen and preserve relationships with our children and our parents. Make the sacrifice and spend the time; it will be worth the investment. You will never get to spend as much time as you and the other person want potentially; but invest in these radically important relationships with your children and, when they are older, your parents.

Remember that wisdom is making the triple-win choice or action – the one where God is glorified, the other person or people are blessed, and you are profited. In this case it is about spending time and interacting with your children or your parent when you might rather be doing something else that is more personally pleasurable or even worldly profitable. But ultimately it is not wise in that it leaves you relationally barren. Wisdom looks for key relationships to build up, making investments in them.

What are the investments that you need to make in your children's lives to deepen your relationship? It might be time spent doing something they like. It might be learning something that they are fascinated by. Make the investment. It will be worth it. Remember, it doesn't matter if you are famous or rich but that your family loves you.

June 18

PROVERBS 18:6
A fool's lips brings strife, and his mouth calls for blows

In this proverb Solomon exposes the things we don't think about. Many times people just do what they want to or what feels right to them at the time. We don't often realize all that comes with doing what we want to do or saying what we feel like saying.

The word *fool* is the Hebrew word *kesil* which means the person who consistently makes wrong choices. This is the opposite of the wise person. The fool makes the selfish and or easy choice. When the selfish person talks, they talk about what they want with little or no regard to how it will sound to others. This behavior often blows up in the face of the foolish person. People get angry as a result. Many times the fool is taken completely off guard and is amazed at how upset people are when all they did was state their opinion or their desire.

This is why Solomon says that strife, fighting, and quarreling come with a foolish person's lips. If their lips are moving, then a quarrel will result because they cannot pre-listen to what they are saying and they are unwilling to be sensitive to those around them. It is easy for a foolish person to accuse the offended person of overreacting.

If people keep reacting to you or you keep getting in quarrels or fights or losing friends, then it is not them – it is you. You are most likely being selfish.

The old saying *sticks and stones may break my bones but words will never hurt me* is just not true. Some of the deepest wounds are words that have been uttered from a selfish person who was unthinking.

Solomon shares this as a part of leadership training. He shares it with the idea: Make sure that you do not have on your team a foolish person who just keeps stirring the pot through their clinging to and spouting their selfish position.

Solomon also shares this to let leaders know that they have to make sure that they are not talking as a foolish person talks. When you rise to positions of leadership, you do not get the right to spout off about your opinions or your selfish desires. Instead, your speech has to be more measured and careful as you now have the ability to wound more people if you were to express your selfish desires or agenda – even in an off-handed way. How many times have we heard tapes, clips, or notes that were confidential comments that were recorded.

Learn the lessons of leadership. Do not slip into foolish talk. Always think the triple-win. What will allow God to get glory, others to win, and you to enjoy benefit? Think wisdom – not what do I really want.

June 19

PROVERBS 19:6

Many will seek the favor of a generous man, and every man is a friend to him who gives gifts

This is an extension of the idea in verse 4 that friendship is built upon mutual benefit. What is the benefit that people gain from being your friend? Are you finding ways to be generous to people you meet? Do people feel that they gain more than they give in being your friend?

What gifts or benefits can you offer to other people? Have some of your friendships become stale because you no longer are generous or beneficial to be friends with?

The word translated *generous* is the Hebrew word *nadiyb* which means noble, liberal, princely, or wiling, generous, inclined. The idea of the word is that those who are of a generous spirit are a little different kind of people. They have the reputation of really helping people and so people ask them. This is what those who are not generous fear. They do not want lots of people approaching them for favors, loans, and help so they say no to everybody. Unfortunately this fear keeps them boxed into a very small world.

The generous person does have to learn to say NO. And this is uncomfortable, but they also have the opportunity to say yes and to feel the wonderful spine-electrifying joy of saying yes. They get to see their contribution make a difference. They get to feel a level of satisfaction that is unknown to the hoarder. Let me challenge you to move in the direction of generosity. You may not have money to share; fine, then share time or give freely of your attention or your skills or knowledge. I have found that the more generous a person is by choice, the more joy and lasting impact they have.

Unfortunately many people want to have a lasting impact and have people ask them for their wisdom but the people never come. The grandkids don't ask how to make wise decisions. The people at work aren't interested in your point of view or ideas on life. Usually it is because they have not felt the impact of your generosity first.

One of the things that I would like to challenge you with is find a way to become generous. We want the results of this verse in our life. We want our children, grandchildren, friends, colleagues, and other Christians to seek us out for our knowledge, expertise, wisdom, and ideas. In order to get to that point, we must begin to be generous with what we do have to offer. Learn to say NO. Become a discerning person when a person is trying to scam you. Tell people what they need to hear not just what they want to hear. The only way to grow in this area is to become generous. Yes, you will be taken advantage of on occasion, but you will learn and you will become a better person for it.

June 20

PROVERBS 20:6
Many a man proclaims his own loyalty, but who can find a trustworthy man?

This proverb presses a truth home that we often don't want to believe. What a person does is more important than what a person says.

proclaims

This is the Hebrew word *qara* which is to call or to call out. It carries primarily the idea that one has a message to deliver. A part of this word is the fact that it is not quiet but a proclamation. It is to more than just a few – either saying it to lots of people individually or in a group.

loyalty

This is the Hebrew word *hesed* which has for centuries been translated love or lovingkindness, unfailing love but has lately been translated loyalty because of an emphasis on the covenantal relationship between God and Israel. It would seem better to realize that loyalty is a part of love rather than try and blunt the clear implications of the word by emphasizing the contractual aspects.

Solomon is helping us see that talk is cheap and many people say they love or will be kind or will work hard (which is love in a business context), but not everyone's proclamation can be trusted. In fact, experience trumps what they say.

find

This is the Hebrew word *masa* which means find.

trustworthy

This is the Hebrew word *emuna* which means firmness, fidelity, steadiness. It comes from a root which is truth, certainty. This is the idea that when something is said by an individual, it will be done. There is no question that what this person says, they will do.

Whether in business or in relationships, we want to be with people who mean what they say and say what they mean. But these kinds of people are not easy to find. But keep pushing.

Two questions come immediately to mind. Are you a person who promises a lot but doesn't come through? Do you wait before you hire someone until after you have discovered what they are really like or do you just believe what they say? Do you hold back your heart, young man or young lady, when you meet someone or do you tend to believe what people say and what people look like?

The first crucial thing is to be a person who others can count on. Second, it is crucial to begin to be someone skeptical of what people say and wait for the actual performance of the promises.

God, through Solomon, is trying to have us not be so gullible. Realize that everyone can paint a rosy picture of who they are and what they will do. But the proof is in the actual performance.

June 21

PROVERBS 21:6

The acquisition of treasures by a lying tongue is a fleeting vapor, the pursuit of death

This proverb reminds us that how one achieves financial security is more important than that one achieves financial security. In our day and age many people have as their number one goal in life to have lots of money. This should not be anyone's number one goal as it will destroy you in the pursuit. This proverb focuses on how you get along in the world; how you pursue financial security.

Solomon uses the phrase "the acquisition of treasure" as a way of saying how you accumulate the funds to build a life. Treasures were anything beyond what you needed to live every day. By this definition almost everyone in America has accumulated treasure.

God is trying to tell us that there is something more important than getting material possessions and wealth. The something that is more important is relationships. If you gain what you want to gain but there is no one with you to enjoy it with, have you really gained anything?

Solomon points out that if you have to use a lying tongue to accomplish a deal or win a big contract or become wealthy, then you are pursuing death. This is a fascinating phrase and a fascinating observation on Solomon's part. He noticed that those who were dishonest in their career path as an integral part of how they lived became a deceptive person; and while they may have accomplished their financial goals, they had a deadly pall covering their life. They became deceptive in their whole life. People separated from them and they were not really able to connect to others because who could really trust them. So while they accomplished the goal they thought they needed to live, they couldn't really enjoy life because their deceptions put a film, a space, a gap between them and others. There is also the possibility that they became deceptive as a matter of course and did not even know their real self any more.

They did not realize that when they pursued financial security through deception, they were putting themselves on an island cut off from truly deep relationships.

Understand that Solomon is talking about lying as a way of life. I remember one woman who used lying her whole life and found that she was cut off from the relationships she valued most. She needed to confess her sin, memorize significant numbers of Scripture about honesty, and work hard at being "cash register honest" in order to repair the damaged relationships in her life.

June 22

PROVERBS 22:6

Train up a child in the way he should go, even when he is old he will not depart from it

There are two ideas that should be explored in this verse:

One, that each child has a way that suits them. *According to their way* is how the original reads. Each child in your family has a pathway that is unique to them. They have been given certain gifts, talents, and abilities that direct them for God's glory in a specific direction. It is that direction that the parents must be sensitive to. God is counting on the parents to watch for the signs of an aptitude and gifting in a particular area. It is not okay to just send them down the path that you went down. What is their path?

Two, that each child must make sure that their path stays within the boundaries of righteousness. The place to learn how to live in a moral sense is with parents. Right and wrong; good and evil; and even good, better, and best is something that parents must instill. The verses that precede this verse and form the odd type of context that Proverbs contains are verses about the reward of humility and the fear of the Lord are riches honor and life. Thorns and snares are in the way of the perverse; he who guards himself will be far from them. It is incumbent upon the parents that they show their children how to be humble and how to live in the fear of the Lord. It is absolutely crucial that parents also show their children the thorns and the snares that are in the way of the twisted; those who live outside the boundaries of the Ten Commandments. Their lives are filled with lies, rape, anger, and insecurity. This type of training is a part of the parents' responsibility.

The other day when our family when to a local swap meet, we had a window on the life of all kinds of people – especially the thorns and snares that are in the path of the perverse. The number of people who were living out a life of trying to get by on the crumbs of sin was amazing. They were bottom feeding. I want my girls to understand that if you embrace that life, you get those consequences or if you embrace a person like that, you get that life.

God has so richly blessed me and my family. We have been spiritually blessed with a sense of God's presence and guidance. We have been mentally blessed by great schools and monies to send our girls to good schools. We have been emotionally blessed by having peace in our home and an "I want to be here" atmosphere. We have been blessed physically by health and an absence of catastrophes. I desperately want my children to understand how to live in the fear of the Lord and live in the bounty of His love. He is a great and awesome God who has saved us from our sins and asks us to live life a certain way within a broad and wonderful plain. It is not narrow and confining but deep and exciting. It does not have the deep sorrow of those who live in inequity outside the boundaries of the Ten Commandments.

June 23

PROVERBS 23:6
Do not eat the bread of a selfish man or desire his delicacies

This is an unfortunate translation of this proverb. It makes it sound like you are to avoid the foolish person for it is the foolish person who is selfish, but the word *selfish* is really the Hebrew word *ra* which is the word for evil or wicked. God is trying to tell us who to avoid and have no fellowship with. It is the person who has moved outside of God's moral boundary structure and is content to live outside of God's Ten Commandments. They practice false religion or magic; they swear constantly; they do not worship God with any of their time; they do not honor authorities; they murder; they commit adultery; they steal; they lie; they covet other people's goods.

Now there are two possible directions that this proverb can go. God can be telling us to never eat anything with this person. Or he could be telling us to not begin a relationship with this kind of person in which we will become aware of what this person has gained from their wickedness.

It would seem best to understand this proverb as prohibiting the relationship rather than the single meal. The New Testament follows up with this idea in 1 Corinthians 5 where it says do not have a relationship with a so-called brother if he is involved with sorcery, idolatry, adultery, swindling, etc. It is the on-going relationship which must be cut off. Eating a meal with a person was a way of denoting a relationship.

The message is the same as 1 Corinthians 15:33 Do not be deceived: bad company corrupts good morals. The company you keep will determine your actions. I realize that everyone says that they will never do what these friends of theirs do, but there is subtle or overt pressure constantly to push past your boundary lines. The only exception to this rule is in order to evangelize them. The Apostle Paul says not to avoid non-Christians but those who are so-called Christians who behave like this.

The point of the proverb is clear. Do not develop on-going relationships with those who are wicked and live outside the boundaries of the Ten Commandments. If this kind of person is your close friend, then there will be pressure to move in their direction. If this kind of person is interested in the gospel, then share the gospel but do not desire their lifestyle.

We do not hear this message of "come out of them and be separate" very much anymore. It has caused many Christians to compromise with the world.

June 24

PROVERBS 24:6

For by wise guidance you will wage war, in abundance of counselors there is victory

The older that I get, the more I notice that people who consistently make good decisions are those who get as much advice as they can. They try and get advice from reliable sources and then evaluate its ability to deal with all the factors.

Many people want to make a certain decision and so begin to lean in the direction of their feelings before they really check out all the directions. If you follow your feelings, then you will often be wrong.

Realize that making a major advance in life is like waging war against your desires and convenient lifestyle. It will take some advanced planning before you just launch into a diet plan or going back to school or moving your marriage forward significantly. It does take time and you will, at times, move in a different direction ultimately than you thought you might at the beginning.

June 25

PROVERBS 25:6
Do not claim honor in the presence of the king and do not stand in the place of great men

It is the height of arrogance to boast of your gifts and abilities in the presence of your leader. This does not endear you to the people above you to constantly be claiming significance and stature in front of them. Most who do this are really trying to get noticed or see themselves as better than their bosses.

It is unfortunate in our culture that this practice of boasting about yourself is accepted and considered the norm – especially in the hiring process. It is the wise man or woman who realizes that even if you have to trumpet your strengths and abilities to get the job, those around you would be more pleased if you toned it down once you got the job.

Let someone else declare that you are worthy of great accolades. I believe that the process of being your own herald diminishes your accomplishments in the eyes of those who see your advertising campaign.

June 26

PROVERBS 26:6

He cuts off his own feet and drinks violence who sends a message by the hand of a fool

This proverb does not carry the power in English as it does in Hebrew. One could call this proverb the dangers of delegation. This proverb is about delegating – to a fool – an assignment whether this is in the home, in business, in government, or any of the matters you get involved in. One must be careful to delegate to those who are not fools at heart.

The word *message* does not convey in our language the whole of the idea in this proverb. It would be better to see it as *assignment*. The owner or authority or leader wants a particular thing done. It is crucial that one not give that assignment to the fool or they will be injuring themselves.

he cuts off his own feet

The first thought in the proverb is that one cuts off their feet. This means the same as breaking the neck in our culture. The assignment will not be accomplished.

and drinks violence

This means that one injures himself in the process of having an assignment handed to a person who thinks selfishly. For the assignment will surely not be accomplished and worst, in the trying, there will usually be some injury to the reputation or client.

If a person is extremely self-absorbed and rebellious, then they should not be hired. They should also not be counted on to accomplish a crucial task delegated to them.

Remember the lesson of the proverb. Selfish, impulsive, and rebellious people are not reliable people to delegate assignments to. One should make sure that you don't raise a fool and don't hire a fool.

Clearly there is a strong message in this whole group of proverbs: Get away from the confirmed fool.

There is a further question that can be asked. Does an assignment given to you get accomplished to the benefit of the person who assigned? Do you move off into a self-absorbed world in which only what you want matters? Have you botched assignments because you always had a better way than what you were asked? Do you keep getting fired? If these are true of you, then it is time to repent of being a fool. You are self-absorbed and impulsive. Learn to submit to authority and move towards wisdom rather than your own way of thinking all the time. I realize that this comes as a shock, but you are acting like a fool. Stop! No longer ask the question what do I want to do? But ask, what is the best thing for those around me? What would bring God glory? These are the questions of a wise person.

June 27

PROVERBS 27:6
Faithful are the wounds of a friend, but deceitful are the kisses of an enemy

When a true friend does have to point out an area of weakness or moral inadequacy, this is truly helpful. A friend really has your best interest at heart and is not doing this correcting for personal advancement or selfish reasons. A friend who has supported you and is positive toward you over a long period of time can, at times, say a hard thing as long as it is clear that the hard thing is truly designed to make your life better. It cannot be just a chance to make their life easier.

We would do well to realize who our real friends are and give them the right to make these kinds of wounds. Every true friend you and I have ever had has known areas where we could make a change that would significantly improve our life. Most of the time we have to ask...

PROVERBS 28:6

Better is the poor man who walks in his integrity than he who is crooked though he be rich

This is one of the crucial value proverbs that needs to be implanted in the psyche of righteous people. Solomon wants people to realize that you will be given options in this world that look like the right thing to do in that you gain wealth by doing it. But the cost will be your integrity. You must be prepared for these types of choices and keep your integrity. The three consistent strong temptations – money sex, and power – are not worth it when stacked against what one loses if they are pursued unrighteously.

The word *integrity* means simplicity and upright. Instead of becoming a duplicitous person, one maintains his integrity. A person must not lie or act righteous even while performing unrighteousness. These ways of gaining money and prestige are corrupting – the person who goes along with financial mismanagement because they will be cut in on the skim. Lack of integrity comes in many forms – pretending to be within the boundaries of the Ten Commandments while living outside of it in various parts of your life. This is a corrupting game that will eventually catch up with you. Get all of your person inside the boundaries of moral behavior.

Now there is a new type of integrity that is really not integrity at all but is really a form of foolishness. This is the idea in some young people that believe "I should be able to say and do whatever I want no matter what I feel." The idea of submitting to someone else's agenda or selling out to the man is then not being true to yourself. Having integrity means that you do not sell out to the impulses of your lower selfish nature. The idea of integrity means not pretending to be righteous when one is really unrighteous. To be unrighteous and open about that is not integrity but wicked. Lying, deceit, and pretense abound in those who pursue their own selfishness.

June 29

PROVERBS 29:6

By transgression an evil man is ensnared, but the righteous sings and rejoices

Trapping evil people is easy; offer them something sinful. One doesn't trap righteous people by offering them sinful opportunities.

Just remember that if you are being tempted to do something that is clearly not right, it is a trap and it will spring on you. You will be free of all the downstream consequences if you turn away before it gets you.

PROVERBS 30:6
Do not add to His words or He will reprove you, and you will be proved a liar

This proverb on not adding to God's words follows a section on God's revelation about Himself. There is regularly speculation about God. This speculation often goes to bizarre lengths in trying to understand God. It is better to realize that God is past figuring out and that anything that we compare Him to He is utterly unlike. As Isaiah says many years later: *To whom will you liken God and to what will you compare Him, has it not been revealed.* The only reliable guide to discussions of who God is, is God's self-revelation in the Bible. Do not go beyond God's self-description in the Bible, speculating upon all kinds of things about God that we do not know.

This proverb has both a large application to every part and aspect of the word of God, but also a particular application to any speculation about the nature and person of God. He has told us what we need to know about Him in the Scriptures, and we would do well to pay attention to His own testimony about Himself. A long time ago I had read a number of theological works about God which caused me great concern. I remember being prompted to just read the Bible and let God tell me about Himself rather than getting all twisted in knots by the speculation and distortions of men. The God who reveals Himself in the plain text of the Bible is more mysterious and more straightforward and more awesome than the speculations of men. I can believe and follow the God of the Bible while the speculations of men about God can create a God that is impossible to believe in and trust. I read the Bible from cover to cover paying special attention to the sections that cast light on who God is and what is He like. What kind of God is He and what does He do? What doesn't He do? The picture that emerged of God was wonderful and terrifying and believable.

Like Agur, I would recommend to you that you let God tell you who He is in the Bible.

There are people who want to add to the Scriptures other books and other writings and treat them as though they are on a par with the Scriptures. This is always a mistake. There have been some monumental works down through the centuries, but they do not compare with the revelation of God through common people as contained in the Scriptures.

This verse does not mean that one should not write about Scripture or provide commentary even as we are doing here. But one should not in any way pretend that our writing is on a par with Scripture. We should always make sure that we go back to the source: Scripture.

He will reprove you

God does rebuke and correct people – their words especially. Words of correction to the Bible will be corrected either in this life or in the Judgment. It will be a frightful thing to have God comb through the things you wrote and point out its error.

Many people are writing thousands of pages of speculation and fantasy about God or His lack of existence or the supernatural realm. Their drivel has no connection to Scripture except to disregard it. These folks will be rebuked by the Almighty.

you will be proved a liar

This is a very strong statement: *You will be proved a liar*. I am aware of numerous groups that have offered up various books as on a par with Scripture. These books will be proven to be inaccurate and without truth. A number have already been shown to be falsifications and having no connection to reality.

What will it be like when God evaluates them and He says, "You said I was like this, but that is clearly not what I am like." Just as He questioned Job, so will God evaluate and rebuke those who speculate about Him beyond Scripture.

I do not want to be in that position.

We would like to know more about the God we worship, but let us not go beyond Scriptures. He has told us all that we can handle knowing or He would have told us more. If we try and close the gaps in our knowledge of God, we will jump into the realm of speculation that will surely distort our understanding of Him.

About Author

Gil Stieglitz is a catalyst for positive change both personally and organizationally. He excites, educates, and motivates audiences all over the world through passion, humor, leadership, and wisdom. He has led seminars in China, Europe, Canada, Mexico, and all over the United States.

Since founding the nonprofit ministry Principles to Live By in 1992 to help people and organizations win at life through Biblical Wisdom, Dr. Gil has been asked to repair, lead, and reinvigorate numerous organizations and individuals. He successfully led a church to 1400% growth in a disadvantaged area. As a Denominational Superintendent in the Western United States he led 50 churches and 250 pastors to over 300% growth. As a Superintendent of Schools he oversaw a school system as it doubled in 4 years. As an executive pastor at a mega-church he rebuilt a staff and added over a 1,000 people. He injects dynamic life-change as a professor at universities and graduate schools on the West Coast and through seminars, sermons, and lecture series. He also partners with Courage Worldwide which rescues young girls who have been forced into sexual slavery in America.

He has a B.A. from Biola University, a Master's Degree and a Doctorate in Christian Leadership from Talbot School of Theology. He has authored over two dozen books, manuals, and development courses including three best sellers. Dr. Gil's resources are available at Amazon.com as well as at www.PrinciplesToLiveBy.com.

Gil and his wife, Dana, have enjoyed over twenty-five years of marriage and reside in Roseville, California, where they raised their three precious girls.

Breakfast with Solomon

Other Resources by Gil Stieglitz

BOOKS

Becoming Courageous

Breakfast with Solomon Volume 1

Breakfast with Solomon Volume 2

Breakfast with Solomon Volume 3

Breaking Satanic Bondage

Deep Happiness: The Eight Secrets

Delighting in God

Delighting in Jesus

Developing a Christian Worldview

God's Radical Plan for Husbands

God's Radical Plan for Wives

Going Deep In Prayer: 40 Days of In-Depth Prayer

Leading a Thriving Ministry

Marital Intelligence

Mission Possible: Winning the Battle Over Temptation

Proverbs: A Devotional Commentary Volume 1

Secrets of God's Armor

Spiritual Disciplines of a C.H.R.I.S.T.I.A.N

They Laughed When I Wrote Another Book About Prayer,
Then They Read It

Touching the Face of God: 40 Days of Adoring God

Why There Has to Be a Hell

Podcasts

Becoming a Godly Parent

Biblical Meditation: The Keys of Transformation

Everyday Spiritual Warfare Series

God's Guide to Handling Money

Spiritual War Surrounding Money

The Four Keys to a Great Family

The Ten Commandments

If you would be interested in having Gil Stieglitz speak to your group, you can contact Him through the website

www.ptlb.com

www.ingramcontent.com/pod-product-compliance
Lightning Source LLC
Chambersburg PA
CBHW021211090426
42740CB00006B/183